INDIAN STATESMEN

INDIAN STATESMEN

DEWANS AND PRIME MINISTERS OF NATIVE STATES

G. A. NATESAN

GYAN

Published by

GYAN

Gyan Publishing House
5, Ansari Road
Daryaganj, New Delhi-110002
Phone: 011-47034999, 9811692060
E-mail: books@gyanbooks.com

Distribution Network
gyanbooks.com
India, USA, Canada, UK, Australia

ISBN: 978-93-7225-249-1 (PB)

First Published, 1927

2nd Impression 2025

Printed at: Gyan Press, Delhi.

INDIAN STATESMEN
Author: G. A. NATESAN

Indian Statesmen

INDIAN STATESMEN

DEWANS AND PRIME MINISTERS OF NATIVE STATES.

WITH SEVENTEEN PORTRAITS

NOTE

NOW that the question of the future of Indian States and their place in the Constitution of the country is being widely discussed, this volume of Indian Statesmen is of more than ordinary interest to politicians and laymen alike. In this new publication we have sketches of Eminent Indian Statesmen, notably those who have been Dewans or Prime Ministers of well-known Indian States. Besides being a record of the lives and achievements of these statesmen and administrators who have distinguished themselves both in British India and in the territories of the Ruling Princes and Chiefs, the book offers an instructive study in the evolution of Indian States. For the lives of these men are so linked with the fortunes of the States which they served that it is hardly possible to draw the line between biography and history. We see the one merging in the other: especially as the early records of these States are little more than the doings of the men who made them what they are. Hyderabad without Sir Salar Jung, Nepal without Jung Bahadur or Gwalior without Sir Dinkar Rao, is inconceivable. Bhavanagar and Oodeshanker, Mysore and Rangacharlu, Travancore and Sir T. Madhava Rao, Pudukottah and Sir Sashiah Sastri are so intimately connected that neither the history of the States nor the lives of the Statesmen can be complete without the other.

It is hoped that this volume recounting the lives and achievements of several distinguished Indians will be welcome not only to the subjects of the Indian States wherein they laboured under the most trying conditions but by all those who feel a just and legitimate pride in the capacity of Indians for Self-Government.

THE PUBLISHERS.

It is hoped that this volume recounting the lives and achievements of several distinguished Indians will be welcome not only to the subjects of the Indian States wherein they laboured under the most trying conditions but by all those who feel a just and legitimate pride in the capacity of Indians for Self-Government.

THE PUBLISHERS.

CONTENTS

SIR SALAR JUNG.

INTRODUCTORY.

FORTY years have gone by since Sir Salar Jung, who made the state of Hydrabad what it is to-day died at the very zenith of his influence and popularity. Since then there have been several changes in the Ministry at the Nizam's Court: but public opinion, as to the genius and statesmanship of Sir Salar Jung, has neither wavered, nor diminished in its fervour and enthusiasm. Some critics have extolled him as "the Saviour of India." One European administrator considers that as a man of business especially in Finance, Sir Salar Jung has not been surpassed by any native of India. Another declares that India is not likely to produce two such men as Sir Salar Jung and Sir T. Madhava Row more than once in two or three centuries. While a third shrewdly remarks that Sir Salar Jung by his diplomatic and statesmanlike skill became one of the foremost administrators in India, and by his noble endeavours contributed to the prosperity of Hyderabad.

HIS FORBEARS.

Since the last days of the Bahmini Kingdom, the family to which Sir Salar Jung belonged had taken a leading part in the affairs of the Deccan. Their loyalty first to the Adil Shahis, then to the Moghul

Emperors, and lastly to the Nizams, was as unflinching as it was sincere and true. The ancestors of Salar Jung belonged to a noble family of Medina. Shaikh Ovais Karani was the first of the line to leave his native country and settle in India. His son held high and responsible offices in the Bijapur Court. It was the time when the Moghul Emperors were forcing their way to the Deccan; the Shaikh's grandson offered his services to the Emperor of Delhi, who appointed him to the Dewani of Shajahanabad and Kashmir. His son, Mohamed Taki, was the first representative of the family to come in contact with Asaf Jah Nizam-ul-Mulk who, at the dissolution of the Moghul Empire, was trying to found a kingdom for himself in the south. Mohammed Taki's son, Shamsuddin, was a great favourite of the first Nizam; his command was in the time of Nizam Salabat Jung increased to 7,000 foot and 7,000 horse with the title of Nawab Munir-ul-Mulk. He was subsequently made the Dewan for the Subahs of the Deccan. Shamsuddin's grandson, Munir-ul-Mulk II married the daughter of Mir Alum, who was the Prime Minister to Nizam Sikandar Jah from 1804 to 1808, and who led the Hyderabad contingent forces to Seringapatam in 1799. On Mir Alum's death in 1808, Munir-ul-Mulk II became the Prime Minister, and held office for 23 years. He had two sons, of whom the elder was Sir Jalar Jung's father; the younger son, Seraj-ul-Mulk, was Prime Minister of Hyderabad from 1851 to 1853. And when he died,

Salar Jung was elevated to the position held by many of his ancestors in Hyderabad at the early age of 24.

EARLY LIFE.

Nawab Mir Turab Ali Khan, Salar Jung, Siraj-ud-Dowla, Mukhtar-ul-Mulk, D.C.L., G.C.S.I., (to give him his full name and titles) was born on the 2nd January 1829. While an infant he lost his father, and when four years old his grandfather, Munir-ul-Mulk II, died leaving the boy in sole charge of his second son, Seraj-ul-Mulk. There is a story related which shows the great affection which Munir-ul-Mulk II had towards young Salar Jung. The latter had an attack of typhoid fever, and for many days his condition was considered to be critical. Thereupon his grandfather, like Baber of old, performed the ceremony which is known among Mussalmans as Tassaduk, and prayed that any evil which might befall the child might be transferred to him, and that if it was the will of God that Salar Jung should die, he prayed that his own life might be taken. Strange to say the boy recovered and the grandfather fell ill and died. The guardianship of the boy therefore fell on his uncle, Seraj-ul-Mulk.

Salar Jung's education till he was thirteen was not regular and continuous. His early training can scarcely be said to have made him fit for the high and responsible position which he was called upon to fill in after life. He was weak, and the pecuniary and other troubles of his family apparently obscured all his future hopes. His grandfather, Munir-ul-Mulk

II had left debts to the extent of 25 lakhs and the then Nizam, H. H. Nasir-ud-Dowla, paid off the debts of his Minister, and took possession of the greater portion of the family estates as security. However Seraj-ul-Mulk cheerfully performed the trust confided to him and gave his nephew such education as was thought fit for a scion of a noble family at Hyderabad. Salar Jung read Persian and Arabic under a private tutor for nearly seven years. The teaching of English was not then in vogue at Hyderabad ; and Salar Jung began to learn this languge when he was 19 years. He worked at it for half an hour every day under an Eurasian private teacher, later on he pursued the study so assiduously till he came to know English as well as his mother-tongue. Towards the end of his life he became a good English speaker, and the testimony borne by Sir Monier Williams is well worth repeating here :—" I conversed with both these great Ministers (Sir Salar Jung and Sir T. Madhava Row) not long since in their own houses and found them capable of talking on all subjects in as good English as my own."

As a boy Salar Jung was fond of riding, and had had many narrow escapes. His uncle had a pet giraffe, and it was Salar Jung's delight to bestride it to the great astonishment of his awe-struck attendants. From his early days, Salar Jung imbued business habits of a very high degree through the exertions of his grandmother. The accounts which the old lady received from her Jaghir villages were sent to Salar Jung, and he had to verify them with the help of the clerks and explain everything in detail to his grandmother—a task which young Salar found by no means easy.

In 1847, Salar Jung was appointed as the Taluqdar (Collector) of some Telingana Districts, which till then were managed by an Englishman named Mr. Deighton. He was thus early brought into contact with the administration of the State, and he found no difficulty in mastering the system of land revenue introduced by his predecessor, and worked it out satisfactorily during the eight months he was in office. By this time the Nizam restored some of the family Jaghirs to Seraj-ul-Mulk, who lost no time to appoint Salar Jung for looking after them. For five years he worked hard to improve the condition of his estates while at the same time to increase their revenue. When in independent charge of his family Jaghirs, he moulded and shaped the high administrative capacity, which he showed in such unmistakable manner in after life.

PRIME MINISTER.

Seraj-ul-Mulk died on 26th April 1853, and as is usual in the then Hyderabad affairs, a political *impasse* intervened. The choice of a Minister became a matter of perplexity to the Nizam. Of the available candidates, the one whom the Nizam least favoured was Salar Jung. The latter was only 24 years old, and he was the nephew of the Minister who negotiated and concluded the treaty by which Berar was transferred to the English control. Salar Jung's candidature was however supported by Lala Bahadur (the State Record-Keeper) and two other favourites of the Nizam. "It is not a Minister," they said to the Nizam, "but your prestige that governs. Siraj-ul-Mulk conducted the administration through the subordinate departments. Lala Bahadur, who did every thing, will as before conduct the affairs of the administration for Salar Jung." Such arguments did not miss the mark, and the favourites won the day. Salar Jung was invested with the office of Minister in full Durbar on the 31st of May 1853. How well Salar Jung knew the difficulties of his new position is seen from the following extract from a letter to a friend of his in England on his accession to power:—

> Without any solicitation on my part or my grandmother's His Highness was pleased to confer the office of Dewan on me at the Durbar the day before yesterday (31st May). I should have been quite content to remain in unmolested possession of my uncle's Jaghirs were it possible without the cares which such an office would impose upon me, especially in the present critical state of affairs here, and I was advised by friends, European and Native, and with too much appearance of truth to reject the advice, that if I declined the office, myself and family would be utterly ruined . . . I shall therefore do my best with God's help to restore some order in the affairs of this country, and endeavour to extricate the government from its embarrassments.

The country was indeed in a deplorable state. The preceding ten years were marked by a series of administrative and financial adversities. Salar Jung's predecessor left a heritage which no statesman could envy. The administrative capacity of the man was put to the greatest test, and it may be affirmed that the new Minister successfully tided over the strain and worry attendant on those who bring order out of utter confusion.

Since his accession to power up to the outbreak of the Sepoy Mutiny in 1857, he found means to introduce many reforms in the State, and this made him very unpopular with those who counted that his youth would be a safeguard for their own private aggrandizement. The very first to quarrel with the young Minister was Lala Bahadur who, experienced as he was in Hyderabad affairs, tried his best to oust him from office. Again and again the prospect of dismissal seemed imminent: but the Nizam had no other subject as capable, upright, and loyal as Salar Jung. As Mr. Sorabji Jehangir has pointed out in his *Representative Men of India*:

> Sir Salar Jung had to wage amidst unparalleled difficulties, prolonged and at times disheartening battles with abuses which had grown hoary with age and whose dimensions were in proportion to the extent of the unwiedly state in which they existed, demanding all the resources of a superior and acute intellect, a conciliatory but firm disposition, administrative prudence and foresight of the highest order, and an intimate acquaintance with human nature, Sir Salar Jung was endowed with these attributes in such a marked degree as to stamp him as an Indian statesman of the highest eminence.

Nor were opportunities for the exercise of his statesmanship wanting.

THE SEPOY MUTINY, 1857.

For in May 1857, the great Sepoy Mutiny broke out near Delhi, and all Mussalmans in Southern India turned their eyes towards the Nizam's capital. The rebellion spread like wild fire in the North. Hyderabad filled with a large population who had only recently been brought under one settled government, and who cherished the memory of the great Imperial House of Baber, was showing its sympathy with the Sepoys, who espoused the cause of the Moghul Emperor at Delhi. Wildest rumours of the dire peril, to which the British were exposed in Hindustan having reached Hyderabad from the north, the city Mohammedans were plunged in a state of intense excitement. Some openly manifested their displeasure to the British Government. The city people assembled in large numbers in the streets clamouring for war against the English.

At such a critical moment the Nizam Nasir-ud-Dowla died; and great fears were therefore entertained in responsible quarters regarding the issue of events at Hyderabad. Salar Jung was then only four years in office, and he so well gauged the situation that he firmly and persistently adhered himself to the definite policy of seeing that Hyderabad did not join in the general revolt, and thus extend the disaffected area far down to the south. He was a Mohammedan and serving a Mohammedan State: to him it was "a trial, the tension and force of which could never be understood by a European and a Christian."

A new Nizam was placed on the Masnad without any loss of time; and the Resident on returning from the installation ceremony found a telegram from the Governor-General announcing the fall of Delhi. He sent for Salar Jung at once, and communicated the news to him. The Minister replied that the news had been known in the city three days ago. To many unacquainted with British resources, the fall of Delhi was synonymous with the destruction of the British *Raj* in India. If Salar Jung had ever wanted to be disloyal to the British Government, he had the best opportunity of disclosing his motive when information reached him about the success of the mutineers at Delhi. What would have been the fate of the British officers assembled in the Nizam's palace on the Durbar day if Salar Jung had only given any sign to show that he sympathised with the mutineers!

The Minister, however, could not keep in check the excited mob in the city. On June 12th, there were found posted on the walls of all conspicuous places, placards with incitements to sedition signed by orthodox Moulvies calling upon the Faithful to be ready to fight against the English. The next day a coloured flag was hoisted at the chief Mosque of the city, and the excited people mostly of the lower orders gathered round it. Two men tried to make a stir by interrupting the preacher, and shouting out: "Why do you not preach the rising of the holy standard?" upon which the cries of "Deen," "Deen" (for the Faith) were heard, and it had no response as the respectable people held aloof from such a scene. The Moulvie was arrested, and the crowds were dispersed by the Minister's orders. A fakir, while openly preaching a Jihad against the English, was promptly arrested and placed in confinement with the aid of a few faithful Arabs, who maintained order in the city. and strict instructions were issued to the guards at the city gate to fire on anyone who attempted to incite the people against the English. "These energeitc measures," says a military officer, "saved South India, for had the people at Hyderabad risen against us, the Mohammedan population of Madras would, it was well-known at the Residency, have followed their example."

The situation was so critical that the Governor of Bombay telegraphed to the Resident at Hyderabad: "If the Nizam goes, all is lost." There was certainly a panic in the above message, but Englishmen in India felt a keen sense of relief when it was found that the Nizam did not and would not go. "Had the Nizam," says Colonel Briggs, "untried as he then was, sided the movement or even openly avowed his sympathy with the mutineers, there can be no doubt that the whole of Southern India would have been in a blaze." But wiser counsels prevailed at the Nizam's Durbar, and Salar Jung's statesmanship saved the situation.

The British Residency at Hyderabad is situated very near the busy quarter of the city and is far removed from the cantonment of Secunderabad. A body of 500 Rohillas with 4,000 disaffected people led by two leaders, Torabazkhan, and Allauddin, marched and attacked the Residency, which was not then protected by any fortifications. The Minister knew of the projected attack, and gave a timely warning to the Resident, Colonel Davidson, who at once ordered for some reinforcements from Secunderabad. On their arrival, they were joined by a party of Arabs sent by Salar Jung. These troops repulsed the mutineers' attack: one of the leaders was shot dead, and several others taken prisoners and deported. Some of the ringleaders were executed, and others fled to Hyderabad with the hope that the Nizam's government would protect them. But the Minister issued orders to hand over the mutineers to the Resident for necessary punishment. A large concourse of people assembled at the chief Mosque with a view to send a deputation of some Moulvies to the Nizam to expound the duties of a Mussalman Sovereign, and persuade him to order the release of all the sepoys who had been imprisoned for attacking the Residency. But it was soon dispersed; a mob collected near the Residency, and broke open two of its gates. Before further injury could be done, fire was opened on them and they were driven away.

Much criticism was levelled against the Resident, Colonel Davidson, for his continued occupation of the Residency in these critical times. But like a true Englishman he said: "I have taken a fancy to lay my bones at Hyderabad. If open force be used I will fight to the last." Besides he added that the non-occupation of the Residency at that time "would have been looked upon as a sign of fear, and the loyal Minister, Salar Jung, would have been left to his fate." But many years after the mutiny, Salar Jung said with characteristic modesty that, but for the courage and hope given by the Residency Officers, he would not have triumphed over the crisis so successfully.

> I have often been complimented as the Saviour of India, he wrote, "but if I was able to be of any use to my Sovereign, and to Her Majesty's Empire in India, the credit of it is entirely due to General Thornhill. Had not General Thornhill been at Hyderabad, I tremble to think what might have become of the Nizam, of the Residency, and of myself. Colonel Davidson was an excellent man and was in every way fitted for the high position he held; but the magnitude of the emergency had taken him so completely by surprise that had it not been for the strong will and stout heart of General Thornhill, he would never in my opinion have tided over the troubles. As for myself, it was entirely General Thornhill's constant counsel and support that kept up my courage and enabled me finally to triumph over the disaffection with which the whole city seemed to be enveloped to an extent which few British officers have any conception of. Next to General Thornhill, though not to be compared with him in point of importance, were the services of General Briggs. His strong arm and undaunted courage were of the greatest service in saving the Residency when it was attacked by the mutinous rabble. I never felt so discouraged in my life as when I saw the services of these two officers passed over without notice.

Sir Richard Temple characterised his services to the British Government on this occasion as "simply priceless." The Governor-General in Council informed him that "the ability, courage, and firmness with which he had discharged his duty to the Nizam and to the British Government entitled him to the most cordial thanks of the Government of India."

In July 1860, the Nizam was presented with British manufactures valued at a lakh of rupees, and his minister articles worth thirty thousand. The districts of Raichur and Dharaseo were restored to the Nizam, and the petty State of Shorapur was added to the Nizam's territory.

INTRIGUES AGAINST HIM.

The attitude which Sir Salar Jung wisely followed during the Mutiny brought on him much unpopularity. A determined attack on his life was made on March 15th, 1859, when he was leaving the Nizam's Durbar Hall with the Resident. A Rohilla, said to have been from Hindustan, discharged a loaded carbine which, though missing the mark, hit one of the Minister's retinue. The assailant then rushed on the Minister with a drawn sword; but fortunately he was overpowered by the Nizam's guards who cut him down immediately.

Salar Jung's passion for reforms in the administration of the State was well-known. But Hyderabadees were slow to recognise it: he grew more and more unpopular with them. In 1861, an attempt was made to remove him from office. The Nizam was made to believe that the Resident was anxious to dismiss Salar Jung. The Nizam in an interview with the Resident made him understand that he would gladly dismiss the Minister. The Resident was surprised to hear the proposal, and dissuaded the Nizam from entertaining any such idea. The conspiracy against Salar Jung was exposed, and the Minister was once again in the good graces of his master. It is said that the Nizam's harem contributed not a little to this change of attitude between His Highness and his Minister. These ladies were, since Salar Jung was made Minister, getting their pensions and allowances regularly—a fact of very rare occurrence in the administrations of the previous Ministers. They in a body petitioned to His Highness pointing out how successful Salar Jung had been as a Minister and threatened in the event of a change some violence to his successor. That Salar Jung had been restored to confidence was evidenced by the presentation of some fine jewels to him by the Nizam at the Ead Durbar; and when the Minister had a fall from his horse, the Nizam was so glad of his recovery that he caused a large some of money to be given away to the poor as a thanks-offering.

In 1866, Her Majesty Queen Victoria conferred upon him the title of the Knight Commander of the Star of India. A year later, once again the relations between the Nizam and his Minister were strained. The Government of India proposed a treaty for the mutual extradition of certain criminals. The Nizam suspected that it was an encroachment on his power, and believed that the Minister was responsible for it. He made no secret of his dissatisfaction with him. At this time one of the two officials whose business it was to act as confidential Vakil between the Nizam and his Minister died. His Highness lost no time in appointing Laskar Jung, a bitter personal enemy of the Minister, to the post. Salar Jung resigned: and the Resident, Sir George Yule, sought an interview with the Nizam, who was much perturbed at what he called his Minister's pride. The Minister threatened to resign more than once, and this His Highness could not stand. He wished that Salar Jung had been more humble and acted as his servant. Salar Jung being persuaded to apologise in a most humble way did so, much to the gratification of his Highness who permitted him to continue in office.

Salar Jung had to clear his course in "the face of a permanent opposition offered by jealous and powerful enemies, and of the most vexatious and senseless interference on the part of his sovereign." "He was kept by the Nizam," writes Sir Richard Temple,

> in a state of thraldom and was almost a prisoner in his own house, unable to move beyond the outer gates of his court-yard without his master's permission. If he wished to give a social entertainment in his summer house outside the city, or attend a parade of British troops, or have an interview with the Resident, he must ask leave, not as a mere formality, but as a request that might be refused or which would be grudgingly granted. I had much business with him, and its transaction was difficult, because to have seen him often would have renewed the Nizam's jealousy, and to have sent him papers in despatch boxes would have been open to the same objection. He did not seem to regard this in the light of a personal grievance as he shared the reverence his countrymen felt for their master. He was seldom admitted to the Nizam's presence, and when he was, he used to be almost pale from agitation. He must have been quite hopeless of conciliating his master, yet he was perfectly loyal, and would have undergone any labour for the welfare of his liege.

In January 1868, another attempt was made on the Minister's life while he was proceeding to the Nizam's palace to attend the Ead Durbar. Two shots were fired at him—one of which went so close as to graze his turban, and the other wounded an attendant. The Nizam warmly congratulated his Minister on his escape, and issued strict orders regulating the possession of firearms by the people.

The would-be assassin proved to be one who had been prejudiced by Salar Jung's administrative measures.

VISIT TO EUROPE.

In 1875, His Royal Highness the Prince of Wales (afterwards King Edward VII) came to India: and among the nobles that formed his suite was the Duke of Sutherland. The Duke paid a visit to Hyderabad as the guest of Sir Salar Jung. When leaving he pressed the great Minister to visit England. Salar Jung accepted the invitation and visited Europe in the summer of 1876. He could not have been quite ignorant of the sort of reception he would meet in England. People would not forget his invaluable services during the Mutiny: his administrative ability and statesmanship were wafted across to distant lands: and his kind and genial personality made him an acceptable friend to many an Englishman.

Lord Lytton, who had succeeded Lord Northbrook as Viceroy of India, landed in Bombay on the 7th April 1876. Salar Jung was present at his reception at the Bombay Dockyards. The next day he sailed for Europe, reaching Rome on the 5th of May. Sir Salar paid a visit to the late King, Victor Emmanuel, at the Quirinal. Three days later, the Pope received him in audience at the Vatican and expressed his gratitude for the facilities allowed to Catholics in the Hyderabad State. After visiting Rome, Naples, and some of the other chief cities of Italy, the party reached Paris on the 13th of May.

Page 16.

SIR SALAR JUNG

Here, Sir Salar was detained for nearly a fortnight owing to an unpleasant accident. On the very evening of his arrival at the Grand Hotel, he slipped on the stairs which resulted in a fractured thigh bone. He suffered great bodily pain not to speak of the vexation of an enforced stay in his rooms, but in spite of it he persevered, says a visitor to him,

> with the equanimity and resignation characteristic of men of his stamp, nationality and faith; but the frustration of his plans would have affected the nerves of any other man . . . Nothing however in Sir Salar Jung's countenance betrayed either pain or anxiety of any kind. Since Sir Salar Jung has kept to his room, none of his attendants (and they were 52) has gone outside the Hotel—not that they are indifferent to sight-seeing, for at Naples, Rome, and Venice they went to look at everything in spite of the crowds which followed and incommoded them. One of them told me that since Sir Salar Jung's arrival in Paris, he has been receiving 20 letters a day in French and English making the strangest applications. Some beg for alms giving a long narrative of more or less voracious misfortunes; others offer all sorts of inventions, merchandise, articles of luxury and fancy; others again ask for an interview; others forward gushing verses expressing regret at his accident; others offer him amusements and recreations of all kinds; not to speak of tailors, shirt-makers, hatters, and shoemakers who not satisfied with writing are constantly stepping into the corridors forcing their cards, prospectuses and samples into the hands, the pockets and almost the turbans of the servants they encounter. Their recital much amused Sir Salar Jung, who however exhibited great satisfaction when informed that this was a Parisian persecution from which he would be free in London. He appears impatient to arrive there, and listens with great interest when the conversation turns upon London or England.

By the end of May he recovered so far as to travel and on 1st June 1876, he left Paris for England and landed at Folkestone, where the Duke of Sutherland was the first to welcome him to the English shores. Sir Salar who was still unable to walk was carried ashore by a party of English sailors, and the Mayor of Folkestone read an Address of Welcome. From that day till he left England invitations, honours and addresses poured thick on him: and the English Press kept up a never-ending chorus of praise of the worth of the great Indian on a visit to England. One of the leading London journals remarked:—

> Our new guest is the man who, when Delhi had fallen, and our power was for a moment in the balance, saved Southern India for England. Even if Southern India had revolted it is possible that by profuse expenditure of men and money we might have conquered it back again, and all the rest of India as well. But, Sir Salar Jung spared us the expenditure of countless lives, and countless millions; and if there was a clear occasion for acknowledging in a fitting manner an inestimable service, such an occasion is presented by the arrival in England of the Prime Minister of the Nizam.

But his stay was made less pleasant owing to the unfortunate accident at Paris, and while confined to his rooms at London, he was visited by the Prince of Wales (King Edward VII), and other members of the Royal Family. On June 20th, the Prince of Wales gave a banquet in Salar Jung's honour when the leading noblemen, statesmen, and old Indian officials were invited to meet him. Next day he went over to Oxford, where the honorary degree of D. C. L. was conferred upon him by the University. On July 3rd, Sir Salar Jung was presented to H. M. Queen Victoria by the Marquis of Salisbury at the Windsor Castle, where he dined with the Queen and other members of the Royal Family. He spent the next day in visiting the Woolwich Arsenal and the

London Docks. On 5th July Sir Salar Jung and his suite attended the State Ball at the Buckingham Palace, and the next day the Marquis of Salisbury (the then Secretary of State for India) entertained him at dinner. Later on Sir Salar had the honour of giving a dinner party at his temporary residence in Piccadilly to H. R. H. the Prince of Wales. Before Sir Salar Jung left London for Trentham, the East India Association presented him with an address recounting his services during the Mutiny and expressing satisfaction at the way in which the various reforms were introduced by him in the Nizam's State. After spending a pleasant week at Trentham Hall with the Duke of Sutherland, Sir Salar Jung travelled over to Scotland, where he received deputations from the Town Councils of Inverness, Dingwall, Tain and Wick. Later on he went to Edinburgh where he and his party drove through the streets seeing all the places of interest in that ancient city.

He returned to London on the 22nd and three days later a special meeting of the Court of Common Council was held at the Guildhall to present Sir Salar Jung with the Freedom of the City of London. The Lord Mayor proposed the toast of Sir Salar Jung and eulogised his services to the Nizam and the English. On July 26th, Sir Salar received deputations from the Manchester Corporation and the Manchester Chamber of Commerce, and owing to ill health had to decline invitations to visit Liverpool and Manchester. His tour in England was like a triumphal march and as one writer says:

> He was entertained by the highest in the land, and yet his success does not seem to turn his head in any way. The house he hired for the occasion, his servants and the whole establishment have been kept up on an almost princely scale but without the slightest ostentation or attempt at vulgar show. His manner is so like that of a well-bred English gentleman that many people cannot understand how or where a native of India who has never been in England seems to have picked up what seems to have been a kind of second nature with Sir Salar.

Salar Jung after a stay of two months in England left London for Paris on his return journey. He was much struck with the marvels of the French capital: but the severe aspect, and the incessant activity of London (as contrasted with the pleasures of Paris) appealed to his imagination.

Leaving Paris on the 3rd August, Sir Salar visited Turin and Milan and took the steamer to India from Brindisi, and arrived at Bombay after an absence of nearly four months. He was not quite recovered from the effects of his accident, and so he was helped over the side of the steamer, when the crew and the passengers cheered him to their utmost capacity. How much the English sailors of the day knew and appreciated Sir Salar is evidenced by the following incident: the steamer conveying Salar Jung and his suite passed a troopship. As soon as the soldiers and sailors knew who was on board they swarmed on to the deck and into the rigging and "three cheers for Salar Jung, the Saviour of India" was the cry followed by such enthusiastic hurrahs which took a long time to subside.

He arrived at Hyderabad on the 26th of August, and was received with the liveliest demonstrations of affection by all classes of people.

THE BERAR QUESTION

H. H. The Nizam Afzul-ud-Dowlah died on the 26th February 1869, and his son Mahbub Ali Khan aged about three years, was placed on the Masnad. Salar Jung and Shams-ul-Umarah—the premier noblemen of the State—were made co-Regents during the minority of the Nizam, and there seemed every prospect of a smooth sailing in the State's progress towards administrative efficiency. But Sir Salar's attitude towards the Berar question brought him in conflict with more than one Viceroy. He fostered so passionate a desire for the restoration of Berar to the Nizam that he expressed his object in a letter to Lord Northbrook:—"Either I must recover Berar or I must be convinced of the justice of the reasons for withholding it or—I must die." Berar had been nominally in the Nizam's possession since 1724, and the dimensions of the province were repeatedly curtailed by grants to the Peshwas of Poona, who laterly were even empowered to collect taxes from the people. Since 1804, the Nizam had the sole authority over the country, but owing to its unsettled state it remained the rendezvous of the lawless. It had dwindled with every political change till in the middle of the last century it was not the Berar of the early Nizams, far less the Imperial Subah of that name. In 1853, upwards of 45 lakhs of rupees became due to the British Government for the maintenance of the Hyderabad contingent. Lord Dalhousie, the then Governor-General, instructed the Resident to ask the Nizam territorial guarantee for the regular payment of the contingent charges, and the liquidation of the debt. After much negotiations a treaty was drawn up, by which districts yielding an annual gross revenue of 50 lakhs were assigned to the British. These included Berar, the Raichur Doab and Dharaseo district. The treaty was signed on the 21st April 1853; and two weeks later Salar Jung was appointed Prime Minister. Ever since he was not at ease over this subject and had two motives to guide him. "The solemn injunctions of his two last sovereigns," says a writer, "had made it a duty of the most sacred obligation upon him to seek its accomplishment. The assignment which was effected in the last hours of his uncle (Nawab Seraj-ul-Mulk) had left a reproach on his family in the eyes both of the sovereign and the people of the country."

In 1866, the Minister addressed a communication to the British Government on behalf of the Nizam claiming the restoration of Berar. The request was not complied with, and Salar Jung was told that "the spirit of extravagant assertion which pervades Sir Salar Jung's letter, unworthy alike of his princely master's dignity and of his own reputation for enlightened statesmanship, leaves the Governor-General in Council no alternative but to require that the future communications of the Hyderabad Durbar shall be framed in a tone more serious and circumspect." There was still hope, and it was based on the statement of the Government of India that the restitution of Berar must remain an impossibility so long as satisfactory arrangements were not made for the regular payment of the Hyderabad contingent from some other source. When the Minister had effected many administrative reforms in the State, he was able to point out "a source" to the British. In 1872, Salar Jung offered to deposit with the Government of India in lieu of Berar, the sum of 12 crores of rupees, the interest on which would be sufficient to meet the cost of the contingent. The Minister noted that this scheme will not only furnish a proper security but also be a deposit of His Highness' treasure, which would enable the Government to carry on some public works out of that source, and also reduce the cost of management. The Government of India were unable to entertain such a proposal since "a territorial guarantee was the fundamental principle of the treaties of 1853 and 1860." After much correspondence, Salar Jung was informed that the Resident would not receive for transmission any correspondence on the subject in future. Whereupon the Regents forwarded an appeal direct to the Secretary of State for India. While in England it is said that Salar Jung influenced a number of British politicians to recognise the justice of his claim. The Secretary of State (Lord Salisbury) affirmed that Berar was not ceded to the British, and that the Nizam's sovereignty over the assigned districts remained unimpaired. His despatch to the Viceroy concluded as follows:—

> Your Excellency has noticed the inconvenience of discussing questions of this kind while the Nizam, on whose behalf they are professedly raised, is himself a minor. In this opinion I entirely concur.

Early in 1877, the co-Regents declared in writing that "they fully accepted the decision of the Secretary of State as conveyed in the above despatch, and would take no steps whatever in the matter during the minority of "His Highness." But Salar Jung was not spared till the young Nizam Mahbub Ali Khan came of age and assumed the reins of government. The subject was therefore shelved till it was re-opened in 1902 by Lord Curzon, when by a new treaty Berar was ceded in perpetuity to the British Government on the latter paying to the Nizam 25 lakhs of rupees per annum.

HIS REFORMS

To sketch the reforms introduced by Sir Salar Jung in the State, is to describe the history of Hyderabad for nearly thirty years. The State at the time of his accession to power had been compared to the England of the Stuarts. The Revenue Administration was in the most deplorable state and the accounts showed a sum of only 18 lakhs of rupees as the net revenue available to the government after paying the troops in the State service. The collection of revenue was carried on what was known as the contract system. The territory was parcelled out for a certain period among contractors called Taluqdars, who were paid at a definite rate for the cost of management. Their sole aim was to make as much money as possible when in power, and therefore much oppression and mismanagement prevailed. Besides certain districts where in the hands of Arabs who had advanced money to the State, and who were empowered to collect the revenue of those districts in repayment of the loans made.

Sir Salar Jung's attentions was first drawn to the maladministration of the Revenue Department. A court was established to adjudicate the claims of the Arabs: and all turbulent men were arrested and punished either by deportation or imprisonment by the Arab Zamindars, whose support was an asset to the youthful Minister. As much of the debts as the finances of the State could allow were disbursed to the creditors. By 1854, Salar Jung was able to recover mortgaged lands yielding a revenue of 40 lakhs, and to disband nearly 4,000 Arabs and Pathans from the State service. The old Taluqdars were forced to submit their resignations, and trustworthy persons were appointed in their places.

In 1856, a Central Treasury was established at Hyderabad, to which all Revenue collections were transmitted. Vexatious transit duties and other minor taxes were abolished. The country was for administrative purposes divided into four parts; and Salar Jung took under his charge the largest division yielding 60 lakhs of revenue.

The traffic in Mahomedan and Hindu children had been going on for a long time, and in 1856, Salar Jung issued a proclamation forbidding the practice under pain of punishment. There were daily robberies and dacoities in the districts; and villages were in many cases looted by armed men. More than once a body of the contingent troops were requisitioned to scare away the besiegers. A special Rohilla Court was established at Hyderabad to try such cases, and several gangs of robbers were imprisoned. There was famine in 1862 and 1866, and Salar Jung took effective measures to relieve the poor and the distressed. In 1867, the Zillabandi system was introduced, and the State was parcelled out into five divisions and seventeen districts.

There was a thorough re-organization of the Judicial, Public Works, Medical, Police and Educational Departments. In the Telugu districts the system of payment in kind was the rule. The Minister abolished it to the great satisfaction of the ryots, and sent a memorandum on the disadvantages of this system to the Famine Commission.

In the beginning of 1882, Salar Jung drew an elaborate scheme for the general management of the administration. This was the last and in some respects the greatest undertaking of the Minister for the benefit of the State. This system was adopted practically *in toto* by his successor, and still remains the basis of administration in the Dominions. To help the Minister, four Moin-ul-Mahams (Departmental

Ministers) were appointed, and elaborate details regarding the powers and working of the Ministers and Secretaries were framed. The Government of India, after a careful and close examination of the scheme, gave it their most hearty and cordial appreciation.

Before Salar Jung's time there were no regular courts throughout the dominions. The Minister established a Court in Hyderabad with a Chief Judge, and four assistant Judges having full powers to try civil and criminal cases. To suppress crime in the districts, *Zilladars* with a fully equipped force were appointed, who either captured or imprisoned all turbulent Rohillas. A special Court to try Thuggee and Dacoity cases was instituted. In 1860, a Court at Hyderabad with a Hindu as its presiding Judge was established to try civil cases among Hindus. Government stamped paper was also introduced; and a stamp office was established in the capital.

Before Salar Jung came into power, the village servants acted as the police; and military troops arrested thieves and dacoits when called upon to do so. Cases of torture were very frequent. In 1865, Salar Jung re-organised the police department. At the head of the administration there was the Inspector-General of Police with *Mohatamims* (Superintendents) and Amins (Inspectors) in charge of districts: the Jamadars and Dafadars worked under them. A Kotwal (Commissioner of Police) was appointed for the Hyderabad city, and the Police Code revised and amended.

In 1875, the Survey department was established on the lines followed in the Bombay Presidency. Education in Hyderabad had been carried on, on the old lines: boys were only taught the Koran and to read and write Persian or Arabic. In 1855, Salar Jung established an Oriental College, where English was taught as an optional subject. Some years later a school was opened in the chief village of each Taluq and one at the headquarters of each District. The department was brought under an Educational Secretary and a Director of Public Instruction. A Civil Engineering College and a Medical School were opened. In a short time the educational charges of the State rose to nearly a lakh and half. In 1880, the school at Chadderghet (in Hyderabad) was raised to the status of a College, and affiliated to the Madras University. With a view to encourage the nobles of the State to study the English language, the Madras-Aliza was instituted which was subsequently re-organised and named the Nizam's College. To train teachers for schools, a normal school was established; and five divisional inspectors were appointed for supervision of the schools in the district.

There was also a re-organization of the Public Works Deparment. Many tanks were repaired, roads and district communications were improved, and several government buildings were erected. In 1874, the Hyderabad-Wadi Railway was completed, and to Salar Jung thus belongs the credit of connecting the Nizam's capital with Madras and Bombay. In 1862, regular postal communication between the capital and the districts was established. There were many mints in the State, but Salar Jung withdrew all the coins and established a State mint at Hyderabad. The Abkari Department showed an increased revenue owing to the suppression of illicit manufacture, and the income of the Customs Department rose to nearly 40 lakhs. Municipalities were established at Hyderabad, Aurangabad, Raichur and Gulburga, where the management was effected by a Council consisting of official and non-official members. When Salar Jung became Prime Minister, the military cost of the State per annum was nearly 80 lakhs; but at the time of his death it was reduced to nearly 20 lakhs. Indeed it would take us far afield to measure all the reforms he introduced in remodelling a State like Hyderabad. Suffice to say that he is in a sense the maker of the modern Hyderabad.

CONCLUSION

In 1871, the Government of India bestowed on Salar Jung the distinction of the Grand Commander of the Star of India; and he received at the Imperial Assembly at Delhi on 1st January 1877, a salute of 17 guns as a mark of personal distinction. Nawab Shams-ul-Umarah died in 1879, and Nawab Vikar-ul-Umarah became the co-Regent, whose death two years later left Sir Salar Jung as the sole Regent of Hyderabad.

In the summer of 1882, Sir Salar Jung paid a visit to Simla to discuss in person certain administrative questions of the State and to arrange for the tour of the young Nizam to Europe in the following year. His stay was very brief not exceeding eight days, and yet he left behind him a very good impression in the highest society that was gathered together in the summer capital of the Government of India. In January 1883, the Regent accompanied the young Nizam on a tour to Raichur, Gulburga and Aurangabad. On return to Hyderabad, arrangements were being made for the forthcoming visit of H. H. the Nizam to Europe: but to the great sorrow of all, Sir Salar Jung died of cholera on the 8th February 1883.

Telegrams and letters of condolence poured in from different parts of India and the United Kingdom. His Excellency Lord Ripon telegraphed a message from the Queen expressive of Her Majesty's grief at the sad news, and also added an expression of his own sympathy. The news of Sir Salar's demise was published in an extra-ordinary issue of the *Gazette of India* edged with a deep black border: "With a feeling of deep regret the Governor-General in Council announces the death on the evening of the 8th instant from cholera of His Excellency Nawab Sir Salar Jung, G.C.S.I., Regent and Minister of the Hyderabad State. By this unhappy event the British Government has lost an exprienced and enlightened friend, H. H. The Nizam a wise and faithful servant, and the Indian community one of its most distinguished representatives." How deeply his loss was felt by all classes of people is to be seen from the following extract from the Resident's letter to the Government of India:—

> I do not know how to express the concern and sorrow which Sir Salar Jung's death has caused to every one here. At present the sense of personal bereavement seems to outweigh the feeling of public loss. Every British Officer who has had the honour of his acquaintance feels his death as he would that of a friend of many years. Those who had the pleasure to serve under him will mourn the kindest, the most considerate of masters. The British Government will lament the death of one whose loyalty and attachment to it, based as they were on an intelligent appreciation of the true interests of the Hyderabad State, were only second to his loyalty and attachment to his own sovereign. Most of all, His Highness for whom Sir Salar Jung had so laboured must grieve his loss. No master had ever a more devoted servant. It seems so hard that he should have passed away before he could see the sovereign whose interests he had so striven for, on the throne.

Sir Salar Jung's appearance was very striking. He was of medium height and slenderly built, and yet he had a commanding presence. His frame though not robust was wiry. He was simple in his habits. His dress was never gaudy, and in his time he was known as the best dressed Indian. He was unostentatious and seldom wore jewellery save on State occasions. He was of free and easy manners, and was easily accessible. Though a Shiah, he did not evince any partiality to one sect or another, and was a thorough liberal with respect to religion. He did not however omit any of the more binding injunctions of the Muslim faith, and it was very seldom that he neglected his daily prayers or the fasts prescribed to be observed in the month of Ramzan.

The Minister left two daughters, and two sons—Mir Liak Ali Khan, and Mir Saadut Ali Khan: the former was the second Salar Jung, and was the Prime Minister of Hyderabad from 1884 to 1887, and the latter a Member of the Council of State and an acting Prime Minister during his brother's absence on tour. His son, Nawab Mir Yusuf Ali Khan Salar Jung III succeeded to the post held so brilliantly by several of his ancestors in 1912, soon after the accession of the present Nizam to the throne of Hyderabad. He however resigned his high office on the 1st of December 1914, that he might take a trip to Europe for the sake of his health. The office of Ministry has since been retained in the hands of H. H. the Nizam himself.

Page 33.

MAHARAJAH JANG BAHADUR

Maharajah Jang Bahadur of Nepal.

MAHARAJAH JANG BAHADUR KANWAR RANA, Prime Minister and Commander-in-Chief of Nepal (1846-1877) can be termed the maker of the modern Kingdom of Nepal. He was well-known to the English as Sir Jang Bahadur, G. C. B., G. C. S. I., owing to his long stay in England in 1850 and to his invaluable services to the English cause in the critical days of the Great Indian Mutiny. In his case, as in that of other great statesmen contemporaries of his, like Sir Salar Jang, and Sir Dinkar Rao, the results of his work have survived him. In his youth he was fiercely barbarous, as suited the then troubled court-politics of Kathmandu; and "even in his old age he retained perhaps a semi-barbaric character." Thus Sir Richard Temple estimates the life and work of that remarkable man :—

When remembrance is borne of the associations in which his youth must have been passed, the awful scenes he witnessed, the massacres in which he participated, the blood he shed—then there is wonder at the moderation and self-control afterwards displayed by him, the discipline enforced by his system, and the public order secured by his stern, yet just, rule. What his feelings may have been originally towards the British no man can now say; but he visited England and returned to Nepal with a conviction from which he never swerved, that it would be well to adhere to the English side, as that was sure to be ultimately victorious. The conduct of the Nepal State during the war of the Mutinies was unsatisfactory on the whole, but there were reasons for fearing that they might have joined the rebellion had it not been for the dissuading voice and restraining hand of Jang Bahadur. (*Men and Events of My Time in India*. 2nd Edition, 1882; pp 308 & 309).

In order to have a right understanding of the personality and work of Jang Bahadur, it is necessary for us to have a clear idea of Nepal and its people, its recent history and polity. Just as Kashmir denotes the geographical extent of the territories of the Maharajah of Jammu and Kashmir, and not the Vale of Kashmir merely, so the term Nepal is used to denote not only the canton of Nepal, but the whole of the extensive dominions of the Gurkhas, covering the entire range of the montane tracts of the southward slopes of the Himalayas as well as a portion of the Tarai belt and stretching from the British territory of Kumaon on the West to Sikkim on the East. The Kingdom has an area of more than 50,000 square miles and comprises the catchment areas of three separate rivers and their affluents, the Ghagra, the Gandak and the Kusi. The bounding mountains of these three great river-basins are Nandadevi, Dhavalagiri, Dayabhang and Kanchanjanga : and from each of these towering pivots there run mighty spurs which form the watersheds between these river-basins. The hill-locked Valley of Nepal is drained by the Bagmati, an affluent of the Ganges and lies between the Gandak and the Kusi basins. "The general character of these mountains is a perpetual succession of vast ridges, with narrow intervening glens, open valleys like that of Nepal being rare." Three longitudinal zones of climate are found in Nepal the lower comprising the sub-montane lowlands; the middle between the Duns and the snow-line; and the upper or alpine. Correspondingly there are three zones of vegetation; the lower region being full of splendid timber trees, such as the *sal*, the banyan and the *pipal*, the central slopes covered with oaks, chestnuts etc; and the upper region producing yews, poplars, hollies, birches, willows etc. The bulk of the inhabitants dwell in the uplands; the spring and autumn are fairly marked; the rainy months from July to August are genial, but the winter is cloudy, damp with rain or snow and disagreeable.

The people are varied in race and origin. In the heights there are the Bhutias, who are Tibetan in race-marks and language, custom and dress. In the central regions we have numerous tribes like the Magars and the Gurungs, the Newars and the Murmis of Nepal proper and the Limbus and the Kirantis of the East. All of these are Mongoloid; and besides there are the Parbatiyas (hill-folk) who are the descendants of the union of Hindus and the hill-women. The central forests and the jungles of the Tarai are inhabited by wild aborigines of whom very little is known. The Parbatiyas, the Magars and the Gurungs form, as the Gurkhas or the Gurkhalis, the dominant race. The chief tribes of the Parbatiyas like the Khas, the Iktharias, the Thakuris, and the Sahis are descendants of Brahmins and Rajputs who were driven into the hills of Western Nepal on the pressure of the Muhammadan invasions and who mixed with the spirited

Buddhist inhabitants. The Khas, or the Parbatiya tribe proper, had their own little kingdom established in the Gurkha Valley to the north-west of the Nepal Valley; and associated with them were the hardy Magars and the Gurungs. These form the military population of the country.

Between the latter and the Khas "there is going on much the same process as formerly obtained in the case of the Brahmins and the Rajputs and the hill-women in general of days gone by, and they also have become Hindus and Parbatiyas."

The people of the Nepal Valley whom the Gurkhas first conquered are the Newars who are the most advanced section of the population and who are either Hindus (Saivamargis) or Buddhists. The Newars have now sunk to a secondary position, but the arts, crafts, trade and agriculture are still wholly in their hands. The Nepal Valley is thus very densely peopled, and its chief towns of Patan, Kathmandu, Kirtipur and Bhatgaon are very populous and crowded—all situated within a few miles of each other.

There are more or less uncertain traditions of the ancient rulers of the valley of which the most important is the *Vamsavali* or Genealogical History of Nepal according to the Buddhistic rescension, written in the Parbatiya with an admixture of Sanskrit and Newari. A copy of this was in the possession of the late Professor Cowell; and a translation made by Munshi Shew Shankar Singh and Pandit Shri Gunanand, has been edited by Surgeon-Major D.

Wright of the Kathmandu Residency (The Cambridge University Press, 1877) supplemented by an introductory sketch of the country and people. It takes us on through the mythological periods and the epochs of the Suryabansi Dynasty and the Thakuri line of Kings, the Karnata Dynasty of Nanya Deva and the Malla Rajas of Kathmandu. The Malla power of the Newars was split up among four branches, ruling respectively at Bhatgaon, Kathmandu, Patan and Kirtipur when Prithvi Narayan Sah, King of the Gurkha Valley conquered it and became master of both Gurkha and Nepal (1765). He overran the country of the Kirantis and the Limbus as far as Sikkim; and he was succeeded in 1775 by his son, Singh Pratap Sah, who in a short reign of three years, increased the borders of the Gurkha kingdom on the west. In 1778 his infant son Ran Bahadur Sah began a long reign. Gurkha politics became from now onwards " one of steady progress as regards arms, and of the disgusting succession of murders and intrigues and atrocious cruelties as regards the court." The army has been always blindly loyal to the constituted authority for the time being, without any sort of distinction as to persons, and hence the Nepal palace revolutions have always been so harmless to the people at large. During Ran Bahadur Sah's minority the queen-mother and the prince's uncle fought 'like cat and dog' for the regency; and sometimes one was in prison, sometimes the other. But " to the honour of both, be it recorded that whichever was out of prison and ruling the kingdom, went to war with all the little neighbours and added canton after canton to Nepal, so that the prince in the nursery took no harm." (Edwardes and Merivale—*Life of Sir Henry Lawrence*: 3rd edition; 1873; pp. 324-325).

In 1791 the Gurkhas entered into a commercial treaty with the English; and in the course of the same year when they were in difficulties with the Chinese, they applied for assistance to Lord Cornwallis. A mission was despatched from Calcutta but it could get nothing substantial beyond another commercial treaty. There was a temporary British Resident at the Nepal Court (1802-03); but gradually the relations became worse between the two states, until finally they went to war in November, 1814. The war was caused mainly by the arrogance of the Gurkhas and their encroachments on British territory; it was ended by the Treaty of Segauli which lost them the greater part of their possessions below the hills. The native chronicler naively states that "a war broke out with the British in the Taryani (Tarai); but depriving them (the British) of wisdom, the Rajah saved his country. Then calling the British gentlemen he made peace with them and allowed them to live near Tambahil." (Wright's *Nepal* p. 265.)

The war was waged in the reign of Girban-Juddha Vikram Sah, the son of Ran Bahadur whose cruelties more than once drove him into exile in

British territory and who was finally killed in a court-brawl in 1807. The new king was a minor; and he was illegitimate to boot; but he was almost the sole survivor out of the barbarous affray that ended in the death, Ran Bahadur being saved by the fidelity of a chief named Bhim Sen Thappa who became regent and ruled the state; and it was Bhim Sen who brought on the Gurkha War of 1814, being puffed up with, the idea that the mountain-fastnesses of the country must prove impregnable to the English. This regent, known usually as General Bhim Sen, was a brave man and a patriot after the Nepalese type. The young king died of small pox soon after the close of the war and was succeeded by an infant son, Rajendra Vikram Sah who ruled until after Jang Bahadur came to power and who was deposed in 1847 in favour of his son Surendra Vikram Sah. Bhim Sen Thappa, the famous general and first Prime Minister of the Sah Dynasty, became the sole power in the state in 1804 and retained authority till 1839. He had to struggle against the jealousy of the queen of the new king and the Pande faction which was the rival claimant to the ministership. But he used his power faithfully and ably; and to this day he is regarded as the first model minister of Nepal history. Bhim Sen died a miserable death in prison, being so tortured and insulted that he cut his own throat. The Pandes now returned to power and held the ministry until "a turn of the wheel in 1843 brought about a great beheading of them, and Matabar

Singh Thappa, nephew to Bhim Sen, became minister." Matabar Singh was a man of mark, possessing the talents, the courage and the vindictiveness of his uncle whose murder he had to avenge. For two years he was in power and took occasion to wreak his vengeance on the Pandes; but he soon became unpopular at court and was treacherously killed by a gunshot in the audience chamber of the King himself. The British Residency's Official Records for 1845 open with the account of the murder of Matabar Singh, "amidst the treacherous cajoleries of the King who afterwards claimed credit for firing the first shot point-blank into his body."

The next year was even more prolific in assassinations and massacres "planned by the queen and the menial of the palace whom she had raised to favour." (Assistant Resident Nicholett's confidential summary, *sub anno* 1846-quoted in W. W. Hunter's *Life of Brian Houghton Hodgson.* pp. 229-230). This murder of Matabar Singh though only one incident in the barbarous history of the Gurkha court, was "the main epic" of the period of the Residentship of Sir Henry Lawrence (1843-45). Jang Bahadur was afterwards regarded as the main actor in this episode. He was a nephew of Matabar Singh; and the British official records of those years frequently mention him as a rising young soldier. He was one of seven brothers, the sons of a *Kaji* or Nepalese official; and soon he rose to prominence, so much so that even his uncle expressed some alarm at the increase of his influence at court and with the army. The Resident Sir Henry Lawrence, mentioned him in his letters as "an intelligent young man, particularly expert in all military matters, but though young in years, profoundly versed in intrigue". After the assassination of Matabar Singh, Jang Bahadur became a prominent member of the Nepal Government, though he was not actually included in the Ministry which was then a sort of coalition of various factious nobles headed by Gagan Singh, one of the chief conspirators and the favourite of the Queen. The King was a mere tool in the hands of the Queen; but shortly afterwards Gagan Singh himself was shot dead in his own house while he was at his devotions. The Rani accused all her enemies in the Ministry and insisted on the King assembling all his ministers and nobles in council in order to find out the assassin. The Queen's party supported by Jang Bahadur and his brothers came heavily armed; but the nobles being summoned in a hurry arrived at the council with no weapons but their own swords. After a stormy debate in which insults and taunts were freely exchanged, Jang Bahadur who had with him the written orders of the Queen, made the signal for the general attack which had been planned beforehand; and in a few minutes 32 of the nobles and more than 100 of the lower ranks were mowed down by the bullets. "The poor King alarmed by the noise of the struggle, mounted his horse and rode off to the Residency. On his return within an hour he found the gutters around the *Kot* (the Council Chamber) filled with the blood of his ministers; and what little power he possessed in the state was gone for ever."

Jang Bahadur, backed up by his brothers and his army, now became after this Kot Massacre, the most powerful man in Nepal; the other Sardars who rebelled against him were again massacred; and in December, the King fled to Benares, while the Rani soon finding herself baulked of her ambition by Jang Bahadur, quickly followed her husband into exile. Several plots were attempted by the exiled King to regain his powers and to assassinate Jang Bahadur. But they all failed, and the only result was that the King was declared by his conduct to have forfeited his right to the throne and his son was proclaimed as the new King. Finally when the royal exile advanced to the Tarai with a small force he was easily attacked and taken prisoner. From this time Jang Bahadur became the undisputed ruler of the land, the old King being a prisoner and the new King being kept under the strictest surveillance and not allowed any power at all. Thus the long record of "plot and counterplot, palace revolution, atrocity and assassination" was ended; and a period of vigorous rule began, "the people at large living meanwhile in complete indifference, satisfied to dwell under a bastard dynasty, and to be controlled *more Indico* by a family of practically hereditary ministers" wielding almost despotic powers.

The Sah Dynasty of Nepal which was thus confined to inglorious obscurity claims its descent from a younger son of the great Mewar dynasty of Udaipur, when that family became scattered after the sack of Chitor by Alau-d-din Khilji in 1303. In the same way the family of Jang Bahadur Kanwar claims "descent from the royal refugees of Mewar, its members having according to their own account, procured the title of Kanwar centuries back from the Rajah of the petty State of Satankote in return for war services." Jang Bahadur's father, Bal Narasinha, was the chief *Kaji* of Nepal and was the person who cut down the murderer of King Ran Bahadur Sah in 1807; and his great grand-father, Ram Kishan Kanwar was the chief lieutenant of Prithvi Narayan Sah, the Gurkha conqueror of Nepal. Jang Bahadur strengthened his position by connecting his family by marriage with the most influential persons in the country. Feeling that he was perfectly secure Jang Bahadur started with a large retinue for England in January, 1850, one of his brothers acting as Prime Minister in his absence. The whole party was much impressed with the power and resources of the English and delighted with the welcome and hospitality they were shown; and the party continued to talk for many years afterwards of all the numerous wonders they beheld. This had a very great effect on Jang Bahadur's attitude towards the British power. Even in 1848, in the course of the Sikh War, he made an offer to the British Resident that he would send eight regiments of Nepal troops to British Assistance. This offer was declined as the Governor-General was suspicious still of the real attitude of the Nepal Government. In 1849 the mother of Prince Dhulip Singh took refuge in Nepal; and this only tended to strengthen the mutual suspicions of the two Governments. But everything was changed after Jang Bahadur's return from England in February, 1851. Shortly after he returned there was a conspiracy against the Minister fomented by one of his own brothers as well as by a brother of the deposed King. The conspirators were arrested and were only saved from death by the intervention of the British Government which consented to retain them as state-prisoners at Allahabad where they were detained for several years.

Jang Bahadur continued in the office of Prime Minister till 1856 when he resigned that post in favour of his brother Ran Bahadur and was himself created Maharaja with power to act as adviser to the King and Prime Minister. At the same time he was given the sovereign right of rule over two provinces. Before this he had waged a two years' war with the Tibetans who had plundered the quinquennial Nepalese embassy to China. After some indefinite triumphs the Nepalese got a treaty by which the Tibetans consented to remit the import duties on goods from Nepal and to permit a Gurkha official to reside in Lhassa to protect the interests of the Nepalese traders.

Shortly before the outbreak of the Mutiny there appeared some symptoms of uneasiness and rebellion in the Nepalese army; but fortunately they were put down without much bloodshed. As soon as intelligence was received at Kathmandu of the Mutiny, the Darbar offered to send troops and even despatched two regiments; but the offer was for the moment declined by the Governor-General and the troops were recalled. It is believed that had the Nepalese troops co-operated, the massacre at Cawnpore would have never occurred. This spontaneous offer of help is thus appreciated by Colonel Malleson:

The independent position occupied by Nepal, the known ability of the man, who though only prime minister, wielded all real authority in the country, the certainty that the overthrow of the British could scarcely fail to offer great opportunities to an able general commanding a compact and well-disciplined army, gave to Jang Bahadur's proposal the appearance of being inspired by a pure and generous friendship. *History of the Indian Mutiny. Vol. IV. cabinet edition, 1889; p. 182.)*

Towards the end of June Lord Canning had to accept Jang Bahadur's offer; and within a few weeks 4000 Nepalese troops had restored order in Azamgarh and its vicinity. In December, Jang Bahadur who had meanwhile reassumed the office of Prime Minister, himself set out with an army of 8,000 men and beating down the rebels at Gorakhpur entered Oudh and advanced to Lucknow where he reinforced Sir Colin Campbell and enabled him to extend his plan of operations. They assisted in the campaign and finally retired into Nepal in May-June 1858. When numbers of fugitive rebels took refuge in the Nepalese Tarai, the Nepalese temporised with them until they had got all the jewels and money out of them. At last in 1859 they organised an expedition which co-operated with the British troops in sweeping the mutineers out. Among the refugees were the Begum of Lucknow and her son, and Nana Saheb. Some say that the Nana fell a victim to malaria in the Tarai; while others maintain that he took refuge in Nepal itself where his wives were given shelter; and for long it was believed that he continued to live in the interior of Nepal. The Begum of Lucknow also took refuge in Kathmandu where she resided for many years.

A large portion of the Tarai was made over to Nepal as a reward for her services; while General Jang Bahadur was created a G. C. B.—an honour of which he was very proud. Had it not been for the personal influence of Sir Jang, the Nepalese would most probably have held aloof or have even sided with the rebels. "Now however all parties see the wisdom of the course adopted and Sir Jang Bahadur's position has no doubt been rendered more secure by the benefits which the country has derived from his policy."

Subsequent to the Mutiny, the relations of Jang Bahadur towards the British Power continued to be equally cordial. He made several alterations in the treaties for the extradition of criminals; but he would not for long relax the jealous rules which excluded foreigners from travelling in and surveying the country, not even allowing scientific expeditions of observation. In 1873 Sir Jang Bahadur was created a G. C. S. I. and in the same year he received from the Emperor of China the title and insignia of *Thonglin-pim-ma-ko-kang-vang-syan* which means "Leader of the army, the most brave in every enterprise, perfect in everything, master of the army, Maharaj." In 1874 Sir Jang proposed to revisit England with a large number of his relatives and even proceeded as far as Bombay, whence he returned on account of an accident.

Sir Jang's position, according to Dr. Wright, was a most astonishing one. His family interests were interwoven with those of almost every important family from that of the King downwards. The King's eldest son, Trilok Bir Vikram Sah was married to his daughter; and the second son to another daughter and niece. As he had upwards of a hundred children the opportunities for strengthening his position by alliances of this type should have been very extensive. Sir Jang's administration was very beneficial to the country; but even he could not interfere with some of the customs and prejudices of the people. He restricted *sati*, but found it impossible to abolish the custom entirely. He was personally not averse to throwing the country open to Europeans, but was afraid to do so on account of popular prejudice which is reflected in a saying.—"With the merchant comes the musket, with the Bible comes the bayonet." Sir Jang also placed restrictions on the custom by which the dishonoured husband was allowed to cut down the seducer of his wife with his *khukri*; he also mitigated to a small extent the severity of the old laws against adultery and breaches of caste rules as well as the barbarity which was practised on the occasion of animal sacrifices. He absolutely prohibited *sati* in the case of women having young children and gave permission to *satis* to alter their minds even in the presence of the fatal pile. He began the practice of having tutors for his children, either European or Bengali. After his return from England, he abolished the old savage code of punishments involving mutilation, stripes etc., and introduced a new system. Only treason, rebellion, desertion in times of war and other serious offences against the state were to be punished with death; besides killing cows and murder.

The administration of justice under Jang Bahadur was fair, and an appeal could always be made to the Council which practically meant the Minister. The standing army consisted in those days of about 16,000 men divided into 26 regiments of from 500 to 600 men each—supplemented by a large force of irregulars consisting mainly of discharged soldiers. All the regiments have been formed on the British model and officered in the same way as the English army. All the higher ranks of the army were filled up by the sons and relatives of Sir Jang Bahadur and his brothers. Practically Sir Jang was the head of every department in the State. He set up an arsenal where rifles and percussion caps are manufactured and cannon are cast and bored.

Sir Jang Bahadur usually resided at Thapatali on the banks of the Bagmati river near the town of Patan. It consists of a succession of squares of gigantic houses inhabited by the minister's relatives and dependents; and the public rooms are described as being large, lofty and well-ornamented with pictures and carvings. He also maintained a huge elephant-court, besides large stables and kennels. A statue of his was originally set up in the centre of the grand monument in the race course at the capital, which was subsequently removed to a new temple built by him. Sir Jang, in spite of his philo-English tendencies was very proud of the independence of his state, and most jealous of any interference with his domestic policy. The British Resident was merely a consul, having nothing to do whatever with the government of the country, and no Gurkha could enter the Residency without permission from the Minister himself and without being accompanied by his *vakil*. Sir Jang used to have a daily report of everything that occurred at the Residency; and it was very difficult for the Resident or any European to obtain information on any subject beyond what actually came under his own observation. Nepal under Sir Jang was a kind of Alsatia for Hindustan as it was very difficult to obtain the extradition of criminals from his state. In fact the Nepalese have always prided themselves on never surrendering a fugitive—except when it suited them.

Sir Jang was always most affable and courteous in his demeanour; and according to Major Wright, whatever might have been his failings, he always bore himself as a gentleman. "He was undoubtedly also a most acute and talented man and it would be well for Nepal," so Major Wright wrote in 1775—"if there were a few more among the rising generation fit to be compared to him."

Nepal under Sir Jang was the example of an independent Hindu state *par excellence* in alliance and co-operation with the British Government. His wonderful career which closed in death in 1877 enabled him to rightly estimate the worth of the English power. It was Sir Jang's great services in the time of the Mutiny that formed the indissoluble tie connecting the two Governments; and the development of the Gurkha Regiments in the British Indian Army after the Mutiny which "forms one of the most remarkable chapters in the history of our Indian Army" was one of the best fruits of that alliance. The idea of having Gurkha regiments was as old as 1832 when the Resident Mr. Hodgson urged it on the attention of Government, but it took shape only as a result of the lesson learned in 1857.

A comparative estimate of Sir Jang with his great contemporaries among Indian statesmen given by Sir Richard Temple in 1880 may not prove uninteresting:—

Of living statesmen among the natives, Salar Jang of Hyderabad perhaps has become Europeanised in his method of administration. But Dinkar Rao of Gwalior was quite original, so was Kripa Ram of Jammu, and more especially Jang Bahadur of Nepal who governed after his own fashion with hardly any tincture of European notions. Madhava Rao of Baroda, too, though Anglicised to some extent, is quite Asiatic *au fond*, and if left to his own resources entirely, would evince striking originality.—*Men and Events of my Time in India*. p. 497.

Sir Jang's tradition has been kept up by succeeding Ministers of Nepal. The fear that his death would be followed by a series of revolutions has been largely falsified. All power still continues in the hands of the Prime Minister; and the present King Tribubana Bir Bikram Sah is much in the same position as his ancestor Surendra. The present Minister, Sir Chandra Shumshere Jang Bahadur Rana who came to power in 1901, practically placed the entire man-power of his state at the disposal of the English during the Great War, in recognition of which help the Indian Government makes an annual present of ten lakhs of rupees to the Nepal Darbar.

RAJA SIR DINKAR RAO*

HIS ANCESTRY

The ancestors of Sir Dinkar Rao the illustrious statesman of Gwalior lived in a village called Devarukh in the Ratnagiri District of the Bombay Presidency. Of this village Vishvanath Hari was the Khot or *Zamindar*. Vishvanath had three sons, Hari, Ramchandra and Bhaskar. Bhaskarpant's son Timaji was favoured by the fates and so found opportunities to make a fortune as well as a name for himself and his family. That was exactly the time when several Brahmins and Mahratta families rose to greatness and distinction. About the year 1745 Timaji found an entrance into the arena of politics at Satara, the capital of the Mahratta Empire and the seat and centre of all the political transactions which have influenced to a great degree the pages of the Indian history. Step by step he rose in the estimation of his superiors and attracted the attention of the Chatrapati, the King of the Mahrattas. The royal favour ensured by an honest and energetic performance of duties, secured for Timaji considerable advantages, pecuniary as well as official. Thus this family emerged out of comparative obscu-

---

* Drawn largely from an excellent biographical memoir by Mr. M. W. Burway of Indore.

rity. Success followed success and at last the family attained a place in the official circle of the Mahratta Empire. Of Timajipant Rajwade's sons, Ramrao and Balvantrao, the former followed in the footsteps of his worthy father and performed the state functions assigned to him with credit. Ram Rao had four sons and of these the eldest Dinkar Rao succeeded his father in the hereditary office of Rajwade.

HIS EARLY DAYS

Dinkar Rao was born at Dewrukha on the 20th of December 1819. On account of the anarchy and chaos preceding the abdication of the Peshwa his family along with many others was reduced to straitened circumstances and consequently his education could not be much attended to. After Raghoba's entrance into the Gwalior service, he brought his family from the Deccan. Young Dinkar Rao was then but eight years old. Here Dinkar Rao picked up a little knowledge of Persian and finance along with Marathi. At fifteen his career as a student terminated and he embarked on his official career.

Dinkar Rao entered the service of Maharaj Scindia at the age of sixteen under the auspices of Bhausaheb Potnis. As Secretary to this influential officer of the Scindia's Court, the young man had many opportunities of measuring the power of the different parties in the state and of acquiring an intimate acquaintance with the state affairs. In this position Dinkar Rao continued to remain for a long time. Day by day his ability in the discharge of his official duties attracted the attention of the other members of the Gwalior Durbar and this circumstance stood him in good stead afterwards.

Raghoba's services in the settlement of the Amba District went a long way in ensuring the success of his son and in securing the sympathy of the influential courtiers in his selection to the vacant Subhaship, the dangers of which post were not at all unknown to the young officer. After being confirmed in the Subhat of Amba, this energetic officer, equal to the responsibilities of the task, set to do his best in ameliorating still more the deplorable condition of the district. In this he followed the footsteps of his sagacious father. During the days of his probationership, Dinkar Rao had taken advantage of every leisure hour to acquire a sound knowledge of administrative details, and had even gone the length of writing a small treatise connected with the conduct of state-affairs.

During the troublous period, 1800-1852, it was not always possible for a man of mere ability and integrity to rise and come to the front in the arena of native politics. Dinkar Rao was then the ablest man in Gwalior. Good fortune favoured him also. There were at this time sympathetic officers of the type of Shakespeare and Malcolm who were always ready and eager to appreciate native talent and merit. Dinkar Rao had caught the eye of Shakespeare and Malcolm. Major Shakespeare was now promoted to the A. G. G. ship at Indore and Major Malcolm had succeeded him at Gwalior. Before relinquishing the charge of the Gwalior Residency the Major had left on record his high opinion regarding Dinkar Rao's honesty and ability and the sound work he had done in Tawarghar.

INTERNAL FEUDS

The most difficult problem that lies before the reader of Dinkar Rao's life for solution is his elevation from the Subhaship of Amba to the Premier-ship of Gwalior, one of the most powerful States in India. While on the one hand the ability, integrity and assiduity of Dinkar Rao created a favourable impression about him in the minds of Sir Richmond Shakespeare and Colonel Malcolm, on the other, the chaos and confusion, which had been prevailing in the Gwalior administration since a long time and which had now assumed a most serious and chronic form, served a great deal to persuade the British Government to put at the head of the administration an officer of the state thoroughly honest and familiar with the administrative work rather than a big sardar sufficiently powerful to do mischief and so sufficiently disqualified for the position.

The internal administration of Gwalior was more or less persistently neglected after the death of the great Mahadaji Scindia. Daolat Rao, Mahadaji's successor, was, as has been just said, an incapable ruler and fitted as little for improving the administration of the state as for controlling the unmanageably large forces of Scindia. The terrible defeats which the Gwalior army had to suffer from the English in the great battles of Assaye, Laswari and Argam, had well-nigh destroyed Scindia's military greatness, but still there was sufficient vitality in the Scindia's kingdom to withstand such disasters.

In the reign of his successor Jankoji Rao, the army grew more dangerous to the peace and sound administration of Scindia's dominions. This chief's short reign terminated on the 7th of February 1843. The great Jayaji Rao Maharajah, the greatest and the best of all those who came to the Gadi after the demise of Mahadaji, ascended the throne at the age of nine only. From 1842 to 1852, the History of Gwalior is full of the intrigues and feuds between the rival parties and the disappointment of the British Political Resident in restoring peace and good administration in the vast dominions of the Maharajah Scindia during the minority of this Prince.

At this time there were two principal parties in the state. One of them was headed by Mama Saheb and the other was under the auspices of the famous Dada Saheb Khasgiwale in whom the Mama Saheb found a Tartar. The British Resident, aware of the magnitude of the danger in case of an outbreak of civil war, wrote to the Governor-General of all those dark movements carried on by Khasgiwale and his foes. The danger was really a serious one. Lord Ellenborough followed a master-piece of policy in desiring to settle amicably the Gwalior affairs. His advance towards Gwalior was indeed with a noble purpose, though unpleasant occurrences did take place notwithstanding these precautions.

The British Government then came to the conclusion that Dada Khasgiwale was at the root of all the present disturbances and dissensions in the dominions of Scindia and an obstinate enemy of all peaceful prospect for the great state. No delay was now allowed to be made in securing the person of the Khasgiwale, who was, after a great deal of ado, sent to the Governor-General's camp. This step was considered to ensure the peace of Gwalior, but the uncontrollable army of Scindia baffled all the sanguine hopes of the Ranee (the Queen Regent) and the Governor-General. In fact both the Ranee and the Maharajah were quite helpless and unprepared to quiet the torrent of hostility which some of the powerful Sardars harboured towards the well-intentioned interference of the Governor-General. Active preparations were begun for facing the British arms and the unmanageable army of Scindia, confident of a certain victory, thought very lightly of the coming calamity. An important and memorable battle took place on the 28th of December, 1843. The Gwalior army sustained two defeats.

The interview between Lord Ellenborough and the Maharajah, delayed by these obstacles, came off on the 30th December 1843 when his Lordship informed the Maharajah of the decision of the British Government to keep the state in its integrity. Gwalior was for the first time, subjected to the influence of the subsidiary system. A treaty was formally concluded on the 13th of January 1844. It was agreed upon, among other important things, that a council of Regency consisting of six members should be appointed to carry on the administration with the advice of the Resident in important matters: Sirdar Ramrao Phalkay as President; Sirdar Bhow Potnis, Udaji Khatkay, Deo Rao Mama Jodhav, Raja Balvant Rai, and Mulaji as Members.

It will, therefore, be easy to understand from the foregoing paragraphs why and how Dinkar Rao, who was undoubtedly the ablest and most honest man of his time in Gwalior, became successful on account of the existence in the state of rival parties, who were every now and then ready to fly at each other's throat, and thus proved the source of much unnecessary bloodshed and unmitigated suffering to the rayat at large. As we will see later on, Dinkar Rao destroyed the possibility of a recurrence of these open as well as subterranean dangers at the risk of great trouble and much unpopularity.

The Council of Regency were dragging on a futile existence, when the last vestige of vitality passed away in the person of Sardar Ram Rao Phalkay. Once more there was a reversion to the old and chaotic state of things. Again there was a very intricate question before the Durbar and the

Resident accredited to the Court of Scindia. Colonel Malcolm was equal to the occasion. He had the courage of his conviction and was a man who could not but do everthing to place the Gwalior administration in as good a condition as it lay in his power to do. The consideration of a capable successor, who would introduce a good administrative system into the state, now claimed the attention of the Durbar and the Resident.

Sir Richmond was long ago raised to the post of A. G. G. for C. I. and had left a very high opinion on record about Dinkar Rao's enlightened and large-minded views, his honesty and administrative capacity of which there was a living proof in the District of Tawarghar. His successor at Gwalior, Colonel Malcolm, bore even a higher testimony to Dinkar Rao's ability. Consequently, there remained no doubt as to the choice of a capable Dewan.

HIS DEWANSHIP

A grand Durbar was held at Gwalior early in the spring of 1852. Prior to this, Dinkar Rao was summoned from Ambah by Colonel Malcolm with the cordial approval of Sir Richmond Shakespeare. In the presence of all the Durbarees and Sirdars, Colonel Malcolm intimated to the assembly the determination of the British Government to appoint Dinkar Rao as Dewan of Gwalior. Dewan Dinkar Rao, soon after the assumption of the high office, embarked upon the onerous task of introducing a systematic and happy civil administration into the state.

The difficulties that beset the path of Dinkar Rao in the administration of the state were of a very severe nature. There were stubborn enemies—open and secret. The Maharajah was a minor. The Sardars were powerful and generally opposed to any curtailment of the tortuous absolutism they enjoyed. The official circle was permeated with a self-seeking tendency and any the least encroachment on their power was tantamount to courting a serious danger. There were, to all intents and purposes, no well-founded laws and so a systematic administration was conspicuous by its absence. Men too, who could be trained to the new order of things, were to be found with difficulty in the state. Much less could then the new system which the Dewan was to introduce be understood and appreciated or supported by the existing batch of officers. The greatest difficulty, however, lay not in the incompetency but in the intentional and systematic attempts of the Gwalior Officialdom to hinder the Dewan in any reforms he might think of introducing. Of these adverse circumstances the Dewan was not unaware. He foresaw such difficulties but they served only to enhance his determination to pursue his task.

REFORMS IN THE REVENUE ADMINISTRATION

The Dewan directed his attention first to the Revenue Department with great zeal. He brought about radical changes in the whole Department. The whole state was divided into three divisions, Malwa, Esagar and Gwalior, for administrative purposes. Each division he placed under a Sir Soobha (Commissioner). Under him were Soobhas or Collectors of Districts (zillas.) Each Soobha had under him the Kamasdars (Tahsildars or Mamlatdars) and Naib Soobhas and so on. A Revenue Code was prepared for the guidance of the Revenue officers and work was enjoined to be carried on strictly in accordance with the rules and regulations contained therein.

The Districts (the zillas,) upto this time, were given to Ijardars (Farmers of Revenue) for a fixed sum to be annually paid by the Ijardars to the Durbar. The new Dewan destroyed this pernicious system, root and branch, and introduced a more or less Ryatwari system. Leases were distributed to the Rayat, fixing the amount of assessment they were to pay to the state, and the period for which these leases were to continue was a long one, say, from 25 to 30 years.

JUDICIAL REFORMS

The regular Judicial administration of the state, like the Revenue, owes its existence to this Dewan. The Sudder Adalut at Gwalior began its systematic work under his auspices. The Chief Justice or the Judge of the Sudder Adalut, the Naib Sir Soobha Foujdari, and the Naib Sir Soobha Dewani, Naib Soobhas Foujdari and Dewani, and the Munsifs had their respective duties clearly defined, and for their guidance there were rules and regulations embodied in a Judicial Code. The salaries of the Judicial officers were as liberal as those of the Revenue officers. One great flaw, however, remained in this system—perhaps unconsciously. The language of the Courts, which ought to have been either Hindi or Marathi, was allowed to be Urdu. This is the only fault we have to find with the otherwise laudable Judicial system, which came into existence in this great Dewan's happy regime.

OTHER REFORMS.

Schools were, founded at his instance in every important town in the Maharajah's dominions.

With a view to ensure the security of property and to suppress crime, an efficient Police Department was created. Gangs of robbers and Thugs, who infested the trunk roads, were brought to book. Dacoity was thus suppressed. At that time there were no railways and mails were carried by runners. Sometimes it so happened that these runners were attacked and the mails looted. But the system of road-chowkies put a stop to these pernicious inroads on the mails and the runners.

All servants of the state received their pay regularly—a reform very praiseworthy and tending greatly to official purity and a conscientious discharge of official duties. He resolved to bring the prevailing extravagance under control. His chief object was to make the expenditure consistent with the income of the state. He effected this by reducing wholesale the scale of expenditure and with a praiseworthy spirit of fairness reduced his own salary to Rupees 2,000, though the Dewan usually received more than double that amount.

Thus in less than five years Dinkar Rao had changed the whole aspect of affairs. It was a change from a violent misrule to a reformed and enlightened regime of peace and order. The whole country was settled amidst the beginning of an era of peace and prosperity. The greatest boon, Dewan Dinkar Rao conferred, was on the class of cultivators and the *Zamindars*. For, none were so much oppressed, none suffered so severely during the past mal-administrations as did the Gwalior peasants.

In the beginning of the year 1857 an event, which was then considered to be of great political significance took place, *viz.*, the visit of Maharajah Scindia to Calcutta in company with the Resident Major Macpherson. Maharajah Jayaji Rao left Calcutta exceedingly pleased with the hearty and generous hospitality of the kindhearted Lord Canning. A close intimacy existed between the Maharajah and Lord Canning throughout the incumbency of the latter, and it was only owing to this fact coupled with the influence of Dewan Sir Dinkar Rao, that Scindia remained steadfastly loyal to the British rule in India in the fateful year 1857-58.

THE GREAT INDIAN MUTINY

The name of Dewan Dinkar Rao is so insepar-ably connected with the Indian Rebellion or Mutiny of 1857, that we must notice that most important and terrible event in some detail. The reasons for our doing this are various. Gwalior, under the control of the Dewan, played the most conspicuous part in the Rebellion. Every one of the Historians of the Sepoys' Revolt is certainly of opinion that had Dinkar Rao and his master, the young Maharajah Scindia, been less zealous in the opportune help they rendered to the Government, the British Indian Empire would have had to face almost insurmountable dangers and difficulties. No state in India possessed such an excellent army as Gwalior did. It occupies also a very advantageous strategical position. Its power of doing mischief as well as good was inexhaustible. Under a bad man, Gwalior would have become dangerous to itself and the whole of the British Indian Empire. There was another element of danger in the heart of this great state. The memories of Maharajahpore and Panhyar were not yet extinct. There was yet a party in the state hostile to the growth of the power of the English.

Sir John Kaye the historian of the *Sepoy Revolt* has to say as follows :

A man of Maharajah Jayaji Rao's character, if he had fallen into bad hands, might have been dangerous to himself and to others. Fortunately, however, he fell into good hands—hands that gently but firmly restrained the restlessness of his nature. At the most critical period of his life, he had Dinkar Rao at his elbow. That great native statesman who had shared with Salar Jung of Hyderabad, the glory of being the Abul Fazal of the nineteenth century, and from whom the best of our English administrators have learnt many lessons of wisdom, exercised a benign influence not only

RAJA SIR DINKAR RAO

over the Government of the Gwalior territory which he reformed and consolidated, but over the personal character of Maharajah Scindia himself.

The great Rebellion of which so much had been said and in which Jayaji Rao and Dinkar Rao took such a conspicuously loyal part first broke out at Meerut and spread like wild fire into the remotest parts of India. The Lieutenant-Governor of the North-Western Provinces and Oudh, which were the centre of the calamity and the rallying place of all the disaffected but brave soldiers, had to bear the brunt of the whole action. Mr. Colvin was in imminent danger. Maharajah Jayaji Rao and Dinkar Rao, on hearing of Mr. Colvin's distress, at once sent the fine body-guard of Scindia to the assistance of the Lieutenant-Governor at Agra. Jayaji Rao and Dinkar Rao also succeeded by various artifices in retaining in a state of inaction the over-whelming number of soldiers, now quite ready and impatient to join the ranks and thus to augment the strength of the mutineers whose power had already become very formidable. It was at this time that both the Maharajah and the Dewan were able to save the several hundreds of British soldiers and officers and their families who found little or no shelter in the British territory adjoining the Gwalior dominions. Several officers and ladies were concealed in the cellars of the Palace of His Highness and their lives were kept secure from the danger of the revengeful gaze of the wild mutineers. Gwalior is therefore called "The Friendly Haven" to which helpless British officers and ladies came running with sanguine hopes of shelter throughout the continuance of the Rebellion.

The Peshwa's hopes of receiving Scindia's aid proved false. Jayaji Rao, to whom the Rao Saheb and the Rani of Jhansi had addressed a friendly letter requesting his aid against the English, defied them and declared his intention of fighting the rebels. They both attacked Gwalior. The victory of the Peshwa's army was complete and Gwalior lay at the mercy of the victors. This important event took place on the 1st of June 1858. The Peshwa Rao Saheb and the Rani entered Gwalior with all the pomp and circumstance of a victory whereupon the Peshwa was formally crowned king of the state, and several Durbars were held for conferring rewards on many a favourite.

The Gwalior Contingent Force broke out into open rebellion on the 14th of June 1857. Their spirits were greatly raised by the exaggerated reports of successes and victories in the North and West of Gwalior. The Resident, Major Macpherson, being in great danger, hastened to consult Maharajah Jayaji Rao and Dinkar Rao with regard to the safety of the European families at Gwalior and Morar. Major Macpherson and Sir Dinkar Rao arrived at the conclusion, to which the Maharajah gave consent, that unless the European ladies and children were carried to the Agra fort, their complete safety was an impossibility. At last the Major left Gwalior in company with the ladies and children and attended by a strong escort supplied by the Maharajah Scindia.

The brave but misguided mutineers thought that the British power would suffer irretrievably owing to the withdrawal of the Resident to Agra. They further beguiled themselves by the vain hopes that the Scindia may now be persuaded to support the cause of the mutineers. The political Agent had full influence over Scindia's Dewan or Prime Minister, the celebrated Dinkar Rao. The Minister in his turn influenced his master and thus Major Macpherson from the interior of the fort at Agra, ruled the course of events at the court of Gwalior.

We had left the Peshwa and the Rani of Jhansi in the full enjoyment of their victory over the Gwalior forces. The Maharajah had already fled to Agra where Dinkar Rao, after providing for the safety of Baizabai and the Ranees, joined his master at no distant date. Sir Hugh Rose had been ordered to take Gwalior and re-seat the Maharajah on his ancestral throne. In pursuance of these instructions, the illustrious General Sir Hugh Rose's army arrived at Gwalior on the 17th of June 1858. An engagement soon took place between the forces of the British General and those of the Peshwa. The Rani of Jhansi met with a heroic death, and her body was burnt with great pomp and splendour. The forces of the rebels were completely routed and the Peshwa, overwhelmed with grief caused by the Rani's death, left Gwalior, despairing and disheartened. On the 20th of June 1858, 19 days after the flight of the Maharajah from Gwalior, Jayaji Rao was again placed on the throne of his forefathers. The disturbance was fully quelled at Gwalior, and General Sir Hugh Rose restored order in the capital of Scindia. A new treaty consisting of ten articles was made by the Maharajah with the British Government and it was formally ratified by the Governor-General Lord Canning at Benares on the 12th of December 1860.

With regard to the part played by Scindia and Dinkar Rao in the mutiny, Colonel Malleson, C.S.I., author of the 'Indian Mutiny,' and of 'The Native Princes and their States' etc. bears the following testimony: "Had the ablest member of the Council of India been at his ears, he could not have inspired him with counsels more calculated to prove beneficial to the British cause than those which he (Jayaji Rao) and his minister Dinkar Rao with the instinct of truly loyal nature, followed of their own free will."

BRITISH GRATITUDE TO SCINDIA

Henceforth the Gwalior Durbar had not much to do with the mutiny. At least they had no direct connection with the transactions connected with it after the re-installation of the Maharajah on the 19th of June 1858, though the final overthrow of the mutinous chiefs and soldiers had not been accomplished for a long time after that date. When the rebellion had been completely quelled and order was restored in the disaffected districts, Lord Canning left Calcutta for a grand tour with the object of inspiring still greater confidence in the minds of the Native Sovereigns and securing their complete good-will, which had been of so invaluable service in the disastrous times. In the Grand Durbar held on the 30th of November 1859, His Excellency took advantage of the opportunity by expressing on behalf of the Sovereign, his warmest feelings of gratitude to the Maharajah Scindia for the beneficial measures adopted by His Highness for saving the British Empire in India, as well as for His Highness's kindness and hospitality to the helpless ladies and officers, who had flocked for shelter to his palace. Later on, His Excellency enumerated in the course of his speech all the good services rendered by the Gwalior Durbar to the British Government in its hour of great peril, and at the conclusion of the memorable Viceregal oration, informed the Maharajah that in grateful recognition of these brilliant services, the British Government was pleased to confer on His Highness a territorial reward worth about three lakhs of rupees per annum. The right of adoption was also received by His Highness along with all the Indian Princes. The Gwalior Infantry was allowed to be increased from three to five thousand soldiers. His Excellency bestowed an appropriate meed of panegyric on the illustrious statesman Rajah Dinkar Rao, who not only had helped the British Government in saving their Empire but had saved Gwalior from the greatest danger that could ever befall it. In recognition of the eminent services performed in 1857, His Excellency conferred on the worthy Dewan a Jhageer of 5,000 rupees per annum. This reward is certainly but a meagre recognition of the Dewan's valuable exertions. The Maharajah, however, made up the insufficiency of the reward by conferring on the Dewan a splendid Jhageer, yielding a net revenue of 60,000 rupees a year.

HIS RESIGNATION

It is not to be supposed that the action of the Dewan could be left unchallenged. Already a "microscopic minority" now almost extinct had poured forth a torrent of sharp vituperation on the conduct of Maharajah Jayaji Rao Scindia and Rajah Sir Dinkar Rao during the Mutiny. They believed that a very suitable opportunity had arrived in 1857 for asserting independence and founding a native rule in India, and they condemned Jayaji Rao and Dinkar Rao. No reasonable and farsighted man can say that the Maharajah and his able Minister erred in any way. The path that they pursued, as we have already pointed out was thoroughly free from reproach. There was, however, only one plan which would have been of great utility in avoiding the terrible bloodshed that took place and in ensuring the peace and safety of the North Indian Provinces at less cost as well as in silencing the clamours of the discontented parties. These men painted Dinkar Rao in as black a colour as they could. For a long time these sinister attempts were not attended to. But the greater the disregard of the Maharajah to these men's counsels, the stronger became their determination to devise new methods for destroying the Minister's influence. Every art was used. The Maharajah, a proud Mahratta Prince in the prime of his youth, was even told to his face that the Dewan was the real master and the Maharajah a mere puppet in his hands. These frequent attempts, repeated every now and then and by every possible means, began ultimately to gain ground. The Maharajah endeavoured to check the minister's powers unreasonably or to put other harassing conditions upon the performance of his official duties. For some time such a state of tension continued between the august master and the honest minister. At last, however, the crisis came. The misunderstanding between the Maharajah and the Dewan deepened day by day, and at last the latter openly spoke of resigning. Often the Resident would interfere in the matter and bring about a reconciliation, for the Resident well knew that the state required the guiding hand of such a Minister for a time at least. But the poison, poured into the Maharajah's ears, was such as to be above all cure. In high wrath His Highness left Gwalior for Sipri, 30 kos from the capital, saying "Either Dinkar Rao or I would rule in Gwalior." The Dewan at once proceeded to the Maharajah's camp. Though His Highness was in high wrath, the Dewan ushered himself into the royal presence and tendered the resignation of his office, enhancing the effect of such a timely and well-suited action by an opportune speech of a few sentences, couched in the most appropriate terms. The Maharajah was a little appeased. His Highness even went to the length of saying that such a hasty resignation was not required. But the Dewan's mind was made up. His decision was the outcome of deep thought, and once made up it was never to be withdrawn. After presenting his resignation, the Dewan returned to Gwalior and related to the Resident the account of his trip and the details of his resignation.

The great Jayaji Rao ever afterwards entertained a sincere regard for his faithful Dewan whose services he frequently utilised in effecting the settlement of intricate questions connected with his State. The Dewan whose fame had already spread far and wide, was at no distant date prevailed upon in spite of himself, to tender his weighty advice in a more exalted position of public utility in the Supreme Council at Calcutta.

IN THE SUPREME COUNCIL

Lord Canning who knew perfectly well the high value of Sir Dinkar Rao as an administrator, was sorry to hear of the Dewan's undeserved treatment and could not allow the great Dewan to remain without any public appreciation of his great talents. He therefore, offered him a seat in the Supreme Council, an honour then enjoyed only by ruling sovereigns. Rao Rajah Dinkar Rao took his seat in the Supreme Council along with the Maharajah of Patiala and Maharajah Deo Narayan Sing of Benares in 1862.

We would only briefly show the amount and nature of the work performed by the Rao Rajah in the Council at Calcutta. As a well-wisher and friend of the Indian Princes, he had to undertake the supervision and reconstruction of the administrative machineries of several important Native States. He was known all over India as an eminent administrator and his fame as such compelled him to yield to the urgent pressure which was brought to bear on him by the Maharajahs of Dewas, Rewah and Dholepore, in whose affairs he had to interfere. The urgent appeals of these Maharajahs were more or less seconded by those of the political officers accredited to their courts, and to shirk from such a duty would have been improper, at least against the etiquette which prevails in the aristocratic circle in India.

SIR DINKAR RAO IN DHOLEPORE

The first Prince who solicited Dinkar Rao's aid in reforming his state affairs was the Rana of Dholepore, a small but very important principality, which has an historical interest worthy of a cursory notice at least. In 1857 Bhagvant Sing rendered good services to the English and saved the lives of several European officers and ladies. His Dewan Deoraj Hansa gave him much trouble. The Dewan attempted in 1862 even to depose Rana Bhagvant Sing, and for this treachery the Rana placed him in custody. There was thus a great deal of disorder and intrigue in the state on account of the refractory spirit of Dewan Deoraj Hansa.

Rao Rajah Dinkar Rao was then appointed with the cordial approval of the Government of India as Superintendent of the Dholepore State. A Superintendent is generally like a special Political Agent for the state with full powers of administration. The first duty of a minister is to place the finances of a state on a sound basis as well as to improve the Judiciary. Reform, therefore, in this direction, was undertaken. Other branches of the administration were also attended to. Intrigues and plots were put down with a strong hand, and the partisans of Dewan Deoraj Hansa prevented absolutely from working any further mischief and chaos.

SIR DINKAR AND THE REWA STATE

Before the expiry of a long interval, this veteran administrator was requested by another and a more important State for the amelioration of the deplorable condition of its affairs. Rewa was in chaos and Dinkar Rao was prevailed upon to go there. On assuming the reins of the Rewah Government, he directed his attention to the reform in the Revenue department. The assessment was made with generosity and justice. The amount of dues to be paid by the *Zamindar* to the State was fixed for a settled period and the pesantry was distinctly told that they were to pay not a farthing more than the amount specified in the pattas (leases). Much of the system of administration introduced in the Raj resembled that introduced in Gwalior a few years before, and the laws and regulations were more or less the same as contained in the famous Dastur-ul-Umal.

The total revenues of the State amounted to about twenty lakhs. Half of this was portioned out to the Bhayyats, the kinsmen to the Maharajah and the noblemen. The other half was then utilised for purposes of the State. About two lakhs of this were absorbed by the civil administration; the palace received three lakhs: four lakhs were to be disbursed on the state army and one lakh was to be kept as reserve fund in the state exchequer.

HIS SERVICES TO BARODA STATE

We now pass on to consider Sir Dinkar's connection with Baroda. In 1863 Malhar Rao Maharajah had, it is alleged, attempted to poison his elder brother, the ruling Gaekwad Khandeo Rao Maharajah, who, coming to know somehow of the criminal intention, placed Malhar Rao in custody at Padra. After the death of Khandeo Rao, the British Political Resident, accredited to the Baroda Durbar, released Malhar Rao and placed him on the Gaekwar Musnad. This Prince had little or no aptitude for turning out a good ruler. Although there must be some exaggeration in the reports spread about Malhar Rao, it is recognised on all hands that Malhar Rao was a lewd Prince of no competency. Sir Lewis Pelly issued a proclamation announcing that there existed a strong suspicion about Malhar Rao Maharajah's attempt to poison Colonel Phayre, that the charge would be gone into before a

High Commission and that the Mahratta rule would be continued in Baroda irrespective of the result of the enquiry. This was followed by another proclamation, setting forth the charges on which the enquiry was to proceed. The High Commission, which was appointed to conduct the enquiry, consisted of the following members, all men of note and mark and eminently fitted by their august position to try an august criminal.

(1) Sir Richard Couch, Kt. Chief Justice of the Bengal Presidency.

(2) His Highness Maharajah Jayaji Rao Scindia, G. C. S. I., G. C. B., C. I. E.

(3) H. H. Maharajah Sawai Ransingji of Jeypore.

(4) Rajah Sir Dinkar Rao, K. C. S. I.

(5) General Sir Richard Meade, K.C.S.I.

(6) Mr. Melville, Bengal Civil Service.

Mr. Jardine of Bombay served as secretary of this Commission.

The Commission began its business on the 23rd of February 1875 in a magnificent building in the Residency. The accused Prince was provided with a seat on the dais and he watched the proceedings, with a mournful gravity. It may well be conjectured that the Rao Rajah Dinkar Rao was especially active throughout the course of the enquiry; for he was well acquainted with judicial proceedings and consequently took every trouble to consult law, equity, experience and common sense, all of which had to be brought to bear on such a novel enquiry.

To Sir Dinkar Rao is due, we believe, the credit of having saved the Prince from the charge of a heinous crime. Though Malhar Rao was weak, he was not, it is alleged, wicked nor had he made for himself a great name for wanton cruelty. Yet the Prince's danger was not gone. A proclamation announced to the whole of India that Malhar Rao was to be deposed for misrule (on the 19th of April) and deported to Madras by a special train where the unfortunate Gaekwar died on the 20th of July 1882.

FURTHER HONOURS

Honours naturally came thick on Sir Dinkar Rao. In 1875 H. R. H. The Prince of Wales paid a prolonged visit to India. It was at Agra that H. R. H. received Sir Dinkar Rao with every mark of courtesy and kindness. The interview between the Prince and Sir Dinkar Rao lasted for a long time and H. R. H. showed to the Veteran Minister every mark of royal appreciation of the eminent statesman's conspicuous services to the Indian Empire. The Prince of Wales presented a large book, Louis Rouselet's 'Indian Princes' with the following inscription on it,—"To His Excellency Rajah Sir Dinkar Rao with the kind regards of Albert Edward."

The Imperial assemblage at Delhi took place in the cold season of 1877. On such an occasion Sir Dinkar Rao, it need scarcely be mentioned, was duly invited. Rao Rajah Dinkar Rao received the great title of Musheer-i-Khas Bahadur as a personal distinction, though afterwards this title was made hereditary along with that of Rao Rajah during the regime of Lord Ripon.

MORE SERVICES TO SCINDIA

Maharajah Jayaji Rao Scindia had adopted a child in 1865 and named him Ranoji Rao. This child turned out very mischievous and signalised his short-lived career as heir-apparent of the Gwalior Raj by taking part in plots and intrigues against his sovereign and father, Maharajah Jayaji Rao. Sir Dinkar Rao's services were availed of by the Maharajah and the adoption was cancelled after a great deal of trouble, mental as well as physical. This event proves conclusively that the Maharajah had every confidence in his late Minister. The joy of Maharajah Jayaji Rao was unbounded when H. H. saw that the adoption was cancelled by the Government of India.

The rendition of the Gwalior fort took place in 1885. But long before this, since the visit of the Prince of Wales in 1876 or even a little earlier, the Maharajah had expressed a strong desire to get back the Fortress at any cost. Sir Dinkar Rao was entrusted with the task of having this ambition fulfilled. Through the aid of this illustrious statesman as well as the unswering loyalty of the Gwalior State, this desire of the Maharajah was duly fulfilled during the Viceroyalty of Lord Dufferin who visited Gwalior in 1885, and personally told H. H. that the Government of India were glad to meet with the wishes of the Gwalior Durbar in this respect.

The last appearance of Sir Dinkar Rao in Gwalior was in the December of 1894, when H. H. Madho Rao Saheb Scindia was invested with powers of administering the State. Sir Dinkar Rao was given a special seat of honour in the grand Durbar held on that auspicious occasion. Now and again the British Government also honoured him with special marks of appreciation. Thus his last days were spent amidst the peace of his home surrounded by his two sons (who also rose to distinction in the service of Gwalior) and a large host of relatives. Wealth and fame were his and the love and respect of a whole generation of his countrymen. On the 2nd January 1896 in his 77th year, Sir Dinkar Rao died peacefully in his residence at Allahabad.

HIS CHARACTER

Sir Dinkar Rao was the last of that illustrious trio, which has been so prominently identified with having saved the British Empire in India. Maharajah Sir Jang Bahadur G.C.S.I., G.C.B., and Nawab Sir Salar Jang, G.C S.I., had long ago joined the majority. Dinkar Rao's uncommon industry and irreproachable honesty of which we have already spoken in detail, were the main causes of his coming to the top of the service and we must also add that it was in no small measure due to Sir Richmond Shakespeare's unerring judgment of Sir Dinkar's character and ability.

And Sir Dinkar fully deserved the choice. Dinkar Rao's public conduct was spotless; his private life was saintly. He was a man who heartily loved reticence. His lofty gravity was never marred by a free use of the organ of speech. But his words always carried a meaning with them. In fact his reticence had become proverbial. But his speech was always charming, animated, full of meaning and gravity. A low joke or an unworthy word never came out of his lips. He was possessed of exceedingly polished, courtly and dignified manners. His very appearance showed that he was a man not belonging to the ordinary run of humanity. He always carried with him that justifiable and truly becoming sense of his august position, and his striking personality always commanded awe and reverence.

Dinkar Rao wielded a boundless influence with the Government of India and the Indian Princes. There were only two other Premiers, Maharajah Jang Bahadur and Sir Salar Jang that enjoyed such a position, along with Sir Dinkar Rao. But even to these two great men Sir Dinkar Rao was superior in one respect at least. In intellectual attainments and administrative ability, Dinkar Rao outshone Maharajah Jang Bahadur and Sir Salar Jang, though of course in all other respects, these three great Premiers were equal.

Page 81.

DEWAN RANGACHARLU

Dewan Rangacharlu

INTRODUCTORY

DEWAN RANGACHARLU was among the forerunners of a new age,—the age of nationalism and self- government. It was some three years after his death that the Indian National Congress met for the first time. It was many months after the Mysore Representative Assembly was started that Lord Ripon's Government introduced their famous measure of local autonomy. His was the age of W. C. Bonnerjee and Dadabhai Naoroji, the political reformers; of K. T. Telang and M. G. Ranade, the religious and social reformers; of Dwarakanath Mitter and Badruddin Tyabji, the jurists; of Rajendra Lal Mitra and Iswar Chandra Vidyasagar, the scholars; and last, but not least, of Sir T. Madhava Rao and Sir Salar Jung, the saviours of Indian States,—all the first fruits, so to say, of Western culture in India. More or less contemporaneous with him beyond the seas were Bright and Gladstone, Lincoln and Mazzini, Mill and Tennyson. The great Liberal principles of which these giant-figures were the exponents in the West found their political expression here in India in Rangacharlu, and his compatriots.

* Largely drawn and revised, from his sketch of the Life of *Dewan Rangacharlu*, by Mr. D. V. GUNDAPPA, Editor of the *Karnataka*, Bangalore City.

EARLY LIFE

A man of the people in origin as well as in temperament was Cettipaniam Veeravalli Rangacharlu. He was born in 1831,—the year in which the British took possession of Mysore, after deposing the Maharaja,—in a village in the Chingleput District, Madras Presidency; and if intelligent and respectable parentage is a fortune, he was indeed fortunate. His father Ragavacharlu, a Sri Vaishnava Brahmin of the middle class, was a clerk in the Collectorate of that district. Among his close connections who won distinction in life may be mentioned the late Mr. Vembakkam Rama Iyengar and Sir V. Bhashayam Iyengar. His father was keenly alive to the benefits of English education and was therefore anxious to send him to Madras; but his income being modest, his ambition seemed almost impossible of attainment until, by the death of a relative, he got, it is said, a considerable sum of money; and Rangacharlu secured, besides, the patronage of Mr. Raghavachariar, the first Indian Magistrate in Madras. Rangacharlu's youth was marked by an unusual degree of preçociousness. He was diligent in his studies, and distinguished in his class and was the pet of his teachers. He came under the influence of Mr. E. B. Powell, one of the pioneers of modern education in Southern India, who had awarded him a scholarship; and he took the Certificate of Proficiency in 1849. Mr. Powell always took care to inspire his pupils with a high sense of their patriotic duties:

> Let each educated Native, then, regard himself as a teacher, either directly or indirectly, of his less fortunate countrymen. As he meets with success in his path of life, and his sphere of influence consequently widens, let him exert himself the more strenuously to secure to others the advantages which have placed him in the position he occupies.

This injunction was never lost upon Rangacharlu. At a public meeting held in Madras in 1875 to do honour to his retiring master, he owned that

> the best effects of his mode of training and the high standard of duty which he set up before the eyes of his pupils are visible in the marked success which attended the career of his students who now occupy the foremost ranks in every department of the public service and some of whom fill the highest public positions, commending themselves to approval, less perhaps by their ability than by their honest devotion to their duty. . . . . . I have now only to add that these most useful labours commencing with the first efforts ever made to promote the intellectual advancement of the people by means of liberal English Education, and continued without interruption over the long period of a quarter of a century have enabled him to effect a great national change, and thus entitled him to the position of a great national benefactor. He may be said to have formed the moral character and intellectual aspirations of a whole generation of men, and to have thus placed the future advancement of the people on a footing of certainty and progress.

AS REVENUE ADMINISTRATOR

Education being over, he successfully passed the Public Service Examination and took up service as a clerk under Mr. Ellis, Collector of Madras. After some time, he was transferred to Chingleput and then to Salem. Experience in the lower ranks of office gave him a deep insight into all the details of revenue administration; and the corrupt practices prevalent therein excited his moral indignation. As a result came out, in 1856, that bold and outspoken paper "On Bribery" which might well be taken as the first manifestation of his popular fibre and popular sympathies. Among those whom it attacked were, it appears, some of his own kith and kin; and every page of it bears testimony to his deep-seated suspicion of red-tapism. It pointed to (1) the inadequate pay of the native servants, (2) the insufficiency of the superior educated and moral agency, (3) the imperfections of the revenue system, and (4) errors of the administrative officers, as the causes of official malpractices and also suggested some remedial measures. It put forward a plea for the formation of popular assemblies in all important towns and for the starting of a "native paper" to voice forth public opinion, disseminate correct notions regarding the nature of the British Government and check the irregularities of public servants. The pamphlet was at first intended for private circulation, but was after two years given to the public, under the pseudonym of "A Native Revenue Officer," at the instance of "a gentleman who is deeply interested in the intellectual, moral and social improvement of the native inhabitants,"—probably Mr. N. G. Taylor.

From Salem he was sent to Saidapet as Tasildhar and from there to Nellore as District Sheristadar. In 1859 Mr. Taylor, President of the Inam Commission and afterwards of the Railway Commission, selected Rangacharlu as his Special Assistant. In this capacity, he crossed the sea on an official journey to Calcutta, along with Mr. Taylor, laying aside the objections of his relatives and co-religionists. This sign of a mind emancipated from superstitious homage to blind custom created no small stir in orthodox circles at the time. His "excellent judgment" and "wonderful capacity" were of great service to Mr. Taylor; and when the latter became, later on, a member of the Viceroy's Council from Madras, he used to consult his old colleague on all points of importance and quote his opinions in the debates.

VILLAGE RE-ORGANIZATION

A great deal is said nowadays about village re-construction, though little has been accomplished yet in that direction. Rangacharlu, when he was Special Assistant Inam Commissioner in Madras, drafted a scheme of Village Panchayats which is admirably adapted for the moral and material advancement of village communities even to-day. The constitution of the Village Municipal Corporation according to his scheme adumbrated in his memorandum of 1860 is as follows:

> Every village shall have, according to the size, from 3 to 7 or more headmen who shall form its Municipal Corporation. They shall be appointed by the election of the landholders above a certain grade. But where there are considerable numbers of other tradesmen, such as weavers, or of Paiyakari cultivators with large and distinct interests in the village, they shall be allowed the election of one of the headmen. The election is to take place periodically once in 5 or 7 years in the presence of the Collector, or his deputies, during the Jamabandy Settlement, vacancies alone being filled up in the interval. The headmen, so elected, shall propose for the approval and confirmation of the Collector—one of their number to be their chief or Munsiff.

Rangacharlu was fully aware of the wants and weaknesses of village communities. He recognized that "the tendency of the administration is to split up communities and to destroy all social distinctions" save that of the official class. The consequence is that public opinion ceases to exercise any influence as an incentive to good behaviour. The people are incapable of any movement for social good, while numerous petty and uncontrolled authorities become focuses of litigation and corruption. Rangacharlu held that:

> The surest remedy to these various evils is the revival of the village municipalities, who, as they are matured, will gradually relieve Government of many minor duties which it cannot profitably undertake; and maintain their interests against official oppression, more effectually, than a distant authority. Society itself will be brought into a healthy working order. A new field of distinction, honour, and influence will be open to men becoming good and esteemed members of society. Their example and influence will exercise a beneficial effect upon their neighbours. Evil propensities will find a check in public opinion, and injured parties will at once appeal to the sympathy of their fellow-villagers. The energies of Government officers will not be wasted in tracing out truth, nor will the morals of the people suffer by attempts to conceal it, in every petty concern of life. Social improvements and public works of utility can be undertaken with facility by the recognized leading men of the community instead of looking to Government for everything; and officers of Government interested in these matters will know where to work, and whom to persuade and advice. A new school for official training will be opened, in which the principal members of the village communities, can enter without quitting their own avocations, or degrading or demoralizing themselves, and an official class with landed interests in the country and with a well-tested reputation for respectability and good conduct amongst the people will become available for the higher revenue and judicial offices, while to men retiring from public life, the village offices will open an honourable and agreeable position, in which they can spread blessings of peace amongst their fellow-men.

In 1864, Rangacharlu was appointed the Deputy Collector of Treasury at Calicut.

MYSORE IN TRANSITION

It will be remembered that in 1831 Maharaja Sri Krishnaraja Wodayar Bahadur III, G.C.S.I.

of Mysore was dethroned on account of alleged maladministration. But the stout-hearted Maharaja pleaded "not guilty," and kept on petitioning and vigorously agitating through an expensive agency in England, for 36 long and weary years, in order to redeem himself from the unwarranted dishonour and be restored to his rightful position. At last in a Despatch dated the 16th April 1867, the Secretary of State communicated to the Government of India that

> Her Majesty desires to maintain that (the Maharaja's) family on the throne in the person of His Highness' adopted son, upon terms corresponding with those of 1799......If at the demise of His Highness, the young prince should not have attained the age......for his majority, the territory shall continue to be governed in his name, upon the same principles and under the same regulations as at the present time.

This wise and just decision was not a little due to the powerful advocacy of the Raja's cause by Liberal statesmen, among them being our own Dadabhai, the Grand Old Man, and the eminent philosopher who later presided at the India Office with conspicuous sympathy and foresight. In the course of a telling article in the *Fortnightly Review* of September 1866, Lord Morley wrote:—

> If there is any credence to be attached to the reports of the most impartial and experienced Anglo-Indians, the incorporation of Mysore is just one of those measures most likely to pave the way for renewed disaffection and its disastrous consequences. . . We have abandoned our legitimate influence in the West in order to annex in the East. We preach moral suasion in Europe so that we may be free to practice material repression in Asia. We make ourselves despised in one continent in order to make ourselves hated in another.

In the meanwhile, a telegram dated the 28th March 1868, from the Commissioner of Mysore to the Secretary to the Government of India announced:

Maharaja died at 11 o'clock last night. Regiment from French Rocks arrived at Mysore and occupied Fort gates. All is quiet. Valuable property sealed up; and ladies and servants received expression of condolence and assurance of protection.

IN THE SERVICE OF MYSORE

Previous to this, Sir Richard Temple, Secretary to the Government of India, had, hearing of the Maharaja's serious illness, instructed Mr. L. Bowring, Commissioner, that "the young Maharaja should be treated personally as successor to the late Maharaja, and suitable arrangements regarding the Palace and the household should be made." Accordingly, the Commissioner reported on the 7th April that he "had an interview with the young Maharaja and the Ranies," that "schedules of all property belonging to the late Maharaja have been obtained and a complete inventory will be made," that "considering the laborious nature of the duties entailed, a first-rate native will be required" "to assist Major Elliot in scrutinizing the establishments and invoicing the property" and that "the advice of an experienced native would be very useful on such an occasion." On 5th May following, Mr. Bowring wrote:—

The Government of Madras have, on my application, been good enough to transfer to me the services of Mr. Rangacharlu, a Deputy Collector of that Presidency, for the purpose of aiding Major Elliot in the laborious duty before him. Mr. Rangacharlu served for a long time under the Hon'ble Mr. Taylor in the Inam Inquiry of Madras and I have little doubt that that gentleman will testify to his remarkable aptitude for business and his high character. I have no hesitation, therefore, in soliciting the confirmation of Government of his appointment to the post referred to.

On May 23, the Government sanctioned the appointment on a monthly salary of Rs. 800. About three months later, we find the Commissioner reporting "the successful accomplishment of the reduction and revision of the Palace establishments of the late Maharaja of Mysore, a laborious duty which, owing to the judicious arrangements of Major Elliot, the Superintendent, who was ably seconded by Mr. C. V. Rangacharlu, has, notwithstanding its formidable nature, been performed so as to command the acquiescense of all those concerned in it." Major Elliot himself had written :—

> In laying before the Government the result of what has now been accomplished and which will greatly facilitate our labours in the settlement of what remains in the Department of Property and Debts of His late Highness' affairs, I cannot avoid anticipating the close by placing on record the very high opinion I have formed of the value of Mr. C. Rangacharlu's services in the success which has attended our proceedings in the accomplishment of what may safely be termed the most important part of the task committed to our charge. His untiring energy, unwearied patience, judgment and sagacity have been applied with so much tact and research to the very last closing of the lists that I attribute in great measure the almost absence of complaint or manifestation of discontent to the persevering scrutiny which, through his valuable assistance, has been brought to bear on each individual case.

Again, the same officer wrote :—

> It is matter of considerable regret to me that I have been compelled by the state of my health to relinquish the charge without for a short time at least having any opportunity of watching the working of the Palace departments under the new regime; I am satisfied that what remains to be done as well as what further explanation may hereafter be required in regard to the past settlements and the principles followed in obtaining them will be readily attended to by Mr. C. Rangacharlu to whose value as a public officer I have again, at the close of my labours, to record my testimony and beg to commend him most strongly to the favourable consideration of Government as one eminently qualified to do honour to the highest branches of public service. To his able assistance I have been much indebted throughout the whole of this, in many respects, delicate and most fatiguing and intricate

inquiry, and I am desirous that Mr. Rangacharlu should receive the credit which he so justly deserves for the ability energy and great accuracy in the details. . . . ."

This was in November 1868. In December next, the Government of India appointed Lieutenant Colonel J. Heines to be Guardian to the minor Maharaja of Mysore and suggested to the Commissioner that " it would conduce to good order and management to place, under the Guardian, a highly qualified native gentleman who might be of much use in regulating and controlling the affairs of the household and who might, from his knowledge of native habits and character, give valuable advice and suggestions to Lieutenant-Colonel Heines. Such a qualified person, His Excellency in Council believes, is at this moment available in C. Rangacharlu. . , . ." The suggestion of course took effect. In 1869, Lieutenant Colonel Heines was succeeded by Lieutenant Colonel G. B. Malleson; and an official paper of August 1871 states:

Associated with Lt. Col. Malleson and now with Mr. Gordon, his successor, in his important work, are Mr. Rangacharlu and Mr. Jayaram Rao. . . . . Mr Rangacharlu had already earned the good opinion of Government by the meritorious assistance which he rendered to Major Charles Elliot.

RETRENCHMENT IN MYSORE ADMINISTRATION

In 1874, Rangacharlu wrote a characteristic paper on "Fifty Years of British Administration of Mysore" which was published in London and created considerable sensation among the Parliamentary friends of India. It was only a fragment; but as it fearlessly exposed the shortcomings of British rule,

—how it was expensive without being adapted to the special circumstances of the State and how certain individuals were fattening at the cost of the public,—the remaining portion of it was not allowed to see the light of day. A deserved honour in the form of a C. I. E. came to him in 1870, and in the next year Chief Commissioner Mr. Gordon appointed him his Revenue Secretary. About 1880, some baseless slanders were set afloat to the effect that Rangacharlu was a selfish alien and that he was responsible for the alleged disappearance of certain valuables from the Mysore Palace. It was almost inevitable that many should have turned Rangacharlu's enemies when he was engaged in the onerous task of purifying the Palace and reforming its administration. As many as 6,000 persons who were maintained at a needless expense of Rs. 38,000 a month were, in all, thrown out of employment in the course of his retrenchment. These and the others who were prevented by him from exercising their undesirable influence on the young Prince and the Ranies made common cause and employed all sorts of devices to defame him. There were also some who thought that they had claims of their own for the office of Dewan which was certain to come into being before long and was likely to be conferred on their rival Rangacharlu. Even some honest and respectable folk were for a time deceived into a belief in the groundless reports circulated by these interested people, so much so that popular feeling ran very high against Rangacharlu at one time. But nothing ever shook the trust that had been reposed in him by the British Government as well as by the young Maharaja and his real well-wishers.

AS DEWAN OF MYSORE

When the long, wearisome and arduous process of making a statesman was thus going apace, Prince Chamarajendra Wodayar was growing to the age of majority and becoming fit to assume the charge of his territories. He was intelligent, noble and patriotic. A careful training, in which Rangacharlu himself had taken no mean part, had developed in him all the graces of conduct requisite in a ruler of men; and the influence of the high-minded British gentlemen of those days as well as his own peculiar circumstances had instilled into him a profound sense of his exalted duties. In fact, on his worthiness depended the sole chance of success for any one who would become his minister,—especially for Rangacharlu. "The most disastrous famine of which we have any record" had laid the people low, ruined trades and industries, and driven the State into heavy indebtedness. Amidst these trying conditions it was that the Government of Mysore was transferred, on March 25, 1881, to His late Highness Sri Chamarajendra Wodayar Bahadur, G.C.S.I. On the same day, "placing trust and confidence in the loyalty, ability and judgment of C. V. Rangacharlu," His Highness appointed him "to be our Dewan for the conduct of the executive administration of the said territories." On the same date was formed also the Maharaja's Council with Mr. T. R. A. Thamboo Chetty (Judge) Mr. Poorna Krishna Rao and Mr. A. Ratna Sabhapathi Mudaliyar (both retired officials) as members, and the Dewan as President, "to submit for our consideration, their opinion on all questions relating to legislation and taxation and on all other important measures connect-ed with the good administration of our territories and the well-being of our subjects."

Undaunted by private foes and public adver-sities, Rangacharlu went on with his work of re-con-struction :

> To reform the abuses of a personal and autocratic—(in the present case bureaucratic)—*regime*, to revive education, to improve the sanitary condition of towns and villages, to open commercial communications, and altogether to raise the political and moral status and character of the people committed to their charge......................at the same time to keep on good terms with the English Residents who are not always the most amiable and to protect the Rajahs themselves against the corrupting influences of their little courts and harems.

These, in the words of Professor Max Muller, used with reference to another Native States reformer, are the functions that fall to the lot of a Dewan ; and "few Prime Ministers even of the greatest States in Europe had so many tasks on their hands." The Professor continues :—

> The clock on the tower of the Houses of Parliament strikes louder than the repeater in our waist-coat pocket ; but the machinery, the wheels within wheels and particularly the spring have all the same tasks to perform as in Big Ben himself. Even men like Disraeli or Gladstone, if placed in the position of these native statesmen, could hardly have been more successful in grappling with the difficulties of a new State, with rebellious subjects, envious neighbours, a weak sovereign and an all-powerful Suzerain, to say nothing of court intrigues, religious squabbles and corrupt officials.

Such indeed, with perhaps some slight modifications, was the situation in which Rangacharlu found himself. But his adamantine will and nerve of steel stood him in good stead. He skilfully husbanded the resources of the state, economised expenditure, carried out a convenient redistribution of taluks and districts, abolished or transferred superfluous courts and offices, substituted natives—particularly the sons of the soil,—for the Europeans in service, re-organised the several departments of administration, laid down principles and policies for their guidance and, in short, continued the work of administrative reform which he, as Revenue Secretary, had initiated in co-operation with Mr. Gordon. Marks of Rangacharlu's personality are still clearly visible in the working of every branch of the Mysore Government. A few facts of his administration and a few of his leading economic ideas can be gathered from his own two addresses to the Mysore Representative Assembly, the first delivered on 7th October 1881 and the second on 26th October 1882.

(I)

The condition of the Province has been very much affected by the great calamity which so recently visited it. The ruinous effects of the famine will be so fresh in your minds that I need not dwell on them. It will suffice for me to say that it cost us 160 lakhs of rupees, involved the Government in a debt of 80 lakhs and withal deprived the Province of a million (a fifth) of its population and crippled its resources for years to come.

• • • • • •

Governments wishing to adjust their expenditure to the revenues should direct their efforts to a proper retrenchment of the expenditure rather than depend on any vague expectation of deriving an increase of revenue from an impoverished country.

* * * * *

The success of agriculture is dependent on the flourishing condition of the manufacturing industries. The old idea that India must confine itself to the growth of agricultural produce is giving way to the more correct theory that no country can prosper unless its agricultural and manufacturing industries were equally fostered. The cultivation may be expected to revive to the full extent in the next few years.

In the department of education, ... little remains to be done by way of establishing additional schools or stimulating a desire for education; but efforts are being chiefly directed to secure better qualifications in the teaching staff of the Taluk and Hobli Schools and to encourage technical education.

The development of the various industries on which the prosperity of the country is dependent equally demands our consideration; and His Highness' Government will be always prepared to give every attention to any suggestions which may be made upon these subjects. The appointment of a special officer for the purpose cannot be of much service as the experience and knowledge of a single individual can accomplish but little. His Highness the Maharaja is desirous of organizing a large association of private gentlemen who are likely to interest themselves in the matter and when such an association is formed, His Highness' Government will consider it to be its duty to help the efforts of the association to promote the industries of the country.

His Highness' Government regards the opening out of the province by means of railways as a preliminary to the development of its resources. The first line of railways in the Province from Bangalore to Mysore will be shortly completed. * *

Other lines of railway are even more urgently required for the Province.

* * * *

[*Here are suggested various industries which can be profitably worked up in the State.*]

The prosperity of the country can never be assured until the labour of its people yields a surplus over and above the food consumed by them. . . . . Improvement in this respect can only be effected by diminishing the proportion of human labour employed in the production of the country, by the application of machinery and capital. . . . . . At present, population increases at a more rapid rate than production, and increasing want and poverty is the inevitable result.

The wealth and intelligence of the people should be encouraged to seek honourable employment in productive industries instead of looking to the Government service or other equally unproductive professions.

The savings of the Government officials are, no doubt, at present very largely laid out on land. But they are solely employed in the purchase of lands as an investment and not on the improvement of their cultivation.

* * *

But such occasional failure of rains is almost a normal condition of the Province, and the Government must always remain in constant anxiety as to the fearful results which must follow from them. The results of the last famine will show how little can be done by the Government in the matter, notwithstanding its liberal expenditure, without the co-operation of the people. Irrigation works will, of course, receive every attention from the Government, although, excepting the river channels, they are not of much use when the rains fail. As already explained the Government has it in contemplation to provide a complete system of Railways to facilitate the transport of food, and it is also intended to initiate, under proper arrangements to prevent abuse, a system of advances to the ryots for the more extensive digging of wells in the taluks where there are springs in the soil; and as already remarked private efforts for the application of capital and machinery in the cultivation of land will receive every encouragement from the Government. But a great deal must be done by the people themselves to provide against these calamities.

(II)

............I must, however again report that *whatever government or any few outsiders can do must be small compared with what the great mass of the population engaged in industrial pursuits could accomplish* in their several occupations when stirred up by a desire for advancement. When all the world around is working marvellous progress, the 200 millions of people in this country cannot much longer continue in their long sleep, simply following the traditions of their ancestors of 2,000 years ago and earning a miserable subsistence, ready to be crushed on the first occurrence of a famine or other calamity. Steam began to be utilized in Europe as a motive power in manufactures only at the beginning of the present century. India then used to export cloths to England. Now England, notwithstanding a severe competition from the other countries of Europe and America supplies the greater portion of the world with cloths and other manufactures. These are not the fruits of any large individual discoveries which alone can attract the attention of the official mind, but the result of numerous individual men devoting their intelligence to effect small discoveries and improvements from day to day in their several occupations which in their aggregate produce such marvellous wealth and general prosperity. What then may not be accomplished if the large population in this country once entered on a similar career of progress?

Comment is needless. It only remains to be said that Rangacharlu always spoke to the people in the same winning and sincere tone about their occupations, their needs, their difficulties and their prospects.

THE DEMOCRAT

A skilful financier and able administrator as Rangacharlu was, the distinguishing trait of his character was his democratic disposition. He had long cherished the idea of establishing a people's assembly in Mysore with a view to secure the benefit of genuine public opinion for the measures and policies of the Government and to create in the mind of the people an active interest in the affairs of the State; and to this idea he gave practical effect soon after he assumed charge of Dewanship. In the order announcing the formation of the Representative Assembly, dated the 25th August 1881, he expressly stated:

H. H. The Maharaja is desirous that the views and objects which his Government has in the measures adopted for the administration of the Province should be better *known and appreciated by the people for whose* benefit they are intended; and he is of opinion that a *beginning* towards the attainment of this object may be made by an annual meeting of the representative landholders and merchants from all parts of the Province, before whom the Dewan will place the results of the past year's administration and a programme of what is intended to be carried out in the coming year. Such an arrangement by bringing the people in immediate communication with the Government would serve to remove from their minds any misapprehensions in regard to the views and action of the Government and would convince them that *the interests of the Government are identical with those of the people.*"

Many and vehement were the objections raised against Rangacharlu's scheme. It was said that the people were not educated, that they were not accustomed, that they were not prepared, that they were not eager and that they were not fit for representative political institutions. But he heeded them not. He believed that capacity for active participation in politics can be acquired by the people only gradually, and only by actually taking part in it for some time, just as swimming can be learnt by one only by getting down actually into water and remaining there in the practice of that art. He was not blind to the existence of rudimentary civic ideas among the people, as evidenced in their ancient institutions such as the *Panchayat*, and he could see nothing intrinsically wrong either with the brain or with the body of the Indian to render him unfit for "a beginning" in taking some share in the administration of his country. And like the great Liberal, Lord Morley, he held that "no Government can be trusted if it is not liable to be called before some jury or another, compose that jury how you will, and even if its majority should unluckily happen to be dunces."

It is perhaps necessary to add here that the Representative Assembly was instituted not only to secure that the people are made happier and the State more prosperous, but also to prevent the possibility of a catastrophe such as had befallen the State fifty years previously.

For Rangacharlu held that:—

The one great problem to be solved by Indian statesmen is how the people could be roused from the crushing influence of officialdom and stirred up to industrial enterprise and progress.

His Highness' Government is most anxious to do what lies in its humble power, in this direction; but now that a new era of representative institutions and self-government is commencing to infuse new life into the nation, the Government must look to you, as the representatives of the people, to spread these ideas amongst them, and rouse them to a sense of their true interest and importance.

The following extracts from his speech before the Representative Assembly of 1882 contain his opinion on the momentous question of self-government for Indians:

It is gratifying to find that since His Highness the Maharaja initiated this popular measure, the Government of India have resolved upon a comprehensive scheme for extending Self-Government in local matters throughout the British Territories in India. Their Despatch of the 8th May, 1882, which contains their orders on the subject, may, from its earnestness of purpose, its liberal views, and far-seeing statesmanship, be truly regarded as introducing a new era in the Indian Administration. The universal satisfaction with which it has been received throughout Southern India, and, I believe, in other parts of India also, is proof of the appreciation of the boon by the people, and refutes the assumption often made that they are not yet prepared for self-government. If the spread of any high degree of education among the great mass of the people were to be insisted upon as a *sine qua non*, we may have to wait for ever; meanwhile every year, under an autocratic system of government, will find the people less fit for representative institutions. The sprinkling of educated men who are sure to be found in these representative bodies will serve for all purposes of leading and guiding; but what is required in the great body of the representatives is common sense and practical views such as characterized your discussions on the occasion of our last meeting, and which are sure to be possessed by men of ordinary knowledge engaged in industrial and other useful occupations. The real education for self-government can only be acquired by the practical exercise of representative functions and responsibilities under the guidance, as observed by the Government of India, of officers possessed of administrative tact and directive energy, and evincing an earnestness in the success of the experiment. The success in different parts of the country will vary, not so much according to the spread of English education as according to the strength with which village communal ideas still subsist amongst the people. The defects which would require to be guarded against in the working of these representative bodies are a tendency to fall into apathy, and the growth of a factious spirit; but these could be successfully overcome by the counsel and exhortations of the District Officer evincing an earnest interest in the success of the measure. It cannot be too often impressed on the representatives that, in the discharge of the important functions entrusted to them, they are expected to evince a true public spirit, and to be actuated by considerations not of any personal wants or grievances, or, of even those of any particular caste or section of the community, but by considerations of the interest of the public at large. It cannot, however, be concealed that the Government officers themselves require as much education in the matter as the less informed representatives of the people. And earnestness on their part to promote the public interest, not to mention considerations of personal distinction and importance, begets a desire to devise and carry out what appears to them useful work; and this is not unnaturally followed by intolerance of differences of opinion or opposition from others. These have to give way to the higher qualities of a patient and watchful interest in the proceedings of others, which they must be content to guide and direct by advice and suggestions without any abatement of their earnestness to promote the public interest. District officers have to be strongly imbued with the idea that in Municipal and other matters the public interests are better served by diffusing sound ideas on the subject amongst the people, and thereby inducing them to work out the results for themselves, in preference to expecting the Government to do the work for them. Though the objects arrived at may not thereby be accomplished so promptly and successfully as by Government agency, the result will be enduring and will have a spreading influence amongst the people, and will be less subject to those changes which often characterize the improvements initiated by public officers.

* * * * *

I must first point out that we have proceeded here under lines somewhat different from those now proposed to be followed by the Government of India. We thought that a Representative Assembly, like the one in which we are now met, formed of the leading members of the District population coming in direct communication with the Government and discussing and exercising an influence on its administrative measures would be a desirable preliminary to the strengthening of Representative Institutions in Municipalities and Districts. The Representatives thus brought in direct communication with the Government will carry back with them to the Districts a higher status, and a higher tone and sense of responsibility to guide them and their fellow-members on the Municipality and Local Fund Boards, and to encourage them in the discharge of their duties under the varying influence of different District Officers. Moreover, there seems no reason why the influence of public opinion should be confined to Municipal and Local Fund affairs, important as they are, and why it should not be brought to bear upon the various administrative measures of the Government in which the people are equally interested.

The moderation and practical good sense which characterized your discussions on the occasion of our first meeting last year, and the several measures of useful and necessary reform which resulted from them, induce me to place a high value on the practical views of the people on matters immediately affecting their interests, as contrasted with mere theoretical ideas. I venture, therefore, to submit that the liberal measures in regard to Self-Government now inaugurated by the Government of India would be incomplete if the elective Municipal and Local Fund Boards created by them were not further utilised whether by way of deputing a certain number to the Legislative Councils of the Local Governments, or in some other way, as the exponents of public opinion on public matters entitled to respectful consideration from Government.

It will be proper that the whole of the members of the Municipal and Local Fund Boards should be elected by the people. The Government may reserve to themselves the power of appointing, when considered necessary, two or three members, either from amongst their officers or from non-official persons, as the exponents of their views; but the system of Government appointing by nomination half or one-third of the entire number of members, seems uncalled for, and is objectionable as it occasions invidious distinction in the status of the members, and weakens the moral effect of the elective system. The Government ought not to seek to secure a majority in the Board to carry out their views. It would suffice to reserve to it the power of overruling the proceedings of the Boards, or of suspending their functions when they are found not to work satisfactorily.

The trend of recent political thought and reform in this country fully proves the wisdom and the pre-vision of the author of the above speech. The Representative Assembly, which in his time consisted of 144 ryots, landlords and merchants, is now twice as strong and counts lawyers, journalists and other educated men among its members. The general tone of its deliberations has also gone on rising from year to year, eliciting the appreciation of successive Dewans.

VIEWS ON EDUCATIONAL AND SOCIAL QUESTIONS

Advanced as Rangacharlu's political views were, it would be highly interesting at present to know what opinions he held on questions of education. Speaking at the distribution of prizes to the students of the Maharaja's College on 24th March 1882, under the presidency of H. H. the late Maharaja, he said:

Though the requirements of an advancing age cannot permit of any education being left to the chances of individual philanthropy as in former days, and it is necessary that Government should undertake the maintenance of public schools and colleges, care should be taken not to allow them to degenerate into a mere Government Department worked on mere routine, and on more or less mercenary considerations. If educational institutions are to attain their highest success, they ought to be characterized by the public spirit, purity of intentions, and devoted attachment between masters and pupils, which belonged to the older schools.

* * * * *

RELIGIOUS EDUCATION

I wish to call attention to the address lately delivered by His Excellency the Viceroy at the convocation of the Calcutta University. . . . . . . The first point to which I would wish to call attention is His Excellency's remark in regard to the incomplete character of a secular without religious education. . . . . I wish, however, to explain that the defect is by no means of so serious a nature as is generally imagined, and that the results attributed to it are really due to other causes. By religious education it is not meant that educational institutions should become schools of theology, but simply that the religious instincts of students should be kept up. But in this country, where public schools are not Boarding but Day Schools, the cultivation of the religious instincts is more conveniently left to be developed in the home life of the students, according to their respective creeds and beliefs. Great responsibility nevertheless rests on the masters in this matter. Though not required to teach any particular form of faith, it is clearly expected of them to cultivate a proper religious tone amongst the pupils, and to check and correct any spirit of levity such as often results from the discussion of the principles of morality at an early age.

HIGHER EDUCATION

If then Government had to contribute a portion of the cost of these collegiate institutions, whether Government or aided, out of its revenues, it is a necessary contribution not to the students of the colleges, but to the people at large. No nation can thrive without a highly educated class at its head, and the system of Government schools can never be complete without the colleges. So long as these colleges are attended by all classes of people and a well-devised system of scholarships place them within the reach of the more gifted students of the poorer classes, Government must regard that it is the national and not individual interests that are served.

POPULAR EDUCATION

Education is but the means to an end. A desire for it can only spring amongst the people by political ambition, any religious movement or any great industrial changes. This is well exemplified by the existing state of education in this country.

What then is really required is to stimulate a desire for education amongst the great agricultural classes of the people. If this is accomplished, Government will be called upon no more to pay for their education than to feed them. It is of all things most necessary that the status of the agricultural classes should be raised ; and they become sensible of their importance. His Highness's Government, you are aware, is already doing something, though as yet very little, in this direction by getting the representatives of the people to meet annually to take part in the affairs of the State, and when people feel that they have a status, depend on it that they will consider a knowledge of the 3 R's at least as a desirable acquisition. As regards teaching the people the more useful subjects of European knowledge, it is not advantageous to mix it up with their other elementary instruction which is best left to their own indigenous schools conducted according to their ideas and conveniences. What is required is to have a select class of well trained men, who as itinerant teachers would go about the villages imparting instruction in a telling and attractive manner on such special subjects as are considered useful to the people from time to time. Vernacular books on such subjects and indeed a great extension of Vernacular literature, are also required......All these things mean not an increased expenditure of money on primary education but an increasing agency of educated natives interested in the welfare of their countrymen, by whom alone these things could be effected

* * * * *

THE GOVT. AND THE EDUCATED CLASSES

The (Indian) Government have generously opened out to the natives fields of profitable employment. What is more required is that the natives should have a voice in the administration in all its branches, that the conduct of native servants should be judged by their own countrymen and that the uncovenanted service should be better regulated so that the public appointments may be treated as matters of State trust and not personal patronage; and that instead of public influence being entirely engrossed by a purely official class, positions of public influence and usefulness may be thrown open to private gentlemen amongst land-holders and other classes as more or less honorary appointments.

TO THE STUDENTS

It is for you to remove from our race any stigma of the educated classes not proving useful members of society; and your worth will always be judged by the manner in which in your various spheres of life you contribute to the general advancement of the great masses of our people. I congratulate such of you as have attained eminent success in the recent examinations. . . . . I have also a word to say to those who were not so fortunate. Those who have tried and failed have no reason to be discouraged. . . . . . In the battle of life, it is found that those who fail in their school career attain to distinction as largely as those who successfully pass their examinations.

Three days before the above was spoken, Rangacharlu had given expression to his opinions on the education of women at a similar function in the Maharani's Girls' School. This institution was established mainly through his influence and aid in 1881 and gradually developed into the far-famed Maharani's College of to-day.

Rangacharlu said:

LEGISLATION FOR WOMEN

I attach great importance to getting up amongst our leading families numbers of young ladies with a high English education who could feel for the advancement of their sex, and take up the same position in regard to them as that occupied by educated men in relation to their ignorant brethren. We cannot altogether trust in the legislation of men for the softer sex, any more than in the legislation of one class for another. Such legislation is often apt to err as much on the side of extravagance, as on that of despotism, indulging in imaginary ideas of women's rights and other extravagant notions. The happy mean will be arrived at, if we leave to women all that concerns themselves to be judged and determined by the standard of their feelings and ideas on the subject.

The rational, progressive and yet nationalistic character of these conceptions is obvious. And considering the date of their utterance, no one can help admiring the breadth of their author's mind and its openness to the wholesome forces of modern thought. Especially the last paragraph quoted above marks him off as a staunch liberal in social matters also.

CHARACTERISTICS

We have characterized Rangacharlu as a democrat. He was also an autocrat in some respects; and in none more so than in the way in which he dealt with officials of a questionable character. He would fine them, transfer them over long distances or dismiss them summarily and even arbitrarily. His ear was always eager for reports regarding the conduct of officials. He had a shrewd way of collecting information about mofussil affairs, through the leading men of Taluks and Districts and through the rural population. When news of some wayward or tyrannical officer reached him, he would himself set out, if possible, to the scene of tyranny, or send out spies, or summon the accused person himself to his presence. If the last was the case, the very reception accorded to the accused would suffice to strike terror into him and turn him to the path of rectitude. If his guilt was proved, there was no escape for him from an exemplary punishment. If malpractices had not been as rampant as they really were among officials in those days, Rangacharlu's treatment of them could have with reason been disapproved as unduly harsh.

An episode narrated by a reliable informant of those times shows how even as a young man Rangacharlu was far above the temptations of money. Once when he was a Revenue official in the Madras Service, he had been out on a *jamabandi* tour along with the Collector. The Tahsildar of a certain place, it seems, went to him with the customary *nuzzur* (offering) in order to buy exemption from his strict official scrutiny. But Rangacharlu reproved the man severely and sent him back. The Tahsildar's friends and counsellors construed this as a sign of dissatisfaction, on the part of Rangacharlu, at the smallness of the offering, and advised him to double the amount if he was really anxious to retain his appointment. The Tahsildar consented; and without anybody's knowledge, had the enhanced sum placed beneath Rangacharlu's pillow on a certain night. When Rangacharlu woke up the next morning and had the bed rolled, what should have been his surprise to find rupees flying about there with nobody to claim them! He at once saw through the trick, sent for the Tahsildar and greeted him with a volley of harsh words. The Tahsildar collapsed and took home his ill-gotten money only after receiving from the incorruptible Sheristadar of the Collector a solemn assurance that he would not report the occurrence to the Collector except in general terms.

Once Rangacharlu received information from a visitor that a certain Deputy Commissioner was in the habit of getting provisions etc., through the Amildars while on circuit. This not only placed the Amildars in a false position in demanding and obtaining payment for the articles supplied, but it implied an altogether inadequate estimate of the status of Amildars and of the consideration and respect which should have been shown to them by their superior officers. The Dewan started forthwith to that particular District and obtained, in the course of his interviews with the people, corroborative evidence which compelled the Amildars to make a candid confession. Thereupon, the Dewan issued an order, which is said to be in force even to-day, strictly prohibiting the objectionable practice.

The Dewan's surprise visits, his vigilant scrutiny, his uncompromising independence and his awe-inspiring personality kept the officers always on the alert. The moral tone of even the incorrigible Palace servants had become improved under his influence. Many of those that had been deprived by him of their sinecures in the Palace sought his advice as to their future careers and followed it with very fortunate consequences.

His was a life of untiring activity. He travelled often; and while travelling, he was not fastidious about his retinue and paraphernalia. He could not adhere mechanically to one programme of business, and would not confine himself to one topic or one language in his conversation. His brain knew no rest, and work seemed to be his rule of life. And this blessed contagion of restless, public-spirited work, he transmitted freely to those around him. A writer says:

> If the archives of the Secretariat at Bangalore could be explored, a number of his minutes and memoranda might be brought out to guide and instruct the younger generation. The very G. O's issued under his authority or committed to him by the Chief Commissioner to be drafted are instructive and relate to almost every branch of the administration.

Rangacharlu was, as we have already seen, a great friend of the cultivator, and this friendship he sometimes carried to such an extent as to seem offensive to the official classes. When at a meeting of the Representative Assembly, an official referred tauntingly to the poor intellectual attainments of the ryots, he retorted by applauding the ryots' strong common sense and wide worldly experience which were sadly lacking in the official. When some one else remarked that, if the Dewan continued to show so much consideration and leniency to the Representatives, the day would soon come when the officials would have to bribe them, instead of their taking bribes from the people, as had been the case till then, Rangacharlu replied that he would heartily welcome such a day. He would not have countenanced the idle contention that Mysore is a *Swaraj* State and that there is no gulf there yawning between the tax-payers who are producers and the tax-gatherers who are consumers.

He deplored the false ideas of authority and prestige that were then, and are even now, associated with the tenure of public office, and his foremost intention was to make the ryots whose status at the time of the Rendition was inferior to what it was in the neighbouring British districts, feel (i) that they possessed complete rights of property in their lands, (ii) that the fruits of their labour were entirely theirs, and (iii) that Government servants could not use them and could not command their services as they pleased. As to how much Rangacharlu was able personally to contribute towards the realisation of that intention, we have only to heave a heavy sigh of sorrow remembering that cruel death snatched him away within less than two years since he took over the Dewanship. He passed away on the 20th of January 1883. The event happened at Madras whither he had been to recover his health which had been shattered by official cares and ceaseless toil. But he had already laid the foundations and prepared the plans for the future edifice. As his successor declared before the Representative Assembly in 1883.

> The present policy of His Highness' Government is in the main, based on the lines so ably chalked out by him in many of the public speeches, both here and elsewhere; and I have no doubt that the great example which he has set us in his unwearied solicitude for the welfare of the people will long continue to encourage us in the discharge of our onerous public duties.

We have it on the authority of Lord Curzon that the Rendition of Mysore was "a great experiment. For, if the result had been failure, then a cruel rebuff would have been administered to the generosity which dictated the proceeding, and the cause of Native States and of Native Administration throughout India must have suffered a lasting recoil." His Lordship however, acknowledged "unhesitatingly" that the State has been "well served." Towards this happy result, Rangacharlu's indirect and invisible contribution is perhaps not less valuable than what he personally and directly contributed.

SIR K. SESHADRI IYER*

INTRODUCTION

MORE than two decades have passed since Seshadri Iyer crossed the frontier of mortal life. It may be safely assumed that an opinion which has gradually settled itself during these years regarding his earthly career is not likely to suffer a great change in spirit and essence at any future date. From men of Lord Curzon's eminence down to the simple-minded denizens of a Mysore village, all are now agreed that he was a "remarkable" man. Every one admits,—Mysorean, Madrassi or any body else,—that Sir Seshadri Iyer possessed a splendid power of intellect and an indomitable strength of will, and that he used these gifts, on the whole, for the benefit of those whose affairs he was called upon to manage.

EARLY LIFE

Seshadri Iyer was born in 1845 (1st June) and died in 1901. His life was thus cast in a period of nascent nationalism and self-government in India and of rampant, though towards the close somewhat impotent, Liberalism in England. He came of a respectable Tamil-speaking Brahmana family of the Palghat country. The original home of the family was

---

* Largely drawn and revised, from his sketch of the Life of *Sir K. Seshadri Iyer*, by MR. D. V. GUNDAPPA, Editor of the *Karnataka*, Bangalore City.

the village of Kumarapuram. But Seshadri Iyer's father, Krishna Iyer, had settled down in some modest position at Calicut. Seshadri Iyer lost his father at the tender age of six months and grew under such protection as his poor, widowed mother could afford. He had also an elder brother who was to some extent helpful. Seshadri's early life can by no means be termed as one of affluence or happiness. It is not seldom that adversity has been the nursery of greatness.

At school his career was brilliant. He had a wonderful head for mathematics, and his general intelligence and eagerness to learn secured for him many coveted prizes. He took the degree of Bachelor of Arts in 1865 and started in life early in the following year as translator in the Collector's Office in his native town of Calicut.

Rangacharlu, the keen-eyed observer of men and merit, who, later, was destined to precede Seshadri Iyer as Dewan of Mysore, was now Deputy Collector at Calicut. Seshadri Iyer was soon the recipient of his friendly attention and felt naturally the elevating influence of that superior personality. Thus was formed a friendship which, stopped only by death, achieved much that was good to the young and rejuvenated State of Mysore and served greatly to enchance the reputation of modern Indians in the domain of statesmanship.

SERVICE IN MYSORE

Rangacharlu came to Mysore in the month of June 1868. Before September following, he made a name for himself by "untiring energy, unwearied patience, judgment and sagacity." His "able" and "valuable" services in the laborious task of setting right the affairs of the Mysore Palace earned for him a considerable amount of influence and importance. Capable men who could also rise above the corrupting influences of the official atmosphere were then wanted for service in Mysore, and Rangacharlu proposed Seshadri Iyer as a candidate. The recommendation was immediately accepted. On the 30th of October 1868, Seshadri Iyer entered Mysore service as Judicial Sheristadar in the Superintendent's Office, Ashtagram Division.

Ascent was both easy and rapid thenceforward. Ability combined with diligence pushes itself to the front in ways not to be dreamt of by mediocrity. Such was the case with Seshadri Iyer. Within ten years since his advent in Mysore, he found himself at the head of a district. He had now served as Judicial Sheristadar, Public Prosecutor, Judicial Assistant Commissioner and Comptroller to the Royal household, for varying terms. He had also qualified himself for promotion in service by taking the B. L. degree (1874) and by getting through some departmental tests. He was appointed Deputy Commissioner in February 1879 and posted to Tumkur. He was transferred to Mysore in August 1881 and remained there for eighteen months. In all these several capacities, Seshadri Iyer discharged his duties as a man of honour and as one who knew his business.

THE RENDITION OF MYSORE

On the 25th of March 1881 took place one of the happiest events in the annals of Mysore as well as in those of British supremacy in India,—an event not less glorious than the most magnificent military triumph,—namely, the Rendition of Mysore. Amid universal rejoicings, His Highness Sri Chamarajendra Wodeyar Bahadur was installed on the throne of his forefathers and invested with powers of administration. Rangacharlu was on the same day made the Dewan and President of the Consultative Council. His position was by no means a cushion of roses. The task was stupendous, the resources slender and the atmosphere uncongenial. Many were the men who regarded Rangacharlu as an alien, an adventurer, and an upstart. But subsequent history and his own private correspondence prove beyond the possibility of a doubt, that Rangacharlu was a true friend of the people, a selfless patriot to whom good government was a religion, and a stastesman born to the position he held, as it were. He had to reconstruct an entire State on new plans and principles, with inefficient assistance and an impoverished people, surrounded, moreover, by hosts of enemies. His chief concern therefore was to gather around himself the most capable and trustworthy men in service. Seshadri Iyer was of course the first among these. He was taken on special duty and entrusted with the work of drafting certain regulations and rules. He did this work in his own thorough fashion, which can be discerned in every handiwork of his. Rangacharlu who was as generous in rewarding as he was fastidious in judging, took Seshadri Iyer into his confidence and even appointed him to look after the current work of his office during a brief period of his absence from the head-quarters.

AS DEWAN OF MYSORE

But Rangacharlu had but laid out the plans of the contemplated edifice when (20th January 1883) he was called away by the resistless arbiter of things mundane. It was at this crisis that Seshadri Iyer was asked to take up and continue the work left by his master so soon after he had begun. This opens the longest and the most interesting chapter of Seshadri Iyer's life.

The position of the Minister of an Indian State, like most positions of responsibility, is one of many advantages and as many disadvantages all peculiar to itself. On one side, the people look upon him as the real master of the situation, the sovereign being incapable of independent action. The sovereign treats him with all the deference due to one who can make or mar the reputation of the State, its ruler and all. His successes are eagerly watched and extolled with pride from corner to corner in India. Britain points him out as one of the fruits of her own culture and influence. He has, as a matter of fact, almost unlimited opportunities for doing good and being great. On the other side, he has often to put up with suspicion, misunderstanding and hypercriticism on the part of public critics. He must often be content to follow his sovereign when his own wish would be to lead. He has not infrequently to face jealousy, faithlessness and clannishness among his own colleagues and assistants. He has to keep in good humour the representatives of the Paramount Power who are not always the most amiable and reasonable of mortals. And he must bring contentment and happiness to the large silent masses whose wants are expressed, if at all, only very inadequately by their natural leaders. Such is the position of a Dewan; and its disadvantages were to be felt in more than an ordinary degree when Seshadri Iyer came to it. The Ruler was young; the finances were disheartening; the people were just recovering from the effects of the most dreadful famine on record; the Rendition was being regarded as only an experiment; he was himself comparatively a junior both in age and in service and had to contend with many opponents both open and covert, both honourable and dishonourable. But two fortunate circumstances besides his own self-confidence gave heart to Seshadri Iyer amidst these difficulties. Firstly, he had the hearty support and co-operation of his Sovereign who, though young in years, was one of the most enlightened and liberal-minded Indians of his time. Secondly, he had the inspiring example of a born statesman who had paved the way for him. Addressing the Representative Assembly nine months after assuming office as Dewan, Seshadri Iyer paid him his tribute of affection and reverence in these touching terms:—

I wish most sincerely that the task had continued in the hands of the eminent statesman who addressed you on the last occasion. I am sure you have missed his genial presence during the festivities which have just closed, and I need hardly add that you will doubly feel in this hall to-day the void which he has left. It may, however, be some small satisfaction to you to be assured that the present policy of His Highness' Government is, in the main, based on the lines so ably chalked out by him in many of his public speeches both here and elsewhere: and I have no doubt that the great example which he has set us in his unwearied solicitude for the welfare of the people will long continue to encourage us in the discharge of our onerous public duties.

AN INTERESTING RESUME

It would be manifestly absurd to think of summarizing, even briefly, in what is more or less a *causerie*, all the events of Seshadri Iyer's regime covering a period of about eighteen years. Nor is it necessary, in order to appreciate his character and genius, to dwell at full length on all the details of administrative work accomplished by him in various departments. The principal events and activities of his administration are succinctly narrated in his own annual addresses to the Representative Assembly. A retrospect covering the first eleven years, which formed the best period of his career, is to be found in his Address for the year 1894. He says:—

" The Dewan or the Executive Administrative Head had the direct control, without the intervention of Departmental Heads, of all the principal Departments such as the Land Revenue, Forests, Excise, Mining, Police, Education, Legislation etc. As the finances improved and as Departments were put into good working order and showed signs of expansion, separate Heads of Departments were appointed, for Forests and Police in 1885, for Excise in 1889, for Mujroyi in 1891, and for Mining in 1894. His Highness was able to resolve upon the appointment of a separate Land Revenue Commissioner only in the latter part of 1894, but for several years previously the administrative duties of this Department had been delegated to a single Councillor empowered to dispose of all the ordinary work of the Department and to a Committee of two Councillors vested with the appellate and revisional powers of the Government under the Land Revenue Code in *quasi*-judicial matters. Similarly, the ordinary work of the Departments of Local and Municipal Funds and Legislation had been made over to individual Councillors, and the executive duties of the Education Department had come to be more and more delegated to the Secretary. Thus the administrative policy of His Highness' reign was one of progressive decentralization.

Finance.—His Highness' reign was attended with a remarkable measure of financial success. It began with liabilities exceeding the assets by 30¾ lakhs and with an annual income less than the annual expenditure by 1¼ lakh. During the first three years the revenues from all sources were generally stationary, and in the fourth year there was a considerable decline, due to the drought of that year, but during the next ten years, the improvement year after year was large and continuous.

Revenue.—The measure of financial prosperity above described was secured not by resort to new taxation in any form or shape. It was mainly the result of a natural growth, under the stimulus afforded by the opening out of the country by means of new Roads and Railways, the execution of important Irrigation works, and the general expansion of industries. It was in some measure due also to improved management of particular sources of income.

Gold Mining.—The important industry of Gold Mining took firm root in the State during His Highness' rule. In 1886 a professional examination of the auriferous tracts in Mysore was made, and the results duly published. For the first time, in 1886-87, Royalty on gold formed an item of our State revenue, and it reached the substantial figure of Rs. 7,33,000 last year on a production of gold valued at £8,44,000. A Geological Survey for the complete examination and record of the mineral resources of the country was established in 1894 and is now in full working.

The *Revenue Laws* were codified, vexatious restrictions on the enjoyment and transfer of land were swept away, and the freer relinquishment of unprofitable small parcels of land was allowed. As a means of remedying agricultural indebtedness, a scheme of Agricultural Banks on strictly co-operative principles was introduced last year.

Forests.—The area of Reserved Forests increased from 643 to 1,704 square miles, and 35 square miles of new plantations were formed.

Education—The number of Government and aided schools rose from 866 to 1,797 and the expenditure on them from Rs. 3,15,000 to Rs 8,19,810. The increase in the number of boys was from 39,413 to 83,398 and, in that of girls from 3,000 to 12,000. Eight hundred Primary Vernacular Schools, fifty English Middle Schools, five Industrial Schools, two Normal Schools, thirty Sanskrit Schools, one first Grade English College and three Oriental Colleges were newly established during His Highness' reign.

Irrigation—One hundred lakhs were spent on original irrigation works during His Highness' reign, making an addition of 355 square miles to the area under wet cultivation, and bringing an additional Revenue of 8¼ lakhs.

Communications.—In addition to the expenditure from Local Funds 67¾ lakhs from the State Revenue were devoted during His Highness' reign to new roads and to the maintenance and special improvement of existing ones. The mileage of roads rose from 3,930 to 5,107.

Railways.—At the Rendition the length of the State Railway open to traffic was 58 miles. The addition made to it during His Highness' reign was 315 miles at a cost of 164½ lakhs.

Municipal and Local Funds.—The number of Municipalities rose from 83 to 107, annual Municipal receipts from Rs. 2,76,500 to Rs. 5,63,000 and the annual expenditure on Conservancy and Public Works from 2½ lakhs to Rs. 4,89,000.

Medical Relief.—The number of Hospitals and Dispensaries rose from 19 to 114 and the number of patients treated from 1,30,723 to 7,06,915."

This is a record of solid, strenuous labour directed to a high purpose with all the skill, energy and care that the occasion demanded. It was a process of State-reconstruction, out of scanty material and with not very efficient tools. The Dewan had to bear the brunt of the burden, the Councillors having no definite share in the executive work of the Government. He had, first of all, to establish the finances of the State on a sound footing and Nature helped him considerably in this task. Successive years of timely rains and good harvests served to replenish the treasury. Then, he had to devise or adopt rules and regulations as necessity arose for them. More than 40 legislative measures were put into the statute book during these 11 years. Thirdly, he had to look to the efficient officering, equipment and supervision of several existing departments, and to start fresh ones. Lastly, he had to inauguarte fresh activities for the benefit of the State. All this he did with a thorough grasp of details, a penetrating insight into actual conditions and a firm grip over the instruments of execution. Beginning with little experience and under circumstances which were by no means propitious, he almost completed the work of State-reconstruction within eleven years under the guidance of his noble master, His Highness Sir Sri Chamarajendra Wodeyar, whom ruthless Fate took away from his beloved people towards the close of the year 1894.

THE FIRST PERIOD

Seshadri Iyer's Dewanship may be roughly divided into three periods. The first closes about the year 1886. This was one, as he himself says, of "a severe and sustained struggle, crippled resources on the one hand and increasing Railway expenditure on the other." By a process of judicious economy, he was able to show at the end of this period a surplus of more than 13 lakhs, tiding over a partial drought in 1884. It is to this wise and able management of the State's affairs that Mr. C.E.R. GIRDLESTONE, the highly sympathetic British Resident, alluded when he said:—

> The minister, the other day, publicly referred in kind and courteous terms, to the support given by me to the measures set on foot by the Maharajah's Government for the mitigation of suffering in the threatened parts of this Province; but my support and sympathy would have been of no avail if His Highness had not in Mr. Seshadri Iyer an able, enlightened, and zealous Minister, and if his Minister had not been seconded by energetic and capable officers in the Districts.

Seshadri Iyer's good work had now made for him a name far beyond the borders of the State. He was made a Fellow of the Madras University in 1886 and a C. S. I. in February following. His representations to the Government of India urging that they should waive their right for enhancing the State's annual subsidy by 10 lakhs had the desired result. The enhancement was postponed for another term of ten years.

THE SECOND PERIOD

Now began the period of positive improvement. In 1886-87 was inaugurated a scheme of Tank Restoration, in which the ryot population had to bear its share in the form of work. The Department of Archæology was also started in the same year. An Industrial and Agricultural Exhibition was organized in 1887. The year 1889 is remarkable for a further extension of the activities of the Department of Public Works in the direction of irrigation, roads and bridges and sanitary improvements for the City of Mysore. The next year saw the actual undertaking of the Bangalore-Hindupur Railway line and some attempts for the Industrial development of the State. At this time (1890) was started also the generous scheme of State Life Insurance for the benefit of public servants. The much-debated scheme of competitive exmination for the Mysore Civil Service was launched forth in 1891-92 and the privilege of electing Municipal Councillors was granted to the cities of Bangalore and Mysore the same year. Reform of the Muzrai department was taken on hand at this time. The State had to pass through a severe distress owing to failure of rains in 1891, and measures of relief were concerted on a careful and liberal plan. In 1893 were begun the works for water-supply to the cities of Bangalore and Mysore, which works have made the late Dewan's name a house-hold word. In recognition of these meritorious services, the Government of India decorated him with a K. C. S. I.

The year 1894 is noteworthy, among other things, for a scheme of Agricultural Banks, the undertaking of the old project of the well-known Marikanave, the formation of the Geological Department and the passing of the Regulation to prevent Infant Marriages. A large project of Railway-extension was also contemplated. But all the progress which a series of prosperous years and the careful husbanding of the State's resources had rendered possible, was brought to a standstill by the untimely death of His Highness Sri Chamarajendra Wodeyar Bahadur. The mournful event opened a new chapter in the history of Mysore as well as in that of its Dewan. For the former,—indeed for all India,—it meant the setting back of the clock of progress for half a century, as the late Mr. Ranade is said to have pathetically remarked at the time. For the latter, it meant the stillness of that one voice whose advice alone he was so long accustomed to seek and obey. Henceforward, he had often to enter into compromise with a body which was not altogether agreeable to his inflexible temperament. Doubtless he subordinated his own inclination to duty; he could not, however, completely set aside worry and vexation.

THE THIRD PERIOD

Not long after the passing away of His Highness, the old beautiful Palace at Mysore, rich in its historic associations, was destroyed by a fire (1896), and the year 1898 introduced into the State that most dreaded of Death's minions, the Plague. But the administration continued to be brilliant and beneficent under the "enlightened guidance" of Her Highness the Maharani-Regent whose "unfailing tact and discretion" and "example of public and domestic virtue" (Lord Curzon) commanded universal admiration.

Works of public utility received as great attention as before. The western suburb of the City of Bangalore was laid out in 1896. The celebrated Victoria Hospital and the first Students' Hostel in the State were built in 1897. In 1899 took place His Highness the Maharaja's marriage. The same year saw the opening out of two more extensions towards the North and the South of Bangalore, known as Malleswaram and Basavangudi, as well as the beginning of that magnificent, one might almost say immortal, monument of Seshadri Iyer's brain-power and courage,—the Cauvery Power Scheme. Towards the close of the busy century, a feeling of weariness over took this busy soul. After years of strenuous toil, Seshadri Iyer grew eager for peace, and in August 1900 took a furlough for seven months as preparatory for retirement. She who had been a life-long sharer in his joys and sorrows and to whose goodness people ascribed his prosperity in life,—may be, a freak of superstition, yet significant,—had left his side rendering him lonely in life. After an illness of about a month, he passed away on the 19th of September 1901.

> **Life's race well run;**
> **Life's work well done;**
> **Life's crown well won;**
> **Now comes rest.**

CHARACTERISTICS

Landmarks of Seshadri Iyer's stewardship abound on every side to-day,—and they will long remain so—reminding us of what he was and what he did. Even the hasty birds'-eye-view that we have just taken suffices to impress one with the progressive character of his ideas and achievements. Flourishing Colleges and High Schools, elementary and technical Schools, improved roads and bridges, reservoirs repaired or rebuilt, water and light supply, scientifically organised, extended railway, expanded towns—these were the features of Mysore when he retired from her service. And what he left behind in the form of plans and proposals to be carried out by his successors was itself of no mean value.

More than all these are the despatches and documents which emanated from his pen. They form a treasure in themselves, to be resorted to in times of perplexity by succeeding administrators. The reader might be here referred to the agreement which he concluded with the Government of Madras in 1892 on the question of water-rights. The archives of the Secretariat at Bangalore are full of such minutes and memoranda on almost every conceivable topic connected with the State. They either enunciate principles and policies in a terse, pointed style, or define the rights and obligations of the State or its various factors, proving his wisdom and forethought.

Sir Seshadiri Iyer was an avowed advocate of self-government. His sympathies were with the Indian National Congress, his own Sovereign Prince having given a handsome donation towards its funds. But, like most men whose chief characteristics are energy, courage and self-confidence, he cherished noble ambitions and desired power to attain them. This inborn tendency was strengthened by both circumstance and habit. His own relations with the Representative Assembly and the Executive Council illustrate his position.

In the first year of his Dewanship, he was still under the influence of his democratic predecessor and "begged that they (Representative members) would rapidly educate themselves in the science of administration." In 1885, he spoke highly of their "practical common sense" and of "a fuller representation of the wants and wishes of the people." Five years later, he appreciated their "moderation and intelligence" and the "material help" they had given him, and introduced the principle of election into the constitution of the Assembly. But it had grown strong by this time, and some of its members had even become, to use a modern phrase, "impatient idealists." Scenes and breezes began to disturb its atmosphere, and H. H. the Maharaja, who was a staunch upholder of popular freedom, never cared to intercede between the Dewan and the Representatives. A Standing Committee was formed to carry on the work of the Assembly all the year round, and inconvenient interpellations in regard to Government's doings became common.

With the Royal father of the Assembly vanished that wholesome influence which was compelling Seshadri Iyer to be respectful towards it. His task now became simpler in regard to the troublesome institution. He could deal with it in a manner that would not have been tolerated before. The "so-called" Standing Committee was disbanded. Members were told that Government had the means of knowing what was best in each case and that their evidence was "not of the slightest use." Hard questions and curt replies were substituted for calm deliberation. This unseemly antagonism between the leaders of the people and the leader of the Government raged loud and furious and never came to an end in his life-time.

It might perhaps be said for Seshadri Iyer, that the "advanced party" of the Representative Assembly was a small minority, that it took no notice of the rest of the members who were far behind in the race for political privileges, and that he disregarded the minority in consideration of the condition of this large majority. The basis of such a contention is no doubt partly true. The members, as well as the subjects they brought up, presented a hopeless medley of all shades of opinion and feeling, from the serious to the silly, from a grave constitutional issue to a cringing request for a half-

Page 128.

SIR K. SESHADRI IYER

holiday for some sectarian feast. But Seshadri Iyer's attitude towards the progressivists can on no account be regarded as one of sympathy; it certainly was not such as could have won the approbation of Rangacharlu in whose path he solemnly promised to tread in 1883. The reason for this strange inconsistency is perhaps to be found in the fact that he was instinctively one of those who believe :—

> For forms of government let fools contest;
> Whatever is best administered is best.

So in regard to the Regency Council. This institution was called into being

> because there can be no guarantee that the destinies of Mysore will continue to be guided during the long period for which arrangements have now to be made, by the able minister Sir K. Seshadri Iyer, whose administration was so successful in the past: and inconvenience and danger are foreseen if his assistance were to be suddenly withdrawn, unless there were at the time existing, and in working order, an organized machinery for carrying on the Executive Government. Both for this reason and also because it is desirable to afford the Dewan some measure of relief in dealing with the mass of work which now comes before him as Chief Executive Officer in the State, it is considered by Government to be indispensably necessary that the council now to be constituted should take an active and not merely a nominal share in the administration of affairs.

This meant certain decentralization of power and was hence a source of annoyance to Seshadri Iyer. But it was his good fortune to encounter in the Council chamber foemen, so to say, quite worthy of his steel,—men possessed of knowledge, wisdom and sincerity. The names of Mr. P. Chentsal Rao, Mr. T. R. A. Thamboo Chetty and Sir P. N. Krishna Moorthi are even to-day mentioned with profound respect everywhere in the State. In differing from the Dewan—as they very often did—they had no motive of either embarassing him or advancing their own interests; and many are the good results attributed to their good sense and independence.

Reference might be made here also to the fact that the village courts which, in October 1883, Seshadri Iyer promised to introduce had to wait till October 1913 to obtain legislative sanction. It is rather significant that this measure of self-government was never subsequently thought about.

Seshadri Iyer gave willing help to the growth and development of Municipalities and Local Boards. He had, on the whole, neither a fervid enthusiasm nor a wanton hatred for the principle of self-government. His attitude could be favourable to it; but his aptitude was not for it. He would tolerate and even encourage it. But he would not reckon it as the equal of the officialdom. He would condescend to be its patron; but he would not rise to be its missionary. When so much is said, enough will have been said to place him higher than most of his compeers, both here and elsewhere.

CONCLUSION

In his attitude towards the social and religious movements of his time, he was a reformer of the moderate type,—a rational nationalist as some might say. Sir William W. Hunter's description of him as one who had given his head to Herbert Spencer and his heart to *Parabrahma* discloses his real character.

He encouraged foreign travel, having had a large hand in the institution of the famous Damodar Dass

Scholarships; was largely responsible for introducing the Infant Marriage Regulation and gave his hearty support to women's education. But his heart lay in the *Katha Upanishad.* He was a great lover of Samskrit literature and the Vedanta; and would often snatch a quiet half-hour from a busy day to hear some favourite Vedic passage read. The Oriental Library of Mysore owes its existence to his love of the ancient culture of the land.

Personally he was a generous, estimable man, affectionate towards friends and relatives and full of love for everything good and beautiful. His life is full of lessons for the rising generation,—lessons of aspiration, industry, integrity, perseverance, sagacity, forethought and courage. His intellect and his expression were always characterised by vigour; and stories are still current of how his brain used to be active dynamo-like at all hours of the day and even of the night. He set hard mathematical problems to his "boys," it would appear, at bed time and demanded solutions the next morning. The one word that can express such a personality is—energy.

Sir Seshadri Iyer's eminent services to the State were publicly acknowledged by his successor; and speaking as President of the Indian National Congress at Calcutta, Mr. (now Sir) D. E. Wacha expressed what the whole country had felt about the "distinguished Dewan of the Mysore State":

> In him the country loses an administrator of the highest capacity and most matured experience. He was the latest instance of the Indian statesman who had shown himself cap-

able of governing fully an indigenous State with as much skill and capacity, judgment and discrimination, tact and sympathy as some of the greatest of English administrators who have left their mark on British Indian history. Sir Seshadri has now gone to swell that illustrious roll of modern Indian statesmen. . . "

A fine tribute to the statesmanship of Sir Seshadri Iyer was paid by Lord Curzon in his memorable speech at the present Maharaja's Installation when his Lordship referred to the remarkable career of the *Rajyadhurandhara* who "for 18 years wielded an authority that left its mark upon every branch of the administration." We may conclude this sketch with the no less remarkable words of Lord Hardinge who, in unveiling the statue of the illustrious statesman, fixed his position for ever among the great figures in our history. Said his Lordship:

Sir Seshadri Iyer has thus left a record behind him which marks him out, with Sir Salar Jung of Hyderabad, Raja Sir Dinkar Rao of Gwalior and Sir T. Madhava Rao of Indore and Baroda, as a member of that group of Indian statesmen whose fame has spread far beyond the borders of where they laboured so faithfully and so well and whose names will remain as a lasting example to their successors.

Mr. V. P. Madhava Rao.

MR. V. P. MADHAVA RAO, C. I. E., is one of the most prominent of Indian Administrators of recent times. He has had the unique distinction of having held the high office of Dewan or Prime Minister in three of the most enlightened Indian States, *viz.*, Travancore, Mysore and Baroda.

Mr. Madhava Rao has had the rare advantage of acquiring administrative experience and achieving distinction both under the British Government and the Governments of Indian States. For he entered Mysore service fully over a decade before the Rendition of 1881 and had already risen to a high position in that service when the State passed into the hands of His Highness the late Maharaja Chamarajendra Wodeyar. Mr. Madhava Rao proved a success in many departments of public service and showed beyond doubt that an Indian could fill with distinction any post however onerous and responsible the duties attaching to it may be.

EARLY LIFE

Viswanath Patankar Madhava Rao comes of an ancient family of Mahratta Deshastha Brahmins, long settled in Tanjore, who are supposed to have emigrated from the Satara District to South India, in the wake of the Mahratta conquest of

Tanjore. Born in 1850, he was educated in the Kumbakonam College under the distinguished educationist, Mr. W. A. Porter, and took the B. A. degree of the Madras University in 1869. Even in his College days, he was thought of highly by his Principal, who was much attached to him and who, struck by his "independence of thought," entertained a "high opinion of his personal character."

IN MYSORE SERVICE

In 1870 Mr. Madhava Rao entered the Mysore service as a clerk in the office of the Guardian of His Highness, the late Maharaja, and was soon made Head Master of the Royal School, where His Highness the late Maharaja was being educated under the guardianship of Colonel G. B. Malleson, C.S.I., Mysore being at that time under British Administration. Mr. Madhava Rao was not long in service before he came under the notice of the British officers, who gave him a start in the general administration as Public Prosecutor. Captain T. G. Clarke who was Commissioner of the Nandidroog Division, predicted for Mr. Madhava Rao even at such an early date, a brilliant future and wrote :—

> Colonel Malleson under whom he (Mr. Madhava Rao) served, has also spoken of him in flattering terms and in entering the administrative branch of the service, therefore, he starts with a high promise of obtaining distinction in the public service.

Sometime later, Colonel T. Clerk, Commissioner of the Mysore Division, recorded that "Mr. Madhava Rao's character was good and his abilities were of the highest order." In the course of a decade, when the administration was handed back to the late Maharaja, Mr. Madhava Rao had worked his way up through the different grades to the position of a Subordinate Judge.

A CHELA OF TWO GREAT DEWANS

Mr. Madhava Rao had, from the beginning, the rare good fortune of being associated with the ablest and most popular of the Dewans of Mysore, *viz.*, the late Mr. Rangacharlu. In fact, Mr. Rangacharlu had gathered about him a few of the rising and talented young men in the service. Mr. Madhava Rao was the youngest and the most privileged member of the circle, one of the most distinguished of the others being the late Sir Seshadri Iyer, Mr. Rangacharlu's successor in the Dewanship. In this select circle the various administrative reforms set on foot by Dewan Rangacharlu were freely discussed and given shape to. Mr. Madhava Rao thus came to have intimate acquaintance with the details of administration, even before entering the administrative branches of the service. It is no wonder that, thus equipped, he was able to effect those administrative reforms in Travancore and Mysore as Dewan, which have already earned for him the warm appreciation and regard and gratitude of the people and of the Governments concerned.

AS DISTRICT OFFICER

On the death of Mr. Rangacharlu, Mr. (afterwards Sir) Seshadri Iyer succeeded to the Dewanship of

Mysore, and Mr. Madhava Rao exchanged the Judicial for the Revenue Department and was, in a few years, posted as Deputy Commissioner of the Shimoga District. In Shimoga Mr. Madhava Rao proved himself an executive officer of the best type. His accessibility to men of all grades, his readiness to hear and redress grievances, the interest he took in the welfare of the agricultural population and the many works undertaken by him for improving the sanitation of towns and villages in providing drinking water, in opening out roads and in planting avenues and restoring irrigation tanks and generally looking after the interests of the people, won for him their love and respect. It was when he was Deputy Commissioner of Shimoga that the first town extension in the State was carried out by him in Sagar and the extension was named after the late Maharaja of Mysore. Sir Oliver St. John, the then British Resident, who happened to be touring through the District, formed a high opinion of him and congratulated the late Maharaja of Mysore on having in his service an officer of Mr. Madhava Rao's stamp. As Deputy Commissioner of Bangalore he devised and successfully carried out the system of granting relief to weavers who were almost the first to suffer when famine appeared. This system was subsequently adopted in Madras and has now become a recognised method of relief.

AN INDIAN INSPECTOR-GENERAL OF POLICE

After being a District Officer for nearly seven years, Mr. Madhava Rao was appointed Inspector-

General of Police, and he has laid the Indian community under a heavy obligation to him by having, as the First Indian Inspector-General of Police, helped to dispel the then prevailing idea that Indians were unfit to hold independent charge of any office in which power of organization, firmness, initiative and resourcefulness are essential for the efficient discharge of public duties. As Inspector-General of Police, he re-organised the force, improved its tone and established the well-known Police School at Bangalore, which has done so much useful work since and has served as a model for similar schools in Madras and Bengal. It was in connection with the Police School that Mr. Madhava Rao solved the problem of giving equality of opportunity to the different classes of the community for gratifying their legitimate ambition to serve in the Government of their country. Knowing that the classes who made good executive officers were rather backward in intellectual capacity, he decided to start a training school for the officers and graduated the test for admission so as to permit of young men of intellectually backward communities getting an entrance into it equally with the more forward classes. Accordingly if the candidate was a Brahmin he insisted on his having passed the Matriculation examination as the minimum qualification. For non-Brahmin Hindus he fixed the Middle school test and for Mahomedans he was satisfied if the candidate could read and write and knew some arithmetic.

PLAGUE RELIEF

Such was the reputation Mr. Madhava Rao had acquired for himself as a capable administrator that when Mysore was threatened with plague, the Resident, Sir Donald Robertson, at once recommended him as the only officer who could be entrusted with the delicate and responsible duties connected with plague administration. Her Highness the Maharani Regent, accordingly appointed him as Plague Commissioner in addition to his duties as Inspector-General of Police. This appointment afforded Mr. Madhava Rao an excellent opportunity for giving full play to his powers of organisation and administration.

The difficulties connected with the enforcing of the rather severe measures which were then in vogue, such as compulsory evacuation and disinfection and getting the people exposed to infection to submit to inoculation are now matters of history. In Mysore there was even greater opposition to these measures than in other parts of India, but Mr. Madhava Rao rendered a good account of himself by carrying on the campaign with great humanity and firmness.

For his services as Plague Commissioner the Regency granted him a substantial bonus and the Government of India conferred on Mr. Madhava Rao the Companionship of the Indian Empire and also gave him the Kaiser-i-Hind Gold Medal in the first year of its institution.

AS REVENUE COMMISSIONER AND COUNCILLOR

While still engaged in the arduous work of Plague Commissioner, Mr. Madhava Rao was appointed a Member of the Council of Regency and was entrusted with the Revenue portfolio. In 1901 when His Highness the present Maharaja of Mysore was installed on the throne of his ancestors, Mr. Madhava Rao was specially selected to improve the working of the Revenue Department and was appointed Revenue Commissioner, in addition to his duties as Member of Council.

Mr. Madhava Rao was the first to be appointed as Revenue Commissioner, an office which was created with a view to securing greater and more direct control and supervision for the important branch of the administration which deals with land revenue and allied matters.

AS DEWAN OF TRAVANCORE

After a couple of years' service as Revenue Commissioner and Councillor, Mr. Madhava Rao was, in March 1904, invited by His Highness the Maharaja of Travancore, to be his Dewan. On the eve of his departure to Travancore he was specially entertained by the European community of the Civil and Military Station, Bangalore, in the Mayo Hall. Sir James and Lady Bourdillon attended it and Mr. Madhava Rao who was as great a favourite with the European as with his own community had a splendid send-off. The Resident, Sir James Bourdillon, used to say that Mr. Madhava Rao's career had much in common with that of Sir Dinkar Rao of Gwalior. He was also entertained in the Mylapore Club in Madras, where Sir S. Subramania Iyer and Sir Bashyam Iyengar and the elite of Madras society joined in congratulating him and Travancore on his selection for the Dewanship of that State.

A SCHEME OF LAND REVENUE

Within the short period of two years, as Dewan of Travancore, Mr. Madhava Rao managed to introduce some reforms of a far reaching character. First and foremost, stands the re-organization of the Settlement Department. The scheme of land revenue settlement in Travancore was framed by the late Dewan Ramiengar, C.S.I., and was practically based on the Madras system, but in the hands of his successors the scheme had undergone many changes with a tendency to go back to the former antiquated method of assessment and registration, the result being that operations which were estimated to be completed in nine years at a cost of 15 lakhs of Rupees, had gone on for 21 years and cost the State 49 lakhs of Rupees and yet no taluq had been settled in the proper sense of the term. Mr. Madhava Rao went into the causes of this delay and of excessive cost with his accustomed thoroughness and, although the Madras system was not familiar to him, he with the eye of a practised administrator, was able to detect the weakness of the existing method and framed a new scheme under which he showed that the whole settlement operations could be completed in four years at a cost of ten lakhs of Rupees. The new scheme has since been worked out and has proved an unqualified success. It must also be mentioned that, in introducing the new scheme of settlement, Mr. Madhava Rao was able to abolish the obnoxious system of levying fines on Service Inam Lands, sometimes amounting to 25 and 40 times the assessment, before they were confirmed to the holders, as also the extortionate fines sometimes amounting to 40 times the assessment on what were called "escheat cases."

RE-ORGANIZATION OF FINANCE

The accounts and finances of the State, which were in great confusion, were entrusted to a financial expert and the re-organization of the accounts and audit department within such a short time, elicited the warm approval of the Government of Madras. How antiquated and inefficient the old system was, can be gathered from the single fact that the accounts of eighteen years had not been audited and the advances for the period not adjusted. Within a few months of Mr. Madhava Rao's taking charge of the Dewanship of Travancore, he was able to introduce the British system of daily audit.

EXCISE ADMINISTRATION

Mr. Madhava Rao's energies were directed to other departments as well. A new department called the Excise Department was organised and was made responsible for the management of salt, abkari, tobacco, customs and other items of separate revenue, yielding 45 lakhs or nearly half the total revenue of the State.

EDUCATION

Much had been done for education in Travancore in previous administrations and in fact, Travancore stood first in point of expenditure on education in proportion to revenue and also in regard to literacy. During Mr. Madhava Rao's administration, the principle was laid down that no child in the State, whatever his caste or social position, should be allowed to grow up without the rudiments of education. As a first step towards realising this ideal, free education was given to all the backward classes.

MANAGEMENT OF TEMPLES

Great abuses had grown up in connection with the management of temples in Travancore. Non-Hindus and the lower classes among the Hindus had to pay fines for polluting Hindu temples and sacred tanks without being given a chance to be heard in their defence. In performing the purificatory rites, the priest's decision as regards the ceremonies to be performed and the sums to be spent on the same was final and the civil authorities summarily levied the fines fixed by the priests. Minister after minister had allowed these abuses to take their course without check. Within a few weeks of his taking charge of his new duties, Mr. Madhava Rao had to deal with a case in which unjust fines had been levied from innocent owners of animals and from Christians who were supposed to have polluted a temple. He quashed all the proceedings as illegal and the Maharaja of Travancore was soon persuaded to declare that the practice should be discontinued. The scale of expenses for the purificatory rites was to be fixed by a commissioner appointed for the purpose and thousands of rupees have been saved to the State as the result of this reform.

THE SRI MULAM ASSEMBLY

Another important measure and the one that will stand for ever as a memorial to the far sighted statesmanship of Mr. Madhava Rao's administration of Travancore is the institution of the Popular Assembly which meets and discusses public questions every year at the capital, under the presidency of the Dewan. Mr. Madhava Rao was later on able to secure from the enlightened Maharaja the privilege of election for this unique institution.

TAXATION

But the measure that will ever be associated with his Dewanship and which has benefited the people most and entitled him to their lasting gratitude, is the abolition of what is known as taxation in kind. Under this system the taxes on lands due to Government from the people were payable partly in money and partly in kind. The payment in kind was not a fixed proportion of the actual produce of the land for the year, but a fixed quantity assessed on each field and the ryot had to pay it every year without regard to the nature of the harvests. Even when there was a total failure of the crops, the ryot had to find the paddy payable by him and deliver it into the Sarkar granary. The ryot was compelled to pay nearly 30 per cent. more than the quantity entered in his rent-roll to cover the loss caused by wastage, and damage by rats; and when issuing paddy to the temples and feeding houses, much less was actually supplied to the temples and institutions, than what was entered in the accounts as payable to them. This was managed by the village officials with the help of the low-paid temple servants. There was in this system scope for peculation, fraud and fabrication of accounts. Detection was almost impossible as both receipts and disbursements were shown in money values at rates that prevailed more than half-a-century ago which were more than 500 per cent. below current prices.

The substitution of money payments at a reasonable rate was hailed by the ryots as an immense relief and when the abolition of payment in kind was announced, the Dewan was flooded with congratulatory telegrams and addresses from all parts of the country. While engaged in seeing these reforms carried out, Mr. Madhava Rao was offered in March 1906, the Dewanship of Mysore, the State in which he had spent the best part of his life.

On the eve of his departure from Trivandrum Mr. Madhava Rao was given a magnificent send-off by all classes and communities and presented with an address of which the following is an extract :—

All Travancore knows how energetic your administration during these two years has been, what wholesome and purify-

Page 145.

MR. V. P. MADHAVA RAO

ing influence you have exercised on the service and what monumental record of administrative reform and progress you have initiated and achieved. Among the reforms we need only mention your achievements in the Departments of Finance and Revenue Settlement; and among the boons conferred on the country during your Dewanship stands foremost the Shri Mulam Popular Assembly, the inception of which was due as much to your high-souled administrative policy as to His Highness, well-known solicitude for the welfare of his subjects. With the institution of the Shri Mulam Popular Assembly and the unique political privilege that has been granted to the people of electing their representatives to it, your administration will for ever be honourably and gratefully associated; while for the abolition of taxation in kind and of *Vilayartham Irayili* lands, your name will be blessed with fervour for long generations to come. Short as your connection with this State has been, you have helped us to infuse a new tone and spirit into the administration and to inspire the people with something of your own enthusiasm for progress. While the ability, courtesy and dignity with which you have conducted yourself in your high office, your coolness of head and calmness of demeanour; your invincible rectitude and courage, and your liberal views and high ideals, have won for you universal esteem and regard, your unfailing sympathy for the people has made you emphatically the people's Dewan.

AS DEWAN OF MYSORE

Mr. Madhava Rao's return to Mysore was hailed by all classes of the people. This is what the *Madras Mail* said about his appointment in its issue of the 23rd March 1906.

The recall of Mr. V. P. Madhava Rao, C. I. E., to take the helm of the State which is at last confirmed to-day will meet with general approval. As Dewan of Travancore, Mr. Madhava Rao has displayed not only that energetic insistance on improvement, which all who knew, expected but a wise and statesmanlike foresight and patience, such as mark him out to be numbered with the best of native administrators. Mr. Madhava Rao possesses a personality of considerable dignity, and always commands attention and respect, of energetic character and proud spirit, yet kindly and courteous to all, with a marked talent for municipal administration, a wide and sound knowledge of Judicial, Revenue and Police Departments of the Mysore service he has earned the esteem and respect of all.

Mr. Madhava Rao commences this final and higher stage in his career under the happiest of auspices, with all the qualifications necessary to ensure the complete success of his administration.

RETRENCHMENT AND REFORM

During the three years of his Dewanship the State made considerable progress in several directions. The machinery of Government underwent some notable changes. The Civil Service was re-organised and the competitive system re-introduced on an improved basis. A Legislative Council was established for the first time in Mysore. The first steps were taken for the separation of Executive and Judicial functions. Rules were framed for the more efficient working of the district and taluq establishments. By means of agricultural exhibitions and demonstration of the working of improved implements and through the medium of the agricultural journal, knowledge of scientific agriculture was spread among the rural community. The co-operative movement received his special attention and a large number of societies were brought into existence replacing the agricultural banks which had proved a failure. The financial system was thoroughly overhauled. A famine relief fund was created in 1906-07 without dislocating the finances of the State and every year a sum of Rs. two lakhs is being added to it. A committee consisting of two Councillors was formed with a view to effect retrenchments in the departments in which costly establishments were being maintained without any adequate return for the money spent. Mr. Madhava Rao's policy was one of Retrenchment and Reform and Reduction of Taxation.

FISCAL REFORMS

Among the more important of his fiscal reforms may be mentioned the abolition of the *Halat* tax which was a kind of export duty on supari and bore heavily on the supari industry. The abolition involved the surrender of a revenue of nearly 4 lakhs of Rupees. This was the outcome of about 20 years' agitation started by Mr. Madhava Rao against the oppressiveness of the settlement rates imposed on the supari gardens of the Malnad. It was when Mr. Madhava Rao returned as Dewan in 1906, and had to deal with the Revisional Settlement of Sagar, that he had an opportunity for giving substantial relief to the ryots and carrying out his recommendations in their entirety. The rates were reduced by more than 50 per cent. and the tax abolished altogether.

ALL ROUND IMPROVEMENTS

The result of this far reaching relief was seen in the revival of the industry within a few years and the return of prosperity to the tract. New gardens are springing up and depots for supari have been opened in Shimoga itself since the extension of the Railway to it. The evils of sandalwood monopoly were greatly mitigated and the ryots were given a share in the value of sandalwood growing on their lands. The municipal regulation now in force in the State, which was passed during his administration, bears evidence of his democratic tendencies. He was instrumental in giving a pure water supply to the important towns of Shimoga and Haripur. He was the first to realise the claims of outlying stations to have their requirements in the way of drainage and water supply attended to equally with those of the capital cities. A scheme for the improvement of the famous place of pilgrimage, Melkote, was sanctioned.

It was during his Dewanship that the question of the institution of the Department of Public Health assumed a practical shape and a regularly organised department with a qualified staff of sanitary officers for districts and taluqs under the control of a Sanitary Commissioner was brought into existence and it has demonstrated its usefulness by the good work it has turned out. Indigenous medicine received support, and a college for teaching Ayurvedic medicine was established in Mysore. The third installation of the Cauvery Power Scheme cost the sum of Rupees 12 lakhs, Electric light to the Civil and Military Station, Bangalore, was supplied and formally inaugurated on the 1st January, 1906.

FREE EDUCATION

That important branch of the administration *viz.*, Education, received full attention from Mr. Madhava Rao. It was during his Dewanship that Primary Education was made free, that the minimum pay of the village school master was raised to Rs. 10/-; that manual training and kindergarten were introduced in all the schools, as also religious and moral instruction.

VILLAGE SELF-GOVERNMENT

But the distinctive feature which distinguished Mr. Madhava Rao's career from that of other Indian administrators is the recognition by him of the fact that no substantial or permanent good will result from merely improving the machinery of Government if the people are not trained in habits of self-reliance and self-help. Having been brought up in a district in which the village communal life was still alive although nearly smothered by the over-government of the bureaucracy, his ambition was to see the old village panchayat and village self-government restored to its pristine purity. The utter neglect of the village tanks in Mysore and the hopelessness of getting their repair and upkeep attended to by the Government agency suggested to him the idea of awakening and bringing into full play the old communal spirit which had helped to cover the whole face of India with self-governing village communities and which were described by early British administrators as so many little republics. He worked at this idea long and the presence of the Irrigation Commission at Bangalore afforded him an opportunity of framing a scheme of village self-government by first formulating proposals for the tanks in villages being handed over to a Committee of members elected by the villagers themselves. This is not the place for entering into the details of the scheme but Mr. Madhava Rao gave much thought to it and had the satisfaction of seeing it brought before the New Council in the form of a bill. The Regulation has since been passed. It must be a source of gratification to all well-wishers of village-self-government that a bill on the lines of the Tank-Panchayat Regulation has been introduced in the Madras Legislative Council. The scheme contains the germs of real self-rule, and if worked under wise and sympathetic guidance is bound to restore to India the little self-contained republics of old.

TWO UNPOPULAR MEASURES

Mr. Madhava Rao has had his full share of blame allotted to him in regard to two distinct measures. The first is the Mysore Mines Regulation of 1906. In regard to this legislation no elaborate attempt at justification is necessary. Sufficient answer to the criticisms passed on it is provided by the fact that it is no innovation and the Regulation was based on the facts bearing on the working of gold mines in Australia and South Africa. It must also be noted that he was only responsible for publishing the Regulation, it having been passed during the previous regime. The Newspaper Regulation is another measure that has been disapproved. It is true that certain of its features deserve to be reconsidered and Mr. Madhava Rao himself had prepared an amended Regulation in accordance with a promise he had given in the Representative Assembly but his term was over before it could be passed.

A THREE-YEARS RECORD

It will thus be seen that, on the whole, his three years of Dewanship in Mysore were marked by continued financial prosperity and he had a large share in the retrenchments made and reforms introduced in the different departments of the State. This is what the "Vokkaligara Sangha," an association formed for promoting the interest of the agricultural community of Mysore numbering nearly a third of the total population, said of his Dewanship, in an address presented to him immediately on his retirement:—

> During your regime you inaugurated a number of reforms conceived in a liberal spirit, and there is no doubt, that they will promote the prosperity and the good of the people. The establishment of the Legislative Council for making Laws and Regulations, the organisation of a Department of Public Health for the prevention of disease and improvement of sanitation, the appointment of a veterinary officer to look after the condition of cattle, the publication of an agricultural Gazette for the dissemination of improved knowledge in agriculture, the popularising of the cattle shows and agricultural exhibitions, the gradual displacement of old agricultural banks by Co-operative Credit Societies the creation of a Famine Reserve Fund, the raising of the minimum pay of the village school masters, the introduction of religious and moral education in schools and colleges, the abolition of school fees in village schools in order to place the benefit of elementary education within the reach of the poorest classes, the introduction of Sloyd and Kindergarten instruction into schools, the elaboration of a system of local self-government based on the ancient Panchayat system in connection with the village Tank Panchayat Bill, the abolition of the sandal monopoly and of *Halat* or duty on arecanut are all notable events in your administration for which you have earned the gratitude of the people of Mysore.

OTHER ACTIVITIES

Since his retirement from the Dewanship of Mysore Mr. Madhava Rao toured through the whole of India with a view to study the conditions of the different parts of the Empire. He has been of opinion that for the uplift of India it is essential that facility should be given to the masses to learn Sanskrit, as it is through that language that direct access can be had to the ancient stores of Hindu culture and spirituality. He was of immense help to his Holiness the late Jagadguru of Sringeri, in founding what is known as the Indian Sanskrit Institute in Bangalore, where higher learning in Sanskrit is being imparted under the ancient method. There is a movement on foot to make the Institute the centre for combining the Pandit method with the critical method of Western nations.

Mr. Madhava Rao identified himself with the District Conference in Tanjore and delivered an address at the annual meeting in 1913 at Shiyali. His address created some sensation as it contained a vigorous attack on the land policy of the British Government in ryotwari tracts. He condemned the system of the recurring settlements and said that that system had no justification either in ancient Hindu practice or in the teachings of economic science. His contention, in brief, was that there is no such thing as unearned increment in regard to agricultural land. In the beginning of 1914, he had taken up the question of the necessity of imparting instruction in non-language subjects through the medium of the vernaculars. The society which had been formed under the auspices of Madras Mahajana Sabha invited him to take an active part in the movement and he interested the Bishop of Madras and Mrs. Besant in it and secured their co-operation. One of the reasons which induced Mr. Madhava Rao to advocate the system was that it was necessary in order to bring the light of modern knowledge to the masses and to bridge the gulf between them and the English educated classes. In order to facilitate the making of vernaculars the medium of instruction, it is necessary, in his opinion, to have our provinces re-distributed on a linguistic basis. These and the formation of an Association for the benefit of the young men of India on the lines of the Y. M. C. A., were engaging his active attention in his retirement. He is a life-member of the Y. M. I. A. in Madras. When he was thus engaged in public movements of various kinds, the call came from His Highness, the Maharaja of Gækwar, inviting him to take up the Dewanship of Baroda in March 1914.

MR. MADHAVA RAO IN BARODA

Soon after he took his office, Mr. Madhava Rao presided over the sessions of the local Legislative Council when the celebrated Baroda Purohit Bill was hotly discussed. The object of the Bill being laudable, the need for such a piece of legislation was accepted by a majority of the Legislative Council. Before discussing the details, Mr. Madhava Rao announced the postponement of the discussion on the Bill *sine die*, so that both the people and the Government may have sufficient time to give fuller consideration to the details. Mr. Madhava Rao had a great hand in the modification of some of the objectionable features of the Bill, which he thought would work harshly upon the people affected, and the Baroda Purohit Act as sanctioned by His Highness the Maharaja Saheb, was published in the local "Government Gazette", at the end of the year 1915. On August 4th, 1914, war broke out between England and Germany, and soon after its declaration, Mr. Madhava Rao presided over a public meeting of the citizens of Baroda, when in a neat little speech he voiced the deep and abiding loyalty of the people and appealed to the people to subscribe to the Imperial War Relief Fund. In the year 1915, a Health Exhibition was held in Baroda to promote sanitation under the inspiration of Mr. Madhava Rao. It was the first of its kind in Baroda and was a great success.

In the same year Dr. Harold Mann of Poona, visited Baroda and gave some lectures at one of which Mr. Madhava Rao presided, when he, although the responsible minister of an important state, boldly advocated permanent settlement, and strongly denounced the policy of enhancing the land revenue assessment at every revision settlement.

By a strange coincidence, a few days after, the revision settlement of Mabuva Taluk of Navsari District came for sanction when Mr. Madhava Rao is said to have strongly advocated the cause of the ryots. In the end a settlement for sixty years was granted instead of for thirty years as originally proposed. The rates were heavy, but it was some consolation that they were not liable to be enhanced for at least sixty years.

During the same year, the First Sanskrit Conference was held at Baroda, and a Sanskrit Pathshala was established as a result. The credit for the idea of holding such a Conference was given to Mr. Madhava Rao, by His Highness the Gækwar himself.

In 1916 Mr. Madhava Rao organised the First Music Conference, and it is noteworthy that the sessions of that Conference proved a great success.

Mr. Madhava Rao, prior to retirement, went on a long leave of three months from 8th May 1916 with a reputation for sound statesmanship, independence, and boldness, and as a tactful administrator.

Mr. Madhava Rao is essentially the people's man and as such his views on Locol Self-Government and village panchayats and on the institution of Madhyastha Panchas (conciliators) are quite sound and democratic, as may be seen from his remarks regarding these subjects in the Baroda Administration Report, for 1914-15. In the same Report he advocates the recruiting of the public services of the State by competitive examinations, a view with which all men with practical wisdom will concur. His views on the industrial problems of the State are full of sound statesmanship, and, if acted upon, it is quite certain, the State will very shortly reach a high stage of industrial efficiency. He also advocates improvements of administrative methods by the establishment of administrative research in order to bring the several departments of the State to an up-to-date condition and to remove antiquated methods and generally improve the methods of work.

It can be seen from the facts already set forth, that Mr. Madhava Rao was out and out a people's man. A broad-minded toleration and a large-hearted sympathy for the wants and grievances of the people committed to his charge, and, a keen sense of justice to secure for them their just rights, are the characteristic and outstanding features of his administration. The establishment of the Popular Assembly in Travancore and the Legislative Council in Mysore was undoubtedly the outcome of Mr. Madhava Rao's liberal proclivities.

Mr. Madhava Rao thinks that the Native States are a great national asset and will play a great part in the work of National regeneration. The rulers and the ruled are bound together by ties of common traditions and sentiment, and the Native Rulers are always accessible to the humblest peasant to patiently hear his complaints, treat him with sympathy and then and there redress his grievances if they are convinced that a wrong has been done. The chord of sympathy that binds the rulers and the ruled makes the administration not a mechanical lifeless thing but a living reality to the people. There is greater security of life and property in well-governed Native States like Mysore, Baroda, Travancore etc., than in British India. Native Princes have a better insight into the needs of their country and are enabled to introduce social legislation for the betterment of their subjects. Reforms like the Separation of Judicial and Executive functions and Compulsory Education, for which British India has yet to wait, have been introduced long ago in progressive Native States like Baroda and to some extent in Mysore.

To these views of Mr. Madhava Rao, it may be added that the Native States have afforded the best field for the development of administrative gifts, powers of initiative and organisation in Indian administrators. They have produced such brilliant administrators as Raja Sir T. Madhava Rao, Raja Sir Dinkar Rao, Sir Salar Jung, Rangacharlu, Sir Seshadri Aiyar and Mr. V. P. Madhava Rao himself who would have shed glory upon the cabinet of any European nation had they been born in those countries.

WORK IN BRITISH INDIA

Since his retirement from Baroda Mr. Madhava Rao has found time to devote himself more freely to the political, social or religious movements in British India. On the publication of the well-known Memorandum of the Nineteen Non-Official Members of the Imperial Legislative Council on Post-War Reforms, Mr. Madhava Rao gave his opinion on the subject in an excellent contribution to the *Madras Mail*, from which the following extracts may be read with interest:

> The fortunes of India are inextricably bound up with those of England, and, whatever the short-comings of England may be, it is only through her that India can hope to become a self-governing nation. Anything, therefore, that may weaken England's power cannot but tell on the well-being and prosperity of India. It is, on the other hand, to England's own

interest as an Imperial Power to do everything to strengthen India's position so that she may become a self-supporting and self-reliant nation within the Empire.

What India needs, and is ripe for, is Government of the people, by the people and the full recognition of the principle that there should be "no taxation without representation."

This is a matter of no mere sentiment or aspiration, due to borrowing fine phrases from the politics of the West without understanding their meaning. It is a positive necessity for the well-being of India and for the integrity of the Empire.

Mr. Madhava Rao's interest in social and religious problems in India is well-known. During the Christmas week of 1916, he was invited to preside over the third All-India Hindu Conference at Lucknow. In the course of his presidential address he held:

On social and religious questions the Government take little or no interest. This is of course proper from their point of view. But when the Government becomes truly national, socio-religious questions will become recognised fields of activity for Government as may be seen from the legislation adopted in Mysore and Baroda on the question of infant marriage. But the fact of our having an alien Government now thrown additional burden on the community as it will have to look after its social evolution and the adjustment of social institutions to changing conditions. These functions the Hindu Sabha will have to exercise even on a larger scale when self-rule has been given to India composed as it is of different races and creeds. It is thus that the question of having a Hindu Sabha becomes all-important.

Mr. Madhava Rao's interest in educational matters is no less keen. Presiding in April 1917, at the Jubilee Celebration of the Kumbakonam College, which he left over half a century ago among the very first batch of graduates, he laid stress on the need for scholarship in Sanskrit and announced that he would set apart funds that would yield an annual income of Rs. 100 to be associated with the honoured name of Mr. Porter.

I select Sanskrit, as it holds the key to literature in philosophy and religion which affords the best solution for the problems of life and is calculated to promote spiritual culture in those that study it. The value of this study in the scheme of education will be all the better appreciated just now when there is moral chaos in the western world, where religion, divorced from sound philosophy, has undermined the basis of ethics and led to the promulgation of the doctrine that, where a State is concerned, the eternal principles of justice, mercy and humanity have no place in the dealings of one human being with another. We are better placed than those western people. As far as our education is concerned, we cannot always command the services of men of the ethical greatness of Mr. Porter, but we have in our Epics and Puranas, not to mention the Vedas, examples of lives led, where truth, dharma and justice have been placed above all personal considerations and men and women, born and brought up as gentle princes and princesses have undergone physical and moral sufferings of the most severe character rather than surrender truth or perpetrate an injustice.

In recognition of his ripe experience and varied activities in public life, Mr. Madhava Rao was invited to preside over the Madras Provincial Congress at Cuddalore in May 1917. Thereafter Mr. Madhava Rao became a leading member of the Congress, actively associating himself with the policy and programme of Congressmen and guiding them in their agitation for full fledged responsible Government. He attended successive sessions of the Congress. And when the historic announcement of August 20 opened the road to political effort he threw himself wholeheartedly into the struggle and advocated the Congress cause with his wonted zeal and authority. Doubtless his administrative experience in three principal Indian States gave his counsel an authority which few Congressmen could command. But side by side with his Congress work he continued to take a leading part in the working of the Hindu Sabha of which till his retirement from public life owing to failing health he was an undisputed protagonist. In fact during this period he was ever active on Congress and Hindu Sabha platforms working with equal vigour on behalf of either institutions.

In 1919 Mr. Madhava Rao led the Congress delegation to England to give evidence before the Parliamentary Committee on the Montagu report and he took the occasion to interview leading Statesmen in England and also to educate the British public on the needs and aspirations of India. His advocacy of the Congress cause was all that could be desired. His lead doubtless gave a special weight and significance to the Congress demand as his unique record of statesmanship in three states had established his reputation.

When we have realised all that Mr. Madhava Rao asked for in his scheme we can be fairly said to have achieved that measure of self-rule to which the country has been aspiring.

Mr. Madhava Rao is now nearing four score years. His has been a crowded and eventful life. For some years past he has lived in retirement at Bangalore and seldom taken an active part in public work. Age has wrought its work on him and he is now in the enjoyment of a well-earned rest.

Sir M. Visvesvaraya.

AN ENGINEER-STATESMAN

The outstanding fact about the life and career of Sir M. Visvesvaraya is, that born in a Native State, he devoted a great part of his life to the service of that State; and what is more, contrary to the usual practice his services have been frequently indented upon by other States and by important bodies in British India as well. Dewan Rangacharlu and Sir K. Seshadri Iyer, Messrs V. P. Madhava Rao and T. Ananda Rao were outsiders, while the ancestors of Dewan Purnaiya and his descendant Sir P. N. Krishnamurthi were comparatively recent settlers in the State. Sir Visvesvaraya and his people on the other hand have been residents of Mysore from time out of mind. He is therefore in a sense the first Mysorean to reach the Dewanship of the State. Again it is common knowledge that when things go wrong with the administration of a Native State, the services of a British official are invariably lent to that State. The order seems to be reversed in the case of Sir Visvesvaraya. For on his retirement from Mysore his experience as engineer or administrator has been availed of by Bombay and Karachi and generally by the Government of India. The great Engineer-Dewan of Mysore is to-day an outstanding figure among the statesmen of India.

A Brilliant Educational Career

Mokshagundam Visvesvaraya was born of an indigent Brahmin family of Chikballapur on the 15th September 1861. His father was a Sanskrit pundit and a well-known physician. After finishing his course at the local High School, Visvesvaraya joined the Central College at Bangalore and graduated in 1874. He took his Arts Degree with Mathematics for his optional subject and was selected as a State scholar to be trained as an Engineer, by the late Mr. Rangacharlu who thought it would be a consummation and a pride to train up local men for the various technical professions and posts of responsibility, to obviate the necessity of maintaining a costly paraphernalia of foreign agency. Mr. Visvesvaraya had a very successful career in the Engineering College at Poona; and as he topped the list of successful candidates in 1883, the guaranteed appointment of the year was awarded to him. He thus abundantly justified his choice.

A Successful Engineer

His striking success at College and the University (where besides passing the F. C. E. and L. C. E. Examinations in the first class, he also won the Berkley Prize) led to his immediate appointment as Assistant Engineer in Bombay in 1884. During the next twenty-five years, says one who knows him, he did unceasing work in various professional appointments he held in Western India. He served as an Engineer in the Irrigation Branch in several

Districts of the Presidency, and in this capacity rendered excellent service to both people and Government. Between 1901 and 1903, says the same writer, he designed and constructed a system of automatic gates patented by him at Lake Fife, which is the storage reservoir for the Moota Canal and the source of water supply to Poona City. The design attracted considerable attention at the time. It very soon received the approval of the Government of India and was carried out at a cost of about five lakhs of rupees. In 1903, he devised a new scheme of irrigation, which has since been called "the Block System of Irrigation" to meet the needs of certain irrigation works in the Deccan. This system has also been introduced into the Mysore State in connection with lands irrigated under the well-known Marikanive Dam in the Chitaldrug District. It is acknowledged to be a highly efficacious system in reclaiming new lands brought under irrigation and it won the approval of the Indian Irrigation Commission of 1903. In their Report, the Commissioners state that the general principle on which it is based was sound, and add that the system afforded an excellent illustration of the views which they had themselves set forth. The scheme took three years to be fully introduced in the Deccan, but it proved a complete success, as was acknowledged by the Bombay Government at the time and has since been demonstrated by the returns produced. The success of the scheme enlarged not a little Mr. Visvesvaraya's reputation in the engineering line

Naturally he had the rewards of a successful service and honours coupled with responsibilities came thick upon him. In 1904 he was appointed as one of the three representatives of the Bombay Government to the Simla Irrigation Conference before which he read several noteworthy papers. Meanwhile he had become an Executive Engineer and had acted, besides, as Sanitary Engineer to the Government of Bombay and Member of the Sanitary Board, in addition to his own duties. In 1905, he again acted in this capacity, and was, besides, in addition to his duties as Sanitary Engineer, on special duty in the Public Works Department Secretariat, in connection with irrigation projects. In the same year he reached the rank of a Superintending Engineer. In 1906 he was deputed to Aden to advise the Executive Committee of the Aden Settlement with regard to certain sanitary matters. His good work there was recognized by the bestowal of the K. I. H. medal. After a brief period there, he returned to Bombay as Offg. Sanitary Engineer to Government. Two years later, in the middle of 1908, he went on a world tour and visited most of the countries of Europe and America.

In the Service of the Nizam

While he was on his tour in America he received the appointment of Special Consulting Engineer to the Government of H. H. The Nizam of Hyderabad. The devastating floods of the Musi called for immediate preventive works. He joined the Hyderabad

Service in April 1909 and in six months he worked out a complete scheme for flood protection and reservoir works as well as a drainage scheme for Hyderabad City, all estimated to cost about 150 lakhs. About the same time he prepared at the request of the Resident a report on the drainage of Secunderabad Cantonment. In October 1909 he relinquished his deputation work in Hyderabad and also retired from the service of the Bombay Government. The Government of Bombay obtained for him a special higher pension on the " ground of meritorious service. "

IN MYSORE SERVICE

Already Mr. Visvesvaraya's reputation in Bombay and Hyderabad had marked him out for a distinguished place in Mysore. More than once the Government of Mysore had solicited his services which had won such golden opinion abroad. The circumstances under which his services were requisitioned by H. H. the Maharaja may now be recalled. We are told that when Mr. McHutchin severed his connection with the Mysore Public Works Department in June 1909, Captain Bernard Dawes was appointed to officiate as Chief Engineer of Mysore pending the selection of a suitable successor to the former. It was then that several candidates appeared on the scene and inspite of the overwhelming influence brought to bear in favour of certain individuals, His Highness the Maharaja, in pursuance of a settled policy of advancing Indian gentlemen of the Province to administrative appointments, thought about the propriety of appealing to Mr. Visvesvaraya's sense of patriotism and inducing him to accept the Chief Engineer's appointment in Mysore. Mr. Visvesvaraya closed with the offer, the more so as it was his wish to give of his best to his own State.

He joined the Mysore Service in November 1909 and began his accustomed round of work. He set about it in a cautious way. He had heard of innumerable abuses in the Department. He was not satisfied with the rut and routine of the local men, says one who had watched his career at close quarters. He had cherished dreams of improvement of the Department and its efficiency and of launching forth gigantic schemes of productive works and developing the material and economic condition of the country; but all this he kept to himself as yet.

After making a careful study of the men and materials he had to deal with and after fairly getting the reins into his hands he set about his business in right earnest. He very soon came to realise that the administrators he had to serve were what a fellow-official described as "hoary voluptuaries in politics,"—

men who were only jealous of younger and more vigorous personalities intruding and climbing into their fold and usurping their places. They at once resorted to their old game of throwing cold water over the young enthusiast's schemes and did their best to allay his ardent spirits and degrade him to their own level and include him in their own rank; but he who had travelled all over the world, observed the incessant activity, ceaseless struggle for improvement and rewards of hard strenuous work in other lands would not yield to the "Peace first and progress next propaganda of these local celebrities". It was very soon apparent to those around him that in Mr. Visvesvaraya they had a man of mercurial activity, a man who had adopted for his life's motto "Better wear out than rust out". His painstaking attention to the minutiæ of his business, his wonderful patience, his insistence of a high standard of excellence in work and correspondence and environment, were things to which they had been strangers and such a man was very irksome to work with."

GREAT ENGINEERING WORKS

Immediately after his advent into Mysore, says our chronicler, he had two difficult works to tackle—the slip in the Ramasagara tank bund and the restoration of the breach at Krishnaràjkatte. For both of these he devised suitable designs and made arrangement for their timely and successful completion. Public attention was first drawn to his methods of work by his memorandum on a complete sewerage scheme for the Mysore City. A warm admirer writes thus:—

Simplicity, order, method, thoroughness, perspicuity of style and a happy knack for marshalling statistical information were the characteristics of the man. Whatever reports or memorandum he drew up, whatever addresses he delivered were always characterised by these qualities and cold-steel logic of facts, scientific precision, conciseness of expression intension and compass were evolved by a brain which "scorned delights and lived laborious days." For romance, sentiments, emotion and rhetoric there was no room in a man who seemed to have been disciplined in the School of John Stuart Mill.

CAUVERY RESERVOIR PROJECT

While working at its development he was equally assiduous in pushing forward the necessary action to mature the Cauvery Reservoir Project. He worked unwearyingly at these and by systematic organisation, persistent pressure and unflagging work he carried on a delicate and difficult correspondence with the Government of India and Madras to obtain the necessary sanction for a reservoir across the Cauvery. The printed volumes of his correspondence will show what a doughty champion he was amidst the chaos of discouragements, objections and perfect want of the least moral support from men who ought to have known better. The way in which he carried all obstacles in his way, made it apparent that even as a Chief Engineer he wielded a truly amazing influence with His Highness, the the Resident and the other authorities and his influence soon eclipsed that of his detractors whom he managed to completely throw overboard and many of them wise in their worldly ways soon came to be accommodating. He succeeded in obtaining the sanction of the Government of India to a reservoir of 11,000 mc. ft. capacity. If for nothing else Sir Visvesvaraya is entitled to the profoundest gratitude of all Mysore and the sincere respect of all its inhabitants for thus securing to Mysore one of its most valuable assets, far better and infinitely more valuable than the best gold mine in the world. He also appointed a Committee and matured a scheme of technical education in the State and organised a Mechanical and Engineering School at Bangalore and the Chamarajendra Technical Institute at Mysore.

RAILWAY PROGRAMME

A comprehensive Railway Programme and the formation of a Railway Construction Department next engaged his attention. Such a programme of Railway Construction was drawn up and sanctioned and a special Railway Departmant formed with one of the most enlightened officers at its head and it has already done most valuable work in the last 3 or 4 years.

IRRIGATION IMPROVEMENTS

There then remained the last but not the least important of the developments indicated by him—one that concerns the vital interests of the agricultural population in the State and is of paramount importance to the prosperity of the ryot and the finances of Government. He was most anxious that a detailed policy should be laid down for future adoption and wanted it should be drawn up and published before he laid down his office of Chief Engineer and took up the responsible post of the head of the administration. He worked at it with an amazing persistency and submitted a comprehensive note which was the basis of his work for the relief of the agricultural population. Thus before he came to guide the destinies of the State he had chalked out in great detail the work that would keep him fully employed during the remaining few years of his official life. It was a programme worthily conceived and as worthily executed.

Dewan of Mysore

Immediately after his term of office as Chief Engineer was over he was appointed Dewan on the 10th November 1912. He saw in this high office an opportunity for the fulfilment of many of his ambitions for the State. That was in fact the main reason for his accepting this high office. As we shall see he fully justified the expectations and raised Mysore to the status of a model State which it was his aim to make of her. In his very first statement in reply to a public address soon after his acceptance of office Sir Visvesvaraya said:

> I notice that...............you refer to yet higher honours and rewards for me. It will, I hope, not be regarded as an affectation of modesty on my part if I say that all I have wanted is opportunity for work, and that thoughts of personal advancement have not influenced my actions in recent years. With the important duties now graciously entrusted to me by His Highness the Maharaja, I have all scope for work that I may have ever longed for. The pleasure of working for a few years more, of serving my Sovereign and my country, is enough for me. Their interests will be my constant thought, and their approbation, if I am able to secure it, my best reward.

At the end of six eventful years he was able to prove that so far as the exigencies of the times permitted there has been no discrepancy between the principles professed here and the practice of them.

Constructive Statesmanship

We shall now consider in some detail Sir Visvesvaraya's distinct contributions to Mysore during his six years' Dewanship. His Memorandum on Public Works in Mysore was a notable contribution to constructive statesmanship. He expounded therein the great possibilities of development in the State, adumbrated what steps should be taken to give practical effect to his proposals. He was never for doing things by fits and starts but wanted to proceed on a well-organised and comprehensive programme. He advocated therein a forward policy as regards

(1) Development of industries.
(2) The construction of a reservoir across the Cauvery.
(3) Railway Construction in Mysore.
(4) Technical Education.
(5) Irrigation developments.

all of which he brought to fruition in his regime.

THE MYSORE ECONOMIC CONFERENCE

He gave strong impetus to every branch of the administration, Railways, Industries, Agriculture Education, Banking, Village Re-organization and indeed sought to make Mysore a model State in every respect. Already, during his Chief Engineership was inaugurated the Mysore Economic Conference with its innumerable committees for tackling various problems of State improvement. A word about its organization and working may not be out of place. For it is a unique institution of its kind in India bringing officials and non-officials together, and reaching the expert on the one side and the ryot on the other.

It works on the Committee system, each Committee having a number of members and a Secretary attached to it. It corresponds to a Department of a Government and its work is to thresh out questions or propositions likely to make for advance,

work them up to success and then hand them over to the Departments concerned for their being absorbed into their general routine of duties. Thus there are Committees for Agriculture, Education and Commerce and Industries—corresponding to the three Departments of Agriculture, Education and Commerce & Industries. Each Committee has its own annual budget and is responsible in its turn to a General Secretary of the Conference, who is usually the Secretary to Government in the Agriculture, Education and Industries Departments. Each Committee acts through a Chairman, who is usually a high official of Government. There is, besides, a Standing Committee which meets regularly every month and deliberates on all matters affecting the Conference. The Conference has two Journals of its own—one in English and the other in Kannada which do much propagandistic work. The Conference meets once a year in June, at Mysore when its work is reviewed, as it were, by the Dewan. Propositions of which previous notice has been given are discussed and the work for the coming year is laid down. The members are partly elected. The discussions show the general trend of public opinion in regard to economic matters generally. Those who say that there is little public opinion behind the back of Indian intellectuals when they claim political or economic advancement would do well to attend a session of this Conference. If they did so, they would go away disillusioned to a large extent. The keenness with which subjects relating to improvements in agriculture, education, trade, commerce, industries, etc., are discussed at this Conference has often been an eye-opener to people new to its work. The expert is, in this Conference, brought face to face with the raiyat and has to defend his position as best he may. He is not allowed to reign supreme in his region; his suggestions are subjected to critical examination and their flaws are mercilessly exposed. The result is that the general tendency for debates to degenerate into mere academic discussions is checked and real progress is marked in an incredibly short time. The best official and non-official opinion is brought to bear on the discussions of important public questions in which there is otherwise likely to be a difference of opinion. The power of the purse is also given, and this gives the members and Committees a sense of responsibility which counteracts any tendency towards visionary ideas. Then, again, the harmonious co-operation of all people interested in the progress is secured and thus a step forward is rendered possible.

Such, in brief, is the Mysore Economic Conference, of which the Dewan is the President.

VILLAGE RECONSTRUCTION

In these days of rural reconstruction it is interesting to observe Sir Visvesvaraya's plan of rural improvement. Addressing the Mysore Economic Conference in June 1917 he adumbrated a practical programme to be carried out by the State under his immediate direction. In every self-respecting village the following minimum result was to be insisted on:

(1) At least 10 per cent of the population should be at school. If there is no school in the village itself, the pupils should attend one in the neighbourhood.

(2) There should be a school, or other arrangement, for imparting a knowledge of the three R's to the adult population of the village.

(3) The economic efficiency of every village should be examined annually by preparing rough estimates of production, and no village, where the annual output is less than, say Rs. 33 per head of population should be considered economically safe.

4. There should be at least one trained blacksmith and one carpenter in every village having a population of 300 and more.

5. Every agricultural family should have some subsidiary occupation to supplement its income from the land. Roughly speaking, there should be one minor or subsidiary industry practised in a village for every 250 inhabitants.

6. Every raiyat should be induced to store at least two years' supply of food grains to provide against the calamities of the seasons. The tendency to contract debts, except for productive purposes, should be severely discouraged.

HIS ACHIEVEMENTS

When he became the Dewan of the State every department was overhauled and improved and his vigorous personality was felt in every branch of the administration. The KARNATAKA, on his retirement gave a list of his achievements which may here be recounted :

1. New Mysore Treaty,
2. Establishment of the Mysore University.
3. Larger powers and Half-yearly Session of the Representative Assembly,
4. Expansion of the Legislative Council.
5. Reconstitution of Municipal bodies.
6. Railway extension,
7. Krishnaraja Sagara,
8. Iron Scheme,
9. Bhatkal Harbour Project.
10. (i) Village Improvement (ii) Minor Tank Restoration,
11. Public Libraries,
12. Mysore Bank, Sandal Oil Factory, Paper Factory Scheme etc.

HIS FINANCIAL POLICY

Such a vigorous and aggressive administration could hardly have gone on without some bitter criticisms. The Bhadravati Iron Works and other projects have naturally been assailed as white elephants and critics charged him with extravagance and reckless waste of public funds. But Sir Visvesvaraya held to the maxim "that a Government forfeits its claim to be called national unless it has a public debt. The greater its spending capacity, the more progressive its character will be." And he was never in want of funds for his gigantic projects. In this connection it is appropriate to quote the figures which a writer in the HINDUSTAN REVIEW who was apparently in the know of things, gave in justifying Sir Visvesvaraya's financial policy. But for Sir Visvesvaraya's unflinching resolution, he says, Kannambadi would to this day have been no better than a paper-project. Here are facts and figures justifying his policy :

I—ASSETS AND LIABILITIES

Periods	Assets	Liabilities
(*a*) During Sir Visvesvaraya's Decennium	Rs. 1,194 lakhs.	Rs. 560 lakhs
(*b*) During the Pre-Visvesvaraya Period	,, 672 ,,	,, 335 ,,
Excess of Assets over Liabilities	,, 634 ,,	,, 337 ,,

II—PRODUCTIVE WORKS

Periods	Total Expenditure	Revenue
(*a*) During Sir Visvesvaraya's Decennium	Rs. 354 lakhs.	Rs. 30 lakhs
(*b*) During the Pre-Visvesvaraya Period	,, 339 ,,	,, ,, ,,

"The total expenditure on productive works during the decennium was 354 lakhs. Much of this expenditure has already begun to pay, as the increase in the Revenue from Productive works shows and the rest will bring in its return in due course." (Extract from the Financial Review and Forecast.)

Revenue and Expenditure

(*a*) Growth of Revenue during Sir Visvesvaraya's decennium was Rs. 95 lakhs. To this the principal heads of revenue contributed a little over 53 lakhs and the productive works nearly 30 lakhs.

(*b*) Growth of expenditure during the decennium was 119 lakhs. Of this, making allowance for 45 lakhs added to Departmental Balances and Revenues in 1917-18 the increase in expenditure has been less than the growth of Revenue. (In other words, the actual expenditure was 74 lakhs.)

(*c*) Excess of Revenue over Expenditure Rs. 95-74 or 21 lakhs (during the decade there was an extra-ordinary expenditure of 74 lakhs on account of War.)

Retirement and After

Sir Visvesvaraya retired in January 1919 after six eventful years of service during which Mysore had made for itself a name second to none among the premier States of India; nay more, it was held up to as the model of an efficient and progressive administration which it would be wisdom on the part of British Government to follow and copy in certain important directions.

Page 176.

SIR M. VISVESVARAYA

His services to Mysore were duly appreciated by His Highness the Maharajah as evidenced by the following *Gazette Extraordinary* announcing his retirement with effect from the 10th June 1919. The *Gazette*, after recounting his previous record goes on to say of his nine years' work in Mysore:

> During all this period Sir M. Visvesvaraya laboured with unwearying zeal and single-minded devotion to increase the material resources of the State. His administration as Dewan has resulted in important and far reaching developments in education, irrigation work, railway communications, and industries and has laid the foundations for a prosperous and progressive future for the State. Sir M. Visvesvaraya carries with him in his retirement the esteem and best wishes of H. H. the Maharaja and all classes of his subjects.

As a mark of appreciation of Sir M. Visvesvaraya's valuable services His Highness was pleased to grant him a special pension of Rs. 1250 a month. Indeed Sir M. Visvesvaraya drove the chariot of the State for six years with remarkable success. His single-minded devotion to the interests of Mysore, his marvellous energy and driving power coupled with his genius for organization and uncommon industry, as well as his clear perception of the goal have enabled Mysore to attain a measure of progress which could not have been achieved with a less gifted person as the head of the executive Government. In the speech which he made subsequent to his retirement he said: "It is occasionally stated in private circles that I am pro this and anti that community. Time will show that I have tried to hold the scales even." That was the true key-note of his administration. After retirement Sir Visvesvaraya did not cease his activities; indeed they had a wider field for their operation. His is perhaps one of the most active brains of the age and we always see him at his comparatively great age (he is now 66) busy with schemes of public benefaction. He travelled again in Europe and America and the East to refresh himself, to add to his stock of knowledge, to see the advance that the West has made in the intervening years and find the means whereby his own countrymen could be redeemed from poverty and decadence.

"RECONSTRUCTING INDIA"

His plans of Reconstructing India are embodied in a book of this name (published by P. S. King & Co., Ltd. London) which is packed with information on all topics of public interest and full of cogent reasonings. His deductions have something of the definiteness and finality of a mathematical proposition and in spite of all his enthusiasm and characteristic idealism are never vague nor merely soothing. His suggestions for political, social and economic reforms are so many and so various that they afford ample material for the statesmanship of the future. New ideas on co-operation and agricultural improvement, on domestic economy and labour saving devices, on home insurance and compulsory education, schemes for the uplift of women and the depressed classes, and work for unemployment, methods of progressive political and cultural association besides means for the progressive realisation of economic and political freedom for social and material well-being—all find their place in this amazing book of ideas. Nor are they mere dreams of a retired Dewan. They are the fruits of years of practical experience as administrator and wide knowledge of world conditions applied to the needs of this country, with due regard to its peculiar conditions. We see in them the marks of a statesman who is himself a practical idealist. His is indeed a rare combination of genius with method, and industry, keenly sensitive to public interest.

EDUCATIONAL IDEALS

Sir Visvesvaraya believes in the efficacy of education to renovate the country. He deplores the present condition of illiteracy and accuses the Government of apathy with regard to this most important item of national programme.

One of the, greatest deficiencies which India has to make up is her lack of facilities for securing education. To-day three villages out of every four are without a school-house, and about 30,000,000 children of school-going age are growing up without any instruction. The officials have been so opposed to compulsory education that, until quite recently, they were disinclined even to permit Municipalities willing to bear the cost to introduce such a system. No wonder that barely seven per cent. of the Indian population can read and write, whereas in progressive countries eighty to ninety per cent. of the population is literate."

" The provision for technical and commercial education is meagre in the extreme.

Lack of liberality in this respect, and absence of official encouragement of indigenous enterprises, have kept Indians from developing new and expanding old industries and extending commerce. At the same time, the world-competition has made it impossible for the indigenous industries to thrive. Indians have, therefore, been driven more and more to the land."

HELP TO INDUSTRIES

Next to education, industries. He proves that it is a mistake to gauge the wealth of the country by the total output of her commerce. Most of Indian capital belongs to Britishers in Britain.

How backward we are in industrial and commercial concerns is evident from the fact that in 1914, the capital of all the Joint-Stock Companies registered in India and held mainly by Indians did not exceed £60,000,000. "The total capital of all the Joint-Stock Companies registered in India was £471,000,000, the greater portion of it, namely £411,000,000 being of companies registered in England and presumably held by the people of the British Isles."

Sir Visvesvaraya suggests among others the following methods by which Government in India can render direct help.

> The principal Governments may make a start by pioneering some of the larger industries like ship-building, machinery, engines, motor transport, chemicals, paper, etc. and also some of the many key industries needed, with the object of making them a success and subsequently transferring them to the people. There are few technical secrets that are not readily available, or that cannot be secured by the expenditure of money.

HIS SCHEME OF INDIANIZATION

He puts forward a complete scheme of Nation-building modelled on the methods adopted in America where the hetrogeneous immigrants are being "Americanized" by a process of unifying the taste and mentality of the population. Acting on the same principle, India, he says, must recognise

> that certain standards of taste, thought and sentiment are necessary to union, and should devise and carry out a comprehensive scheme of "Indianization," with a view to creating a new type of Indian citizenship and building up an efficient unified Indian nation.
>
> The principal characteristics to be developed in the life and habits of the people under an "indianization" programme should, in essential, be as follows :—
>
> 1. Love and pride of country (nation, province, city, town, or village) ; a high sense of self-respect and personal honour, and a spirit of service, combined with loyalty to the Sovereign and to the British connection.
>
> 2. Use of a common language in every province, and of English as the *lingua franca*.
>
> 3. A minimum of six years' compulsory general education, and a further two to four years' vocational course for every boy and girl, due attention being paid to games and sports and physical development, and to moral discipline.
>
> 4. Training in civics and thrift in schools, and, for adults, in special institutions, or by lectures and cinemas.
>
> 5. Organized effort to eradicate unhealthy ideals and practices known to handicap the Indian and to standardize existing good traits, practices and traditions in the country, and protect them from disuse or decay.
>
> 6. Cultivation of a spirit of initiative and habits of closer association ; uniformity of dress, as far as possible ; acquisition of business discipline and the usages of civilization ; travel among all classes of people, including the establishment of hotels and better railway facilities for the middle and poorer classes.
>
> 7. Equipping all classes of the people with correct ideals and objectives to work for, so that individual and local effort may be in consonance with national objects and aspirations.

8. Training all leading men and women to take part in international life and intercourse.

A Leaf From Japan

Sir Visvesvaraya reviews the problems confronting us, from every point of view, and exhorts us to take a lesson from Japan and America and other progressive countries with a view to develop our resources in the light of modern knowledge and the lessons of experience abroad :—

> Do the people of India propose to profit by the lessons which world experience has to teach them, or will they be content to allow matters to drift and themselves grow weaker and poorer year by year?
>
> This is the problem of the hour. They have to choose whether they will be educated or remain ignorant; whether they will come into closer touch with the outer-world and become responsive to its influences, or remain secluded and indifferent; whether they will be organised or dispassive; an industrial or an agricultural nation; rich or poor; strong and respected, or weak and dominated by forward nations. The future is in their own hands. Action, not sentiment, will be the determining factor.
>
> Nations are made by their own efforts.

President, Indian Science Congress

On his return home from abroad he began to take a more active interest in the affairs of British India. Invited to preside over the Indian Science Congress at Lucknow in January 1923 he delivered a remarkable address in which he summed up the achievements of science and called upon his country-men to march with the times. He is indeed the one statesman among us who is at home in all the technical arts and sciences of this age. He recounted recent advances in physical, chemical, astronomical and electrical sciences and put in a vigorous plea for the organisation of research institutes and research scholars.

Speaking of Indian scientists he remarked :

We may be proud of the galaxy of reputed scientists, who are responsible for maintaining the standard of research at a high level in India. Men like Sir Ronald Ross and the past general and sectional Presidents of this Congress naturally form the pick of the scientific workers in the country. Other leading names may be chosen at random. Sir J. C. Bose in Physiology, Sir P. C. Ray in Chemistry and Dr. C. V. Raman in Physics are representative specimens. Dr. Alfred Hay in Electrical Engineering, Dr. Sudborough in Pure and Applied Chemistry, Dr Harrison, the Howards of Pusa and Drs. Coleman and Mann in Agriculture, along with Dr. Simonson in Forest Research, Mr. Hutchinson in Histology, Sir John Marshall in Archæology, Dr. Walker in Meteorology and Mr. Evershed in Astrophysics are responsible for the high level of scientific research maintained in India. Nor can we afford to forget men like Glenliston and W. F. Harvey of Kasauli, Grig and Row of Bombay who are the leading names in the field of Medical Science.

He urged for the closer co-operation of the work of the many isolated scientific bodies and the starting of one authoritative Indian publication for each science ; and he regards the following problems to be of fundamental importance to the material prosperity of the country.

1. Application of Science to Industry.
2. Application of Science to Agriculture.
3. Population and Food Supply.
4. Low Standard of Living.
5. Undeveloped Resources.
6. Untrained Citizens.

He is convinced that India's poverty is mainly due to her undeveloped resources and untrained population and her lack of elementary education. He said:

> We want vision, we want enterprise and we must abandon "the old and beaten paths" which have paralysed effort in the past. It is now for the Congress to consider what practical action it should take regarding the further development of the Congress itself and the representations it should make to the Government to do their share of the work for the scientific equipment which the country needs. A future Congress should be able to suggest scientific remedies to all the ills referred to and the suggested Advisory Council of Government should advice practical action. The Congress will do the scientific work without prejudice or bias; the Advisory Council will formulate practical remedies. The one body will show what is theoretically possible and the other what may be practically expedient. The Congress should also keep in touch with associations and institutions engaged in similar activities abroad. This will help the country with ready-made solutions to many a problem, and prevent the publication of work now occasioned by our failure to study experience outside India.

He then gave an account of the recent great achievements of Science which included, hydro-electric schemes, long distance transmission of high voltage current, masonry dams, bridges, harbours, sky-scrapers and other engineering wonders of the century and concluded with a comprehensive survey of the internal combustion engine, the advance in wireless telegraphy and telephony, the harnessing of volcanic and tidal energy and the manufacture of synthetic food-stuffs.

AN INDUSTRIAL POLICY

But Sir Visvesvaraya is not a mere theorist He believes in the efficacy of applying Science to

Industries. In an article in the INDIAN REVIEW for August 1923, Sir Visvesvaraya wrote on "The Urgency of Industrial Awakening" outlining an industrial policy for the people and Government of this country. No policy could be regarded as complete, he wrote, which does not provide for the following:—

Protection.

Other helps from the political power of Government.

Enlisting co-operative power of the people represented by Chambers of Commerce, manufacturers' associations, &c.

Financial assistance, Government loans, bonuses on manufactures exported, &c.

Help from the banking power of the country.

A comprehensive system of Technical Education.

Provision for Original Research.

Experimental and Demonstration stations.

Pioneering key industries.

Starting industrial museums and holding exhibitions.

Industrial Survey, Census and Statistics.

Reviews and stock-taking by Responsible Ministers and members of Government (annual and periodical).

These facilities are afforded in all the British Dominions and he demanded that the people of India should not be bereft of them.

Three out of every four persons in the country, he wrote,

> are dependent for their livelihood on agriculture; the soil is overtaxed and large numbers of the rural population are without adequate employment for three to six months in the year. There is no census taken of production, no attempt made to frame estimates of income and wealth, such as are available in the Dominions, and there are no statistics of unemployment maintained in times of distress as in the United Kingdom. If such information were available, it would show that production had not kept pace with the growth of population, that the standard of living for the vast majority was appallingly low, that employment was rife in all grades of life and that it rose to calamitous proportions in seasons of scarcity.
>
> The country should be awakened to these truths and a strenuous effort made in the direction of industrial equipment and diffusion of general and technical knowledge. For this purpose, both Government agencies and people's associations should spread a correct knowledge of the conditions under which industries thrive in foreign lands, and jointly strive to utilise all material resources, all talent within the country, and all inventions and discoveries that come from abroad.

PRESIDENT, ECONOMIC ENQUIRY COMMITTEE

It was not long before he was offered an opportunity to conduct an official enquiry into the economic conditions of the country, under the auspicies of the Government of India. On the 4th February 1924 the Council of State in a resolution on the subject of an enquiry into the economic conditions of British India urged the appointment of a Committee. This was approved and confirmed by a resolution in the Assembly in September, and in January 1925 the Government of India announced the appointment of such a Committee with Sir Visvesvaraya as-

Chairman. Nothing could have been more appropriate. The terms of reference were:

> To examine the material at present available for framing an estimate of the economic condition of the various classes of people of British India; to report on its adequacy; and to make recommendations as to the best manner in which it may be supplemented, and as to the lines on which a general economic survey should be carried out with an estimate of the expenditure involved in giving effect to such recommendations.

The Committee submitted their condensed Report in August 1925. It is needless to say that the document is one of absorbing interest and of profound import. It is hoped it will serve as the basis of a considered policy of industrial and economic development in the future.

A PRACTICAL REFORMER

Sir Visvesvaraya's pre-eminent interest in administrative and industrial reform should not make us forget the importance he always attached to social reform. Healthy social conditions are necessary for social well being, and he holds that it is the duty of the state to provide such conditions. He is by no means indifferent to the duty of the individual citizen in the matter of wholesome conditions of civic life but a well ordered state should always keep an eye to the requirements of the average citizen. He warns the country against the danger of creating slums in urban areas; but he is sternly against the cry of "back to the land."

CONDITIONS OF TOWN LIFE

For he believes it is yet possible to develop urban life without the slums and the concomitant miseries of modern industrial cities. He would have all the advantages of civilized life for the dwellers in towns. For he says that "Parks, playgrounds, theatres, museums, art galleries and other means of public recreation and instruction should exist in every urban area, together with readily accessible railway and tramway facilities, boulevards and other means of transit and communication."

At present, urban areas are allowed to grow up without regulation or organization. Serious attention needs to be given to the question of housing not only the industrial workers, but the people in general.

"In order to raise the standard of living, a desire for better housing must be aroused and the people taught to appreciate the advantage of substantial masonry houses with tiled or terraced roofs. Such dwellings promote the health and comfort and therefore the efficiency of the people, whilst overcrowding reduces a nation's efficiency and working capacity, and leads to many other evils.'

Domestic Reforms

And then he insists on a high standard of sanitation and civic utilities. He would minimise the waste of human labour involved in the management of house-holds by time-saving appliances. He would give a course of education to women in civics and domestic economy and afford every opportunity " to improve the national working habits so that productive power and earnings may be increased." Sir Visvesvaraya thus adumbrates a scheme of social reform in consonances with the requirements of the age. In order to qualify ourselves for the new type of citizenship we should bring our life more in line with modern conditions. Caste, of course will go and along with it the prejudices and idiosyncrasies of a narrow social outlook. The joint family system he says tends to produce drones. And therefore "Society should take immediate measures to put a stop to this degenerating state of affairs. Begging ought to be prohibited by law, as in Japan, and a suitable allowance made for indigent persons by the State and local authorities or civic organizations. Persons suffering from blindness, sickness, mental disease and other infirmities are better cared for in institutions specially maintained for them. In particular, institutions should be provided for defective or friendless children, facilities afforded for medical examination in schools, and, where necessary, separate hospital treatment for those little ones who require it." He would modify the laws of marriage, sanction the re-marriage of widows, and altogether discountenance the prejudice against foreign travel. He would offer better opportunities to women to educate and improve themselves and facilitate the conversion of the untouchables into respectables. Above all he would urge the need for social discipline in an age in which respect for even wholesome traditions is losing ground under the impact of western education.

Social Discipline

Social discipline can be easily enforced among college-educated young men, but even they will need authoritative guidance from the leading men of the country. Among the rural population, much can be done along the lines of agricultural and craft education but there is no doubt social discipline will come mainly from development of the co-operative movement.

Among the industrial workers, he thinks it must as inevitably come through their own industrial associations.

He recognizes that the necessity of Indian trade unionism must be faced. "The spirit of industrialism will mean the continual danger of anarchy and violence unless the employing class goes out to meet the problem frankly by peaceful methods of negotiation and conciliation."

Such are his methods of social regeneration and they deserve the immediate attention of political as well as social reformers. For to his mind they are closely linked together, and no social progress is possible without political action as political freedom is useless without social well being.

Other Activities

Thus, as we have seen, Sir Visvesvaraya's recent activities have been India-wide and rarely confined to Mysore. He took part in the historic Round Table Conference in Bombay following the poignant fast of Mahatma Gandhi. Indeed wherever there was any special work requiring special talent his services could be counted upon. In response to the invitations of the Corporations of Bombay and Karachi he placed at their disposal his financial genius to set them in order. In either case his recommendations have been thankfully accepted and acted upon. The Corporation of Madras also made a similar request to him to examine and report upon its finances but for some reasons he could not accept it. His hands have been too full with other work to permit him the time and the energy needed for the affairs of this Municipality. Only the other day was published a report of the Back Bay Committee of which Sir Visvesvaraya was a distinguished member. Indeed he has given freely of his ripe experience of affairs and men, and his administrative and financial talents have been ungrudgingly given to the service of his countrymen. And so we see him at his post, now in Bombay, now in London, busy with important schemes, active as ever, giving of his best to the service of his fellowmen. What a splendid record of work is his!

CHARACTERISTICS

We may conclude this sketch of his career and achievements with a brief note from the pen of a Mysorean who writes with intimate knowledge of the character and personality of Sir Visvesvaraya. His countenance, says he, "is not massive and his glance not fascinating. He is middle-sized, thin, unassuming, simple, and modest. He is neat, grave, strict, and remarkably scrupulous. His temperament is analytical and exact, and his statements of facts neither passionate nor ornate, but simply oracular. His speeches are like the steady flow of the river, or the calm breathing of the wind. His striking originality is evinced by the mechanical and economic inventions, theoretical or material, which stand to his credit. His disciplined life and his steadiness of conduct, make him irreproachable, and enable him to enforce obedience even from the unwilling. We rarely see one who has such absolute freedom, such marvellous control over his feelings and passions.

"Sir Visvesvaraya is not good humoured nor is he angry. He is not weak or sensitive nor is he cold or hard-hearted. He is not merciful, nor is he cruel. He does not weep for social reform and the condition of women, as many social reformers do. But his theories of it go farther than any of theirs. He seems the spirit of the twentieth century taken shape and composed of no other qualities but *justice*, *duty* and the idea of *national regeneration*."

Page 193.

RAJA SIR T. MADHAV RAO

Raja Sir T. Madhav Rao*

RAJA SIR T. MADHAV RAO,—"the Turgot of India," as the late Mr. Fawcett justly styled him,—outshone his compeers in intelligence and culture. Peering above his contemporaries in administrative tact and political sagacity, Sir Madhav Rao was an imposing figure in the arena of Indian politics. Towards the close of his life he suffered in the estimation of some of his countrymen and was attacked by some as an enemy to reform and was set down by others as but a mediocre thinker. Two circumstances combined to produce this erroneous view,—Sir Madhav Rao's contributions under the *nom de plume* of "A Native Thinker," and his secession from the Madras Standing Committee of the Indian National Congress. The reflections, which Sir Madhav Rao published under the pseudonym mentioned above, were too cautious, not to say commonplace, for the ardent social reformer; nor were they such as to please the enthusiastic political reformer of the day in any greater degree. To this cause for dissatisfaction was added Sir Madhav Rao's withdrawal from the Congress Committee. Sir Madhav Rao, as is well-known, withdrew because he

* Abridged from an article published in the *Journal of the Poona Sarvajanik Sabha*, on the death of the great statesman.

disapproved altogether of the radical election scheme for the reform of the Legislative Councils in India, which was proposed by the Madras Committee and adopted by the National Congress assembled at Bombay in 1889. The position which he had taken in this respect brought on him attacks from many quarters. Persons, who ought to have known better and thought better, misjudged him as an enemy of the Congress movement,—misjudged the man, who only a couple of years before had acclaimed the Indian National Congress as "the soundest triumph of British Administration and a crown of glory to the great British Nation." It is not our purpose here to examine Sir Madhav Rao's position with reference to latter-day political movements in India. We propose only to take a brief survey of his remarkable career, and to portray, as faithfully as is possible within the limits of this sketch Raja Sir T. Madhav Rao, the administrator, the politician and the statesman.

I

Madhav Rao was born at Kumbakonam in 1828. He was a Mahratta Brahmin by caste and belonged to one of those adventurous families, which in the palmy days of the Mahratta ascendancy in India followed the national flag to the southernmost corner of this Peninsula, settling at Tanjore and making that city the chief outpost of the Mahratta Empire in the South. During the troublous times of the latter part of the last century, when the British Power was making efforts to assert itself in South India, Venkat

Rao, the uncle of Sir Madhav Rao, cast in his lot with the British. Recommended by his official superior to the Resident of Travancore, Venkat Rao entered the service of that State. By his remarkable ability he soon rose there to the post of Dewan. Venkat Rao's brother, Ranga Rao, later on won laurels in the Travancore service. Madhav Rao was the youngest of Ranga Rao's sons. With the advantages of these brilliant family traditions, young Madhav had the rare good fortune to combine the benefit of a careful training under the care of that eminent educationist, Mr. E. B. Powell. The school career of Madhav Rao extended over only half a dozen years, but during that short time he made remarkable progress, and, according to Mr. Powell, showed such proficiency in Mathematics and Physics as would have secured him an honourable position even in the University of Cambridge. But Mr. Powell paid him a still higher compliment by getting him appointed to act for some time for himself as Professor of Mathematics and Natural Philosophy. Madhav Rao was hardly nineteen when he received this substantial recognition of his merits at the hands of his teacher. To this testimony might be added that of a former Resident of Travancore, who said: "he had never met with a native of India who had obtained so thorough a mastery over the English language and so full an appreciation of English views in regard to politics and political economy." Thus equipped, Madhav Rao began life early in 1849 in the Accountant-General's Office at Madras. There he remained for a little over two years, when an offer was made to him to take charge [of the education of the Princes of Travancore. Madhav Rao left British service and accepted the offer gladly enough; for the prospect of making his *debut* on the stage, where his uncle and father had played so conspicuous a part, could not but be pleasing to him. Well qualified as he was for the part he had undertaken, he acquitted himself most satisfactorily, and was four years later (in April 1853) appointed by the Maharaja, with the hearty concurrence of General Cullen, the Resident, to a responsible post in the Revenue line under the Dewan. Two years later the Maharaja recognized his services in the following terms:

> The unaffected zeal with which you undertook and satisfactorily succeeded in improving my nephews by imparting to them useful and liberal education, the ardour, interest and integrity manifested by you in the capacity of a public servant and the skill with which you have been conducting the affairs immediately under your guidance to my full and entire satisfaction are services too valuable to pass unnoticed or unrewarded.

And the Maharaja promptly rewarded Madhav Rao's services by promoting him to the office of Dewan Peshkar or Naib Dewan,—a post next in importance only to that of the Dewan. The work which Madhav Rao did in his new capacity marked him out as a man possessing extraordinary administrative talents. The State of Travancore at this time was hopelessly rotten. Numerous petitions had been sent to the Madras Government by the subjects of the Raja and by Christian Missionaries, complaining of the misrule which prevailed in the State. The police force, it was complained, was a tremendous engine of oppression; prisoners were confined for very long periods without investigation, and many were acquitted after torture and long imprisonment; the regulations of the State were systematically set aside; appeal to the Resident brought no relief, since the Dewan was the Resident's *protege*; convicted criminals were suffered to be at large; the ryots' complaints were unheeded; the system of the forced labour was rampant; incalculable evils arose from the pepper, salt and cardamom monopolies; the higher Government officials were corrupt; men of the worst character were in some cases appointed to responsible offices; every appointment had its price; and, as a consequence, official power was abused, bribes extorted, justice perverted, the weak oppressed, the guilty shielded, and royal favourites amassed large private fortunes. When this distressful tale of anarchy and misrule reached the ears of Lord Dalhousie, he almost made up his mind to annex the State; but a second thought suggested milder measures. Through the Local Government he warned the Maharaja that the contingency of annexation was inevitable, unless averted by timely and judicious reforms. It was on such a scene and at such a time that Madhav Rao began his work of administrative reform. The Peshkars at the time we speak of varied in number from two to four and were all stationed at the headquarters. They did little responsible work and spent their time and energy in intriguing against the

Dewan. Madhav Rao was disgusted with this state of things and suggested to the Maharaja that each Peshkar should be given responsible charge of a separate District, or group of Districts, subject of course, to the general control of the Dewan. The suggestion was adopted and Madhav Rao was appointed to the Southern Division, comprising the very Districts from which complaints to the Madras Government had been most serious and numerous. And before even a dozen months had rolled by, the hand of a skilled administrator was seen at work in these Districts. The Political Officer described Madhav Rao's work in these words:—

> Within the short space of a year, Madhav Rao has called forth order out of disorder; has distributed justice between man and man, without fear or favour; has expelled dacoits; has raised the revenues; and his minutes and State papers show the liberality, the soundness and the statemanship of his views and principles. He has received the thanks of his sovereign; he has obtained the voluntary admiring testimony of some of the very Missionaries, who memorialized to the excellence of his administration.

"Now, here is a man," remarked Mr. Norton, "raised up, as it were, amid the anarchy and confusion of his country to save it from destruction. Annexation, looming in the not far distant future, would be banished into the shades of night, if such an administration as he has introduced into two of the Districts were given to the whole kingdom by his advancement to the post of Minister. He is indeed a splendid example of what education may do for the native." The hope, expressed here by Mr. Norton, was soon realised. Dewan Krishna Rao died in 1857;

and though Madhav Rao was then only twenty-nine years old and had a senior competitor in the field, the choice of the Maharaja fell on him. It was approved by the Resident and finally confirmed by the Madras Government towards the end of 1858. Thus Madhav Rao surpassed the traditions of his family by reaching the high position of his uncle and father at the early age of thirty.

II

DEWAN OF TRAVANCORE

In most cases thirty would certainly be deemed too early an age for so high a trust as that of a Dewan. But Madhav Rao's extraordinary talents and intellectual attainments more than made up for his immaturity of years. The task he had undertaken was one of rare difficulty;—it was that of rehabilitating a rotten State, of reforming and re-modelling an entirely disorganised administration. The picture that has already been presented of the condition of the districts, which Madhav Rao undertook as Dewan Peshkar to administer, did not represent the state of misrule only in an isolated spot; it applied to the whole State of Travancore, as it was at the time we are speaking of. With the public treasury nearly emptied; with payments and collections largely in arrears; with the public service made up, from top to bottom, of an army of voracious place-seekers, with whom corruption was second nature; with peculation, torture, false accusations and compulsory benevolences on behalf of the Sirkar as matters of every day occurrence; with the courts of Justice turned into bazars of corruption; with dacoits and marauders scouring the country by hundreds; and with the so-called Police requiring to be protected against instead of affording protection, the Travancore State was in a perilous plight indeed. When Madhav Rao was placed at the helm, he guided the State bark with such wisdom that it avoided the shoals of danger and entered into the haven of prosperity. How Madhav Rao did this we shall presently describe. Fully as he had imbibed the spirit of Western life and Wstern thought, and perfectly convinced as he was of the benevolent intentions of the British Indian Government towards the subjects of the Feudatory States, Madhav Rao discerned instinctively what was best in the British administrative machinery, and assimilated it gradually and wisely into the State under his control. In his letter to the Governor-General-in-Council, dated 9th August 1879, in connection with the transfer of Mysore to Native rule, Viscount Cranbrook observed:

> The absolute security against internal revolt, which is now enjoyed by native rulers, entails upon them obligations towards their subjects which they cannot be allowed altogether to disregard It is in the gradual and judicious extension in the Native states of the general principles of Government which are applied in British territory that their rulers will find the surest guarantee of their administrative independence. and the best safeguard against intervention on the part of the paramount power.

What Viscount Cranbrook enunciated in 1879, Madhav Rao practically anticipated in 1858. He saw that the country had entered or was entering upon a new era, and that the old ways of thought and life, the old machinery of administration and the old methods of government were unsuited to the changed circumstances and new requirements of Native States. And the very first thing that he did on assuming the reins of office showed what high ideal of Government he had set before himself. Travancore, like most other Native States, was given over to superstition and caste dominance. The Brahmins had dictated different modes of wearing clothes to the different castes, any deviation from which was jealously watched and checked not only by the Brahmins but by the different castes themselves. The Shanars or toddy-drawers of Travancore proved an exception to this debasing servility. The women of these Shanars were, by custom and by age-long religious ordinances, prevented from covering the upper part of their person. When the Queen's Proclamation of 1858 was declared, the Shanars, encouraged by the Protestant Missionaries residing in South Travancore, protested against the practice and openly disregarded the degrading custom to which they had been subjected. The other superior castes pretended to read the great Proclamation as rivetting anew the bonds of custom and spiritual tyranny. They thought the Proclamation guaranteed British non-interference in matters religious under any and every circumstance, and thus gave them the right to do what they liked, provided they did it in the name of religion. Things took a serious turn and turbulent affrays ensued. Madhav Rao was now on his trial as an administrator. His difficulties were increased by the fact that the Resident and the Maharaja did not favour the cause of the Shanars. But Madhav Rao rose superior to caste-prejudices. He saw that the Shanars were right, and that important principles were at stake in the struggle. At the same time, he saw the difficulty of quieting the disturbed state of feelings. There was serious rioting and it was a question how to conciliate the disputants. Madhav Rao went to the scene of the disturbance himself. A detachment of the Nair Brigade had preceded him to the spot. Some of the leaders of both parties were arrested, and without having recourse to extreme measures, Madhav Rao succeeded in restoring peace. The Shanars were granted liberty to dress as they chose, and the Maharaja's consent to this change was secured, though not without pressure from the Madras Government. The Resident, for his want of judgment, was asked to resign, and Mr. Francis Maltby, a man of talents and great official experience, succeeded him in the post. About six months after this appointment, the Maharaja died; and his nephew, Prince Rama Varma, was placed on the *gadi* on the 19th of October, 1860. With this young prince-pupil as his master, and a Resident of high character and enlightened views as his supporter, Madhav Rao began the work of administering the State with vigour and with skill. The most striking feature of the first few years of his administration was his great fiscal reforms, for which he was praised by Mr. Fawcett as "the Turgot of India."

After uprooting oppressive monopolies and reforming the fiscal system, Madhav Rao turned his attention to the improvement of the Public Service. The Travancore Public Service, as we have stated above, was under-paid and, as a consequence, thoroughly corrupt. Madhav Rao removed the main cause of corruption by raising the salaries to a respectable standard. The increase in the cost of the Police establishment was more than cent. per cent., and in the establishment charges of the Judicial Service, it was nearly as great. Next came the organisation of the Public Works and Educational Departments. Under the former head, the expenditure trebled itself in the nine years, 1861—70, and the expenditure on education was doubled during the six years, 1864—70. Besides the legitimate expenditure of the State on its large departments, Madhav Rao had to provide for a very extravagant expenditure of public money (amounting on an average to something like three lakhs and three quarters per annum) especially on the State charities, for which Travancore has always been renowned, for feeding Brahmans gratis all the year round. Notwithstanding these heavy demands on the Treasury, Madhav Rao managed to pay off the whole of the public debt of Travancore amounting to many lakhs of rupees within a few years. During the reign of the previous Maharaja, the State had been brought to the very brink of bankruptcy, and when Lord Dalhousie warned him that if matters were not speedily mended, the British Government would be compelled to resort to annexation as the only remedy, a sum of five lakhs of rupees was borrowed from the Pagoda to meet the exigencies of the moment. This sum, together with the interest which amounted to half as much, was paid off by the end of 1868. This was no small financial achievement. When Madhav Rao assumed the administration, he started with an empty treasury, a heavy debt, and a voracious system of fiscal policy, which ate into the very vitals of the ryots. In a few years, the debt was liquidated; oppressive monopolies were abolished; numerous minor taxes were removed; and the customs duties were greatly reduced. All this involved a large sacrifice of public revenue. And yet, except in the case of the enchancement of the price of salt, for which Madhav Rao, was not responsible, not a farthing was added to public taxation. Salaries were largely increased to improve the tone of the Public Service: large sums were devoted to works of public utility, and to the furtherance of education; a frightful waste of public funds for the purposes of mistaken charity, which Madhav Rao was not free to stop, had to be reluctantly sanctioned; and yet, with all this, the State finances were so carefully managed that handsome surpluses were left to accumulate each year in the State coffers. In 1866, the Secretary of State for India expressed himself satisfied with the financial results of Madhav Rao's administration and congratulated him on his "enlightened and able administration of the revenue department." Comparisons are generally odious but still one cannot always avoid them, and we hope it will be thought excusable if a countryman of Sir Madhav Rao remarks with pride that the great Mahratta statesman, in the narrow field in which he was called upon to work, did with ease and skill what has taxed to the utmost the resources and talents of British Indian statesmanship, which, again, has achieved no better result than barely to make the two ends meet and this with the public debt and public taxation doubled all round.

The success of the financial policy pursued by Sir T. Madhav Rao was not marred by any inattention to the paramount claims of improving the efficiency of the Public Service generally. The reorganisation of the Police Department was taken up by Sir T. Madhav Rao in the early years of his administration. The wants of the Department were: "First, increased pay; secondly, increased strength; and thirdly, more method and discipline." And all these defects were removed in the course of a few years by a steady and watchful attention to details. The administration of justice was placed on a sound basis. The Civil Procedure Code of British India, the Criminal Procedure Code, the Law of Limitation and the Registration Act were introduced one after another with such modifications as the conditions of the State demanded. An experienced judicial officer from the Madras Presidency was nominated to the Post of Chief Justice. Well qualified men were appointed as Zillah Judges; qualified Vakils were admitted to plead in their courts, and the number of Munsiffs was doubled, each Taluka being provided with one Civil Court. The jurisdiction of these Munsiffs, as also that of the Zilla Judges, was defined and enlarged and placed under check by a careful system of appeals; and lastly the Munsiffs were invested with powers to decide small causes finally. No less noteworthy was the reform in the administration of the land-revenue. The Travancore Sirkar does not claim to be the sole land-lord of public land. More than half of the cultivated land belongs to private owners and to Pagodas. The remaining State lands are farmed to tenants, and were, previous to Madhav Rao's administration, subjected to an arbitrary and a constantly increasing rack rent. It was not uncommon for one ryot to dispossess another of his land simply by offering to pay more rent to the State. The feeling of insecurity, to which this gave rise, told heavily on agriculture, and greatly reduced the saleable value of the Sirkar lands. Madhav Rao fixed the assessment on these *State* lands, and their holders were recognised as possessing heritable, saleable and otherwise transferable property in their lands. The ryots were assured that they would be allowed to enjoy their lands undisturbed so long as they paid the prescribed assessment, which was to continue unaltered till circumstances required a general revision. The land-tax, it may be here noted, was fixed very moderately, being in most cases below one-fourth of the net produce. Side by side with this wise measure, regulations were made to facilitate the sale and reclamation of waste lands. The cultivation of coffee, which before Madhav Rao's administration was almost unknown, received great encouragement under the new *regime*. In 1869-70, nearly seventeen thousand tubs of coffee, valued at about three lacs and a half of rupees, were exported, and the export duty on this article brought in something like seventeen thousand rupees. Along with coffee, tea-cultivation also began to flourish. Experiments in cinchona-gardening were also made under Sirkar management. Thus, while a great impetus was afforded to the extended cultivation of lands and the growth of new and remunerative crops, taxation was kept within very moderate bounds, and the security of possession and freedom of transfer were fully guaranteed to all the Ryot-holders of Sirkar lands. As a consequence, the land revenue went on rising year by year. In 1861-62, it brought in a little over fourteen lakhs and a half of rupees to the State treasury; and in 1869-70, this amount rose to no less than seventeen lakhs of rupees.

Since the *regime* of Venkat Rao, Madhav Rao's uncle, no public works of any importance or magnitude had been undertaken by the Travancore State, excepting one masonry bridge. Madhav Rao organised a regular Public Works Department in 186● and he made large grants of State money for pushing on a forward P. W. policy. A trunk road from the Capital to the southern extremity of the State extending over more than fifty miles, was thoroughly repaired. A net-work of branch roads, extending in all to between a hundred and hundred and fifty miles, was laid in South Travancore. Two ghat-roads, together with a road crossing and connecting these latter, were also constructed ,at great expense. To these trunk roads, measuring several hundreds of miles, were added many lines of village and town roads. A large scheme for the extension of water communication was also projected. A splendid iron girder bridge was erected in South Travancore and smaller bridges of the same sort were put up by scores over many rivers and streams in the State. A light-house was constructed at Aleppey. A commodious College building was commenced, and numerous public offices were built throughout the State. Altogether Madhav Rao undertook "great and enduring works" during his ministry, and "estimably enhanced the material prosperity of the country"

"If the public works in Travancore owe to Madhav Rao so much," remarked the writer of the article on Sir Madhav Rao in the *Calcutta Review*, "education owes to him still more. There was but one English school worth the name in the whole of Travancore, and as for vernacular schools there were none. Alive to the great importance of education, as exemplified in his own case, he strove ceaselessly to extend its benefits to Travancore."

We have said in a previous part of this sketch that the State expenditure under this head went on increasing year after year. The old English school was re-organised and a full-blown Arts College was added to it. As feeders to this central institution, sixteen English shools were opened in the districts. In 1865-66, an annual outlay of twenty thousand rupees was sanctioned for the furtherance of vernacular education. In addition to this provision for the education of males, three girls' schools were started. All these additions doubled the State expenditure on education in the course of half a dozen years.

This brief review of the leading features of Madhav Rao's administration of Travancore for fourteen years will give an idea of the high ideal aimed at and the great success achieved by him during this period of his life. In his own words, it was his cherished aim "to provide for every subject, within a couple of hours journey, the advantages of a doctor, a school-master, a judge, a magistrate, a registering officer and a post-master." Progressing steadily towards this ideal, he "banished annexation into the shades of night." He found Travancore a den of misrule ;—he left it "a model Native State." The Madras Government went on complimenting Madhav Rao on his administrative success from year to year and the Secretary of State echoed the praise in no faint voice. In 1862, when Madhav Rao visited Madras in company with the Maharaja, he was appointed a Fellow of the Madras University. When he next visited Madras, following the Maharaja, who proceeded thither for his investiture with the Insignia, of the "Star of India," he received his own Knighthood. Sir Madhav Rao resigned his office a few months after, and the Maharaja settled on him a pension of a thousand rupees per month. The retired Minister settled in Madras with a reputation already made.

The high ideal that Sir Madhav Rao had placed before him, though not fully attained, was well nigh reached. The State was set in order and it was for his successors to perfect the administrative machinery he had so skilfully adjusted. *Cen'est que le premier pas qui coute*, as the French proverb rightly says, and the "first step" taken by Sir T. Madhav Rao in the work of reforming and re-modelling the Travancore State was indeed a giant stride.

DEWAN OF INDORE

After his retirement, Sir Madhav Rao was offered a seat in the Viceregal Legislative Council, but for some reason or other he was compelled to decline the honour. He was only forty-five years at this time. and that was hardly the age for him to retire from public life. He was not, therefore, to remain inactive long. Maharaja Tukoji Rao Holkar offered him the Dewanship of his State. Sir Madhav Rao accepted the offer and went to his new field of activity in 1873.

At Indore he had not much scope for his administrative talents, hedged round as he was in every department of administration by the all-powerful will of the Maharaja. Yet when he left the State, every department of the State showed the work of his reforming hand. It was during his administration that he brought about the reconciliation of Tukoji Rao Holkar with Jayaji Rao Scindia, and thus put an end to long-standing disagreements. While at Indore, Sir Madhav Rao was invited to go to England to give evidence before the House of Commons Committee on Indian Finance, but he was not able to accept the invitation.

III

DEWAN OF BARODA

Just at this time, a storm was brewing in a Native State of considerable importance. Under Maharaja Mulhar Rao, Baroda was realizing all the horrors of despotism. The cancer of corruption had entered into the vitals of all departments in the State and oppression was rampant. Numerous petitions were sent by the Gaekwar's subjects to the Resident at Baroda, complaining bitterly of misrule.

When the bold step of deposing Mulhar Rao Gaekwar was resolved upon, the next question which had to be considered related to the form of the administration to be set up. Annexation was out of the question as opposed to the most solemn pledges given by Government. Lord Northbrook wisely resolved to conciliate public sentiment by discarding the usual plan of setting up a British officer to rule the State during the young chief's minority, and proceeded to try the noble experiment of entrusting the work to a native statesman who enjoyed the confidence of the Government and the good will of the people. Sir T. Madhav Rao was called upon accordingly to undertake the work as being the best and perhaps the only man for the post.

Sir T. Madhav Rao's work at Baroda did not differ in kind from the work he had to do at Travancore twenty years before, but it much differed from the latter in dimensions. Sir Madhav Rao, being the trusted nominee of the British Government, had the disadvantage of going to his work at Baroda with the people around him full of suspicion and fear, for they looked upon him as the representative of an intruding authority. Besides, the tyranny and misrule, which he had to undo at Baroda, was much greater and much more wide-spread than at Travancore, and the difficulty of strengthening the foundations of a good Government were immensely more trying. There were claimants to the Baroda *Gadi*, who were busy in intrigues, fancying that the stars might favour them some time and that they would have their day of good luck. These had to be quieted and ultimately defeated. Sir Madhav Rao dealt gently with these intriguers. He relieved them of heavy accumulated debts, made liberal provision for their maintenance, and treated them with consideration. Madhav Rao had also to face the difficult problem of depriving a large number of the ex-Maharaja's dependants, who had lavish grants conferred on them during the previous *regime*, of their unmerited allowances without at the same time provoking general discontent. This was done by means of cash grants and by giving them in addition a moderate subsistence allowance on condition of good behaviour. Next, there were various complicated pecuniary claims pending against some of the leading members of Mulhar Rao's administration. These were got rid of by summary compromises. There were, again, the complaints of Native bankers to be disposed of. Under the old order of things, rich banking firms were entrusted with the management of public funds on behalf of the State. The allowances of several of these had been discontinued by the late Maharaja and their services dispensed with. These prayed for the restoration of their allowances. Some of them also claimed the restoration of their private property which had been confiscated during the past *regime*. The settlement of these complaints was really a difficult affair, but Sir Madhav Rao did the work with consideration and tact. Equally difficult was the work of settling the claims of jewellers, who complained that their jewels, taken away for inspection, had been neither purchased nor returned by the ex-Maharaja, but were needlessly detained. In deciding these applications, Sir Madhav Rao had to make his way through scattered and uncertain data, and, in many instances, where the circumstances would not brook delay, he had to lay down a rough basis of settlement and order payments with reference thereto, pending a closer scrutiny at leisure. The allowances of some of the near relatives of the late Maharaja had also to be satisfactorily settled or re-adjusted. The claims of some of the members of Maharaja Khanderao's family, who had their allowances stopped by Mulhar Rao and were treated with unjust severity by him, had also to be considered and decided. Besides these complicated claims, there were cases in the nature of private suits, the main complaint in which was that the ex-Gaekwar had misdecided the suit, or that he had unjustly abrogated a decision of his predecessor. The disputes between the Sirdars and their bankers were a further source of vexation. These difficulties were all successfully met by Sir Madhav Rao, and the British officers, who watched events carefully in the early years, were most favourably impressed with the Minister's wonderful tact.

When these difficulties were settled, Sir Madhav Rao undertook the formidable task of forming a well-regulated system of administration. He well knew that it would be unwise to hastily thrust a foreign administration upon the people of the State, and he therefore proceeded slowly but surely. "We have resisted the temptation," he wrote in his first Administration Report,

> to enter upon an ambitious course of legislation. It would be premature to make and promulgate regular and rigid laws. A simple population must be unable to understand and therefore unable to act up to minute, elaborate and intricate provisions. What they desire is substantial justice. What they dislike is a system of technicalities, the object of which is not apparent to their rough intelligence and the action of which they conceive to be only the defeat or the delay of justice.

So that the programme of administration which Sir Madhav Rao marked out was mainly intended to maintain public order and tranquillity, to redress the evils of the past mal-administration; to establish a machinery for the proper administration of justice and create a Police commensurate with the extent of the country; to promote education, to provide suitable medical agencies; to reduce taxation and enforce economy in expenditure; and permanently to keep the expenditure fairly below the receipts, so that a surplus may become available as a provision for adverse seasons and available also for further administrative improvements.

The administration of justice under the old rulers occupied a very subordinate place in the list of public duties. Sir Madhav Rao allotted to it the position and importance to which it is entitled according to the ancient Hindu and modern European ideas. The Public Works Department was brought into being for the first time and adequate resources were placed at its disposal. The finances of the State, which had fallen into utter disorder, were placed on a sound footing, and all existing resources carefully husbanded. Previously revenue farmers made enormous gains and a venal and selfish order of officials favoured them and enriched themselves at the cost of the State and its subjects. Sir Madhav Rao wrote a very telling paragraph on this subject in his first Administration Report. "It was an exchequer," he wrote in the words of Burke, "wherein extortion was the assessor, fraud the cashier, confusion the accountant, concealment the repcrter, and oblivion the remembrancer." Sir Madhav Rao faced this most difficult financial problem with confidence, rescued the finances from all the old embarrassments and confusion, introduced honesty and integrity into the administration and assured the solvency of the State as thoroughly as he had done at Travancore. He placed the land-revenue system upon a sound basis, substituting the ryot-wari for the old farming system, thus making a clean sweep of all the vexatious and extortionate incidents of the latter system. The following was the triangle within which the lines of his financial policy were laid out: (1) to simplify and purify the taxation of the country and to so fix it that it may last unaltered for a good period of years, (2) to fix scales of expenditure for the several departments of the State so that the limits thus imposed may continue unchanged also for a considerable term of years; and (3) to insure in ordinary cases a fair surplus over expenditure, so that a surplus may accumulate and be available in bad seasons to meet extraordinary demands.

It is hardly necessary here to go further into the details of Sir Madhav Rao's internal administration at Baroda, to tell how he evolved order out of chaos, introduced honesty and efficiency into the administration, improved the finances of the State, relieved the people from vexatious taxes, carried out a vigorous Public Works policy, made provision for the protection and education of the people, afforded them medical relief free of charge, placed the administration of justice on a sound footing and assured continuous progress and prosperity all round. We shall content ourselves with only sketching, in Sir Madhav Rao's own words, the broad outlines of the work he did during the five years he was at Baroda.

> It would be false modesty, to disguise the fact that during these five years, our work has been exceedingly heavy and trying, for the fact accounts for our visible delays and deficiencies. It is not simply that we have had to carry on ordinary current business. We have had to investigate and decide a multitude of matters inherited by us, which in number and complexity are probably unsurpassed in any other Native State. We have had to organise the machinery of Government. We have had to carefully consider and carry out vital reforms. We have had to bring under control a vast expenditure in all its dark and intricate ramifications. We have had to rectify our relations with our numerous and diversified neighbours. In this respect, grave and embarrassing aberrations from sound principles had in course of time and neglect, sprung up, and their correction presented peculiar difficulties. We have had to bring them to the notice of the authorities concerned, to explain, to discuss, convince and sometimes to respectfully expostulate. The extra strain thus caused has, however, begun now sensibly to diminish, and it is therefore hoped that we shall be increasingly enabled to devote our time and energies to the development of internal improvements. It must be frankly admitted that there is still abundant scope for our exertions in this direction. All we claim to have done is that we have fulfilled the primary obligations of a civilised Government.

Such is the tale of Sir Madhav Rao's administrative work at Baroda. We would have gladly recorded in detail the strength and completeness of the work he did there, but we must resist the temptation as our space is but limited. There was one feature of his administration, however, in regard to which Sir Madhav Rao has been strongly attacked in some quarters, and it is necessary to dwell upon this subject with more fulness of detail.

It is contended by some critics that Sir Madhav Rao failed to safeguard the interests of the Baroda State, when they clashed with those of the Imperial Government, that he yielded without a protest to the aggressive policy of the British Indian Government, that, in a word, the State was nothing to him if only he could win a smile in high quarters. We think such a charge could only be made by those who are ignorant about the actual facts of the situation. Sir Madhav Rao was not at all responsible for whatever injuries the State might have suffered during his *regime*. Wherever and whenever he thought that the interests of the State were in jeopardy, he protested against outside pressure in the strongest terms possible. Beyond this he was powerless to do anything. He had to yield, as any other politician in his situation would have had to do, when the Supreme Government's ruling was peremptory and inexorable. In most cases, however, his protests resulted in a compromise,—a great achievement, when we remember how difficult it is to get the Government of India to budge an inch from their superior position in their dealings with Native States. So that what ignorant and irresponsible critics have blamed Sir Madhav Rao for is precisely that which brings him out as a high-class politician.

To exemplify our remarks, let us take the salt question. The British Government, besides prohibiting the manufacture of salt in the Baroda State, claimed the right to work salt-pans within the Gaekwar's territory, and demanded the exemption of salt so manufactured from the Baroda duties. Sir Madhav Rao protested that the right to levy these duties belonged exclusively to the State and that the British Government was not justified in demanding exemption. "Apart from the question of right," he added,

> it is clear that the opening by the British Government of salt works within the Gaekwar territory is undesirable. However affairs may have been managed in past years, when neither the ruler nor the subjects had any precise ideas of right and justice, in these days such matters are better understood, and a steady progress (no doubt the result of the close contact with the British Government) has set in towards the definition of the rights of the State and of individuals. Such being the case the opening of the salt works, which will render necessary the presence of the servants of the British Government within the territory of the State, and transactions of various kinds between them and Gaekwar ryots, may lead to collisions and conflict of jurisdiction. It appears to me that there is every reason to deprecate such a source of probable trouble and unpleasantness.

Throughout his tenure of office, Sir Madhav Rao fought sturdily in the interests of the State. A number of instances might be cited, which would make it clear beyond the shadow of a doubt that Sir Madhav Rao endeavoured energetically to safe-guard the interests of the State in spite of cynical aspersions cast on his attitude towards the suzerain power.

Another point on which Sir Madhav Rao has been roundly found fault with was the fact of his having sent for the sanction and approval of Lord Ripon's Government a draft-constitution proposed to be enforced in the Baroda State on the installation of the young Gaekwar to the Baroda *Gadi*. It was contended that Sir Madhav Rao's constitution would have reduced the Baroda State to a mere *Zemindari*. We have no space to discuss that constitution here and show the hollowness and unwisdom of this criticism. It is but fair to note the contention of the adverse critics that enough time had not been given for a constitution to grow from within, and that it was premature to enforce a cut and dry system of alien ideas of Government on an ignorant people. Side by side with this, it is equally fair to remark that Sir Madhav Rao's constitution was entirely the same in spirit and nearly the same in detail as the one promulgated in Mysore when those territories were restored to Native Rule, and we all know how beneficially that constitution has worked there in the best interests of the State.

Sir Madhav Rao retired from Baroda in 1882, soon after the installation of the present Maharaja. He passed his days of retirement at Mylapore, where he died at the age of sixty-three.

IV

We have given a sufficiently clear presentment of Raja Sir T. Madhav Rao, the administrator, the politician and the statesman. Evolving order out of chaos in two, if not three, important Native States, and skilfully sowing the seeds of an advanced system of Government—this was the work of Raja Sir T. Madhav Rao, the administrator. Destroying silently the elements of disturbance and discontent by laying the malcontents under obligations to the

State, and securing for the State under his control the utmost possible good under the utmost possible pressure of the Simla Foreign Office without producing friction, was the work of Raja Sir T. Madhav Rao, the politician. And perceiving beforehand the relations which would come to subsist between the British Government and their Feudatory States, and adjusting accordingly his system of administration so that it may suit the changed circumstances under which Native States had begun or were soon to live, and forestalling, through the force of his extraordinary talents, aided by the high education he had received and acquired, such reforms in the States, placed under his charge, as time would sooner or later have made imperative, as also fore-stalling the relations which increased education in Native States would bring about between the Maharajas and their subjects, and proposing accordingly a constitution which, while preserving what was good in the old order of things, would so fashion the State introducing it as to make it capable of moving with the movements of the age and rising with the rising aspirations of its subject people,—that was what constituted Raja Sir T. Madhav Rao's title to statesmanship.

Sir Madhav Rao, in our opinion, was a greater man than either Sir Salar Jung or Sir Dinkar Rao. These latter did not possess that familiarity with the English tongue and hence with European thought on politics and political matters, which was Sir Madhav Rao's *forte*. Sir Madhav Rao's acquaintance with literature bearing on Native States and policy pursued towards them from time to time by the British Indian Government, as also his knowledge of European views on economics and finance, was, it will be clear to those who study his official writings, simply perfect, and that circumstance gave him a great advantage over the two other native statesmen of his time. He could appreciate better than they could all that was best in the British administrative system. And having the capacity to appreciate that, he could inaugurate, with less difficulty and more confidence, an era of reform and progress in the States which were entrusted to his care. In a way, Sir Salar Jung laboured under greater difficulties than Sir Madhav Rao. His lot was cast amid less enlightened and less peaceful population; so that he could not effect reforms as smoothly as Sir Madhav Rao succeeded in doing. Yet we are not under-rating the great politician of Hyderabad, when we repeat that he was, on the whole, a smaller man than Sir Madhav Rao,—smaller in intellectual attainments and perhaps in talents. Sir Dinkar Rao represents the old school of native politicians, which becomes extinct with him. Sir Madhav Rao was a perfect politician of the new school. Sir Salar Jung plied between the two.

To educated natives, Sir Madhav Rao's life is a rich mine of knowledge and experience. Those who study his State papers will not fail to be impressed with the vast store of information and the keen observation of men and things which he brought to bear on his ministerial work. His life will also teach them to be, especially in politics, more practical than theoretic, more accurate than wordy, more moderate than enthusiastic, more cautious than precipitate.

V

DEWAN ANANDA RAO

In due course the mantle of the illustrious statesman fell on the shoulders of the eldest of his three sons. Dewan Ananda Rao lived to a ripe old age and retired as Dewan of Mysore. Born on 15th May 1852 in Travancore Ananda Rao received his early education in Madras and Trivandrum. He had a brilliant career at school and college having passed his Matriculation, F.A. and B.A. in the first class. He took his degree in 1871 taking a first class in History, Logic and Psychology. After a brief stay in Indore as tutor to the late Maharaja Ananda Rao joined the Mysore service in 1873 as an attache under the British Commission. He served in several Districts as Magistrate and earned reputation for calmness and courage especially in quelling a strike in Mysore. He was subsequently Chief Secretary and Director of Statistics and later rose to be Revenue Commissioner and first Councillor to His Highness the Maharaja. Ananda Rao succeeded Mr. V. P. Madhava Rao as Dewan and his two years' *regime* was marked by peaceful and steady progress though there was no large departure of policy. Silent and useful reforms were enacted. The one great service which earned for him the gratitude of the Mysoreans was that he reserved the Mysore Civil Service for Mysoreans born and domiciled in Mysore. Ananda Rao did much to improve the service and during his tenure of office Mysore also witnessed the birth of the Mysore Economic Conference. Ananda Rao retired after two years of Dewanship and received a special pension from the State. He was also honoured by the British Government with the title of C.I.E. He died on July 20th 1919 mourned by the whole State. Ananda Rao left no children, and he stoutly refused to adopt, holding the view that "fiction cannot be a fact and adoptions are unnatural."

Page 225.

KAZI SHAHABUDIN

Kazi Shahabudin, C.I.E.

AMONG the great Indian statesmen of the last century Kazi Shahabudin deserves a high place. Born of comparatively poor parents he rose by sheer dint of character and ability and persevering industry to positions of trust and responsibility. Like many other statesmen in India he first won distinction under the British Government and latterly devoted himself to the service of an Indian State of which he became the Dewan. By education and training he equipped himself to the high office to which he was called and he proved an administrator of no mean repute even in an age when Indian talent for administration was keenest.

EARLY LIFE AND EDUCATION

Kazi Shahabudin was born in 1832 in the family of an Arab Kuresh in Savant Wadi, a small but historically important Native State in the Southern Maratha country. Like so many of his co-religionists he received his early education in Persian and underwent a course of studies in Islamic theology. Later, he entered the State Marathi School where he attracted the notice of the then Political Superintendent of the State—Sir G. Le Grand Jacob. Closer contact confirmed Sir Jacob's judgment of the character and ability of the youth who had attracted his notice at school.

Thereupon Sir Jacob sent him to be educated at Poona, where having finished his school course Shahabudin entered the Poona College. There also he displayed the same remarkable aptitude for learning which gained for him the friendship and regard of the Professors. Subsequently, says his biographer in the "Representative Men of India," he joined the then newly-opened Engineering School, and in the year 1855 left it, after having passed a "highly creditable examination." He could without difficulty have obtained an appointment in the State Public Works Department; but "there's a divinity that shapes our ends." He preferred to serve under Colonel Jacob as Head Clerk at Bhooj, which placed him on the high road to his future career as a statesman. Shortly afterwards he was appointed Secretary to a Council of Regency—with the Political Agent, the late General Trevelyan, as its President—which was formed to conduct the affairs of the State of Kutch, in consequence of serious dissensions between the reigning Chief and the heir-apparent.

IN THE SERVICE OF BHOOJ

The duties of a Political agent were, as might be expected, both difficult and delicate and the services of Mr. Shahabudin were of especial value to the Regency. For it was a time of great trouble. The Mutiny had broken out and the whole military and other resources of the Bombay Government were requisitioned for service outside the Presidency. It was natural for the people to be uneasy under the circumstances. Fortunately in every respect the hearty loyalty of the Chief, His Highness Rao Desuljee, enabled the Government of Bombay to withdraw the whole of the British troops from Bhooj for service elsewhere, and arrangements had to be made to guard the Residency, the Treasury and the Fort, with the Durbar troops, and to raise with the least possible delay a small contingent under the command of European officers for local service.

The strain on the Kazi might well be imagined and it is no wonder that he continued to possess the utmost confidence of the Political Agent. In fact he was so popular and withal so serviceable to the State at the time that when an appointment in the Education Department was offered to him, the Political Agent directly wrote to the head of the Department that the Kazi could not be spared.

JOINS THE BOMBAY SERVICE

The great services he had rendered were, however, subsequently rewarded by his appointment as an Assistant in the Revenue and Financial Department of the Bombay Secretariat. Here again he speedily came to be appreciated by the well-known Sir Barrow Ellis of the Bombay Service. Mr. Ellis offered Mr. Shahabudin a first-class Mamlatdarship in Gujarat, which he accepted. In this new sphere the Kazi made such good use of his opportunities that within two years after his appointment as Mamlatdar he was nominated a Deputy Collector on probation, subject to passing the Lower and the Higher Examinations at the expiration of one year. He, however, offered himself for the higher examination within nine months, and having passed it "with credit," was confirmed in his appointment, and posted to the Collectorate of Surat, under Sir Theodore Hope, then Collector of that district.

WORK IN KUTCH

The good work done by the Kazi in Kutch, as Head Clerk to the Political Agent, and as Secretary to the Council of Regency, had left its mark, and when towards the end of 1868 the post of Minister became vacant, His Highness the Rao selected him to fill it.

But this office was no bed of roses. In those days intrigues in Native States were frequent. The story of the Kazi's work for the State of Kutch may well be told in the words of Mr. Sorabji Jehangir.

> In addition to conflicting parties and intrigues at the Durbar, the relations of the Prince with many of the Zamindars' called the "Bhayads" or kinsmen, to whom certain rights had been guaranteed by the British Government in the early part of the century had become a matter of controversy between the Political Agent and through him the Government of Bombay, and the Durbar. The relations between the Rao and the Political Agent were greatly strained in consequence of this case, known as the "Bhayad case." Being unable conscientiously to support the policy of the British representative, and rightly unwilling, as a servant of the British Government, to oppose that policy, the newly-appointed Dewan requested to be permitted to revert to his post at Surat, but was dissuaded from doing so by the earnest solicitations of His Highness the Rao. The situation became really grave, and with the view of extricating himself from his embarrassing position he resigned the British service, and resolved, in addition to his ordinary duties as Minister, to prosecute the Rao's appeal in the Bhayad case. His labours, however, being unsuccessful in India, he was dispatched to England in 1869, where he had a fair hearing, which smoothed the way for a satisfactory settlement of the case,

ACTIVITIES ABROAD

While in London he was for three years Honorary Secretary to the East India Company and for two years Professor of Oriental Languages at the University College.

About the year 1871 a Parliamentary Committee, presided over by the Right Honorable Sir M. E. Grant Duff, sat to inquire into the financial condition of India, and first amongst the few natives of the country who gave evidence was Mr. Kazi Shahabudin. On the eve of his return to India in 1873 he received an appointment as attache to Sir Bartle Frere's Mission to Zanzibar for the suppression of the slave trade, and during the short period he was with the Mission he acted as Special Correspondent of the *Daily Telegraph*, contributing some interesting letters, especially on the question of slavery. From Zanzibar the Kazi proceeded to India, and resumed his duties as Dewan of Kutch. There, however, he found a state of things existing which compelled him to resign. After a delay of some months, the Rao reluctantly accepted his resignation, and in March 1874 the Kazi left the State.

IN BARODA

Soon after his retirement from Kutch, Mr. Kazi Shahabudin was invited by Mr. Dadabhai Naoroji, the then Dewan to the unfortunate Mulhar Rao, Maharaja of Baroda, to assist him in the administration of that State, especially in the Revenue and Financial Department.

Owing to the utter incapacity of Mulhar Rao, Dadabhai's administration was a short-live done. The Dewan and his colleagues including the Kazi resigned and left Baroda. But on the deposition of the Maharajah arrangements were made to carry on the administration and Kazi Shahabudin was invited to be the head of the Revenue and Financial Department. The interregnum ceased on the appointment of Raja Sir T. Madhav Rao, as Minister, who was invested with almost full powers of Government during the minority of the present Maharaja. Mr. Shahabudin continued at the head of the Finance Department and became one of the most trusted Councillors of the Minister. In his Administration Report, for the year 1876 Sir Madhav Rao wrote:—

> Mr. Kazi Shahabudin has most successfully managed the Revenue Department. The important officer combines in a rare degree a thorough knowledge of details with a thorough knowledge of principles. His energy and his keen perception make themselves felt through all the gradations of the service over which he presides and his application to business has been such that he has found time to render me valuable assistance in the consideration of important questions not pertaining to his own Department.

Not long after, Shahabudin's salary was raised at the instance of the Minister who again bore testimony to the Kazi's services.

> I need not say that I regard Mr. Kazi's services as very valuable. He has worked hard and incessantly. He has brought great intelligence and experience to bear on his work. His familiarity with the great principles which must govern public measures enables him to rapidly evoke order out of chaos. I have largely consulted Mr. Kazi in making appointments and promotions, and I have observed with much satisfaction that his selection and recommendation of men are just what they ought to be. He is a very reliable and safe judge of merit and

character. Another valuable feature in Mr. Kazi is, that he knows how to secure the cordial co-operation of the public servants he comes in contact with. He is conciliatory, while firm where firmness is required.

Sir Madhav Rao had good reason to speak of Shahabudin in such high terms. For, the latter cordially co-operated with the Minister in carrying out those reforms which have since made Baroda what it is. A regular revenue survey was organised and the anomalous systems of collecting revenue were replaced by an accurate and definitely ascertained system. Large tracts of waste lands were reclaimed according to a very judiciously framed set of rules. The security of life and property was ensured according to a code of rules formed for the guidance of the Police Department. The benefits of education were largely extended. Schemes for making railroads and metalled roads were started. Several large works of public utility were started.

In fine, as an English journal pointed out at the time, it might be said truly that the work begun by Sir T. Madhav Rao had been successfully carried on by Kazi Shahabudin. One particular trait of the Kazi deserves special mention. During his tenure of office in Baroda, extending over a period of thirteen years, he rose high above the general run of officers.

Indeed "Whenever Sir T. Madhav Rao was absent on leave or on duty, the Kazi was put in charge of the Minister's work: no small responsibility when the state of transition through which the Baroda State was passing is borne in mind."

He had no predilection for any particular caste or creed. He appreciated merit wherever he found it, whether in the Brahmin, the Mussalman, the Maratha, the Parsi, or the Gujarati.

HONOURS AND FURTHER SERVICES

Doubtless such services were duly appreciated by the Government who conferred on him a Khan Bahadurship in 1877. Three years later he was made a Companion of the Indian Empire.

The same year he, as officiating Dewan, was invited to a conference with the British Delegate on the question of the Baroda State entering into a Customs Union with the British and the Portuguese Governments in connection with the Anglo-Portuguese Treaty of 1879.

Sir Madhav Rao resigned his office in April 1883, and the Maharaja appointed Khan Bahadur Kazi Shahabudin his Minister, which post he occupied for upwards of three years. Continuous hard work, however, began to tell on his health, and in July 1886 he was allowed to retire on a handsome pension. In July 1886 Kazi Shahabudin left Baroda with the best wishes of the people and the Durbar.

Lakshman Jagannath

BY a curious coincidence, one who was a fellow-student with Kazi Shahabudin was destined in after life to be his fellow-worker and subsequently his successor in office in the Baroda State. The career of Lakshman Jagannath was, in fact, in many respects, similar to that of his predecessor. He, too, rose from humble beginnings by sheer dint of character and ability. His father was an old and faithful servant of Government in the Bombay Presidency. Lakshman was born on the 15th August 1835 and after the usual school course joined the Poona College where as we said he was fellow student with Kazi Shahabudin. Like the Kazi, Lakshman also won the warm appreciation of his professors "for diligence, progress and exemplary conduct." The story of his early career is told with vivid interest by Mr. Sorabji Jehangir in his "Representative Men of India."

IN BRITISH SERVICE

We learn that soon after he left College he entered British service as a clerk in the office of the Superintendent of Police in Poona. He was subsequently employed in the newly created department of the Inam Commission; he afterwards went to Sind where he seems to have successively served as Accountant to the

Karachi Municipality, Deputy Accountant in the office of the Collector of Shikarpur and later Accountant in the Harbour Works. In all these offices he conducted himself with praiseworthy diligence and he naturally won the unstinted appreciation of the authorities. In 1863 we find him appointed a Mukhtiarkar. He then left for Hyderabad (Sind), on promotion and we find the Collector and Magistrate of Hyderabad acknowledging the services of Lakshman Jagannath in terms of admiration of his qualities and talents. We next see him in Karachi as Dufterdar to the Collector. Here too he was found "invaluable." He was confirmed soon after and the Collector Mr. Lambert used these words in commending Lakshman Jagannath to the notice of the Government.

"I have so often expressed my high appreciation of Mr. Lakshman Jagannath's services in this Collectorate, that I can only repeat here what I have said on former occasions. When he came here everything showed the want of efficient supervision; the Tuppudar's accounts had been unclosed for two years, and large balances of revenue were due. He brought the accounts into order the first year, and reduced the outstanding balances to one-half, to less than a quarter the second year, and to trifling sums during the succeeding years of his administration. He took a leading part in introducing the new system of accounts, and he gave me the utmost assistance in drawing up a complete set of village forms on the introduction of the regular settlement. His steady industry, combined with his undoubtedly great ability, enabled him to effect improvements in everything which came under his view, and the assistance he rendered me was invaluable. He is the best Native public servant I have ever had under me."

After ten years' stay in Sind, Lakshman Jagannath was transferred to Bombay, and in 1869 we find him at Sholhapur as Hoozur Deputy Collector. Here he so endeared himself to the people that they called their market after his name—"Lakshmanpet." A year later he was called away to the Belgaum Collectorate. He then passed the Departmental Examination "with credit" coming out first in rank among the successful candidates. After some rapid promotions, he was appointed Income-Tax Collector and subsequently Chairman of the Municipality. To say that Mr. Lakshman Jagannath performed all his duties satisfactorily is to speak very inadequately of all the services he rendered. Whether as an officer of accounts, a Magistrate, or a Chairman of the Municipality, he was a paragon of a public servant. His energy was indomitable, and his judgment, temper, and tact were perfect. Performing his duties with unswerving fidelity, he gained the good-will of all.

Indeed in every office he was employed he won the approbation of his superior officers. These repeated commendations, says the writer of the sketch in "Representative Men of India," brought him prominently before the notice of the Government, so that his name was submitted to the Government of India as that of a person well qualified to appear as a witness before the Parliamentary Committee appointed to inquire into the financial condition of India. The next year (1874)

Mr. Lakshman Rao was selected by Government to fill the responsible and onerous post of Assistant Revenue Commissioner N. D., one till then rarely, if ever, conferred upon a Native. He was scarcely two months in this position when he was indented for by the Baroda State.

IN THE SERVICE OF BARODA

We need not linger long over the circumstances which called him and some others to Baroda. It was a very critical period when all the best available talents had to be employed in tiding over the crisis. Mulhar Rao's misrule had just come to an end. The Commission of Enquiry had recommended certain reforms which had to be urgently carried out in order to stabilise the Government. Dadabhai Naoroji was invited to form an administration consisting entirely of educated Indians. The British Government, says the writer of the sketch from which we have quoted already, was persuaded to afford facilities for the formation of such a Government as the Dewan suggested by lending to the Baroda State the services of such of their officers as might accept posts therein. It was under these circumstances that Kazi Shahabudin wrote to his old school-fellow Mr. Lakshman Jagannath to join the newly formed Government. After recalling past times he said: "This is a fine opportunity for one of your talents to show what educated Natives can do, and to do an immense deal of good to large numbers of the poor." There could be only one answer to this impressive call. Lakshman

Rao took charge of the Navsari District as Soobah, hat is to say, he was invested with revenue and judicial powers equal to those enjoyed by the Collector and Judge of a British District. In fact he was virtually the head of the whole District, responsible for its administration. And by training and capacity he was best fitted for this onerous task which he performed with distinction. But not long after, affairs in Baroda took a serious turn. The alleged attempt on the life of the British Resident brought the administration of Dadabhai to an end and the new Soobah of Naosari was left to fight the battle of reform single-handed. Mulhar Rao was subsequently removed from the *gadi* and Sir R. Meade assumed charge of Government. The crisis over, things took their normal course and Lakshman Rao continued to do his bit to further the work of reform he had begun. Not only in his District but in the head office as well, his work was by no means negligible or slight. He brought to his task no inconsiderable tact, judgment and resource.

To evolve order out of chaos, to eliminate the elements of anarchy, and to introduce peace and contentment among an oppressed people, is a task which, as it falls to the lot of only a few, is also one which calls for the exercise of rare administrative abilities. Mr. Lakshman Rao was by his previous training and varied experience well fitted to undertake such a task, and, as the results prove, he has performed it with credit to himself, honour to the Government which he serves, and with benefit to the ryots and to the State.

Though his work was welcome to the peace-loving citizens of the State he was not left undisturbed by the rowdy elements of the population. The farmers of revenues, whose prosperity depended on the continuance of misrule and anarchy stoutly opposed his reforms and it was not before his iron will was exercised that they ceased to oppose them. We read:

> The ringleader was incarcerated, and this salutary step stunned them all. The land was over-taxed; justice there was next to none. Security of life and property had not been known for years. Mr. Lakshman, therefore, applied himself to remedy these evils. The assessment on land was reduced by nearly forty per cent. A police force was organised. Liberal rules were made to encourage the cultivation of waste lands. These and several cognate measures brought peace and prosperity to the district. The town of Navsari, by its cleanliness and well laid-out roads, attracted visitors, people from Bombay and other districts going there to enjoy their holidays. In the Kadi Division, where Lakshman Rao was subsequently transferred, he had to deal with a dangerous style of outlawry, besides the confused state of Revenue administration and outstanding account work, but he coped successfully with these evils, as was testified to by Raja Sir T. Madhav Rao. He was then called upon to fill the position of the head of the Revenue Department, where he introduced uniformity of procedure in the work of that department. Many irregular taxes, inequitable in their incidence on persons and property, were either abolished or equalised, and a thorough vigilance was exercised on the work of the subordinate officers. Departmental examinations were introduced in the Revenue Service, which was also graded and organised, so that the subordinate officers may be rewarded according to their merits and the soundness of their work.

Naturally Lakshman Rao's vigorous and successful administration drew the attention of the authorities concerned. In August 1886 H. H. Sayaji Rao Gaekwar selected him to succeed Kazi Shahabudin as

Dewan. His administration was marked by quiet and unobtrusive work. Substantial reforms were introduced. Writing of the reforms carried out in his *regime* Mr. Sorabjee Jehangir points out :—

Trade in transit used to be encumbered by heavy Customs duties, which have since been abolished. The system of popular education has been put upon a sound basis, and a liberal expenditure upon it sanctioned. Increased provision has been made for affording medical relief to the people. The Excise Department has been brought more in harmony with that of the Bombay Presidency, which, while securing peaceful relations with the neighbouring British authorities, has also proved financially profitable to the State.

Lakshman Rao's responsibilities were even more onerous than those of other Dewans. The Gaekwar, in consideration of his health, had to be away from the State for long periods. The administration had therefore to be conducted by the Council with the Dewan at its head. The Dewan had always directed the administration with marked ability. So admirable was Lakshman Rao's administration that Col. Berkley, in a letter to His Highness wrote:—

"The work of the administration here has gone on perfectly smoothly since you left. My interference or advice have been seldom needed In your Dewan you have an excellent and loyal servant, who never for a moment loses sight of your interests."

To this may be added Col. Oliver St. John's observations culled from his own letter to the Minister.

"I congratulate you personally on the near return of His Highness, which will relieve you of the heavy responsibility you have borne during his absence. He is to be congratulated on having had so honest and capable a Minister to rule his State during his absence."

No wonder that on February 16, 1887, on the occasion of the Jubilee of Her Majesty's reign the Government thought fit to bestow on him the title of Dewan Bahadur as a personal distinction.

Lakshman Jagannath retired in 1890 with a pension from the British Government and a handsome allowance from the Gaekwar, and he spent a well-earned rest in the historic city of Poona.

Page 240.

LAKSHMAN JAGANNATH

Romesh Chunder Dutt.

EARLY YEARS

ROMESH CHUNDER DUTT comes from a cultured family of Calcutta which was distinguished even in the days of Clive and Warren Hastings. His great grandfather, Nilmani Dutt, was a kind-hearted, broad-minded, distinguished Hindu leader of Calcutta, well-known in the latter half of the eighteenth century. His great uncle, Rasamoy Dutt, was the first Indian who held the high posts—first of Principal of Sanskrit College in Calcutta, and then of Judge of the Court of Small Causes. His father Isan Chunder was one of the first Deputy Collectors in Bengal, when that service was created for the higher employment of Indians by Lord William Bentinck. Miss Toru Dutt a cousin of Romesh Dutt, wrote English verses which were much admired in England a generation ago; and several others of the gifted family distinguished themselves in literary pursuits.

Mr. Romesh Dutt was born in Calcutta in 1848 (August 13,) but his early boyhood was mostly passed in many Bengal Districts, where his father was employed as Deputy Collector. Those were pre-railway days, and Mr. Dutt had always pleasant recollections of long journeys by land and river, and of many villages and towns and Districts visited in his boyhood.

Losing his mother and father soon after, young Romesh and his brothers and sisters lived under the guardianship of his uncle, Shashi Chunder, himself a man of literary pursuits and greatly devoted to English literature. Romesh's successes in the University examinations were marked; he was the first of his school at the Matriculation Examination of 1864; and he stood second in order of merit among all the students of the University at the first Examination in Arts held in 1866. But he never graduated;—an event happened which changed his future life and career.

DEPARTURE FOR ENGLAND

One fine morning in 1868, (March 3,) three Bengali youths left India and sailed for England. One of them, Surendranath Banerjea, went with his father's consent; the two others, Bihari Lal Gupta and Romesh Chunder Dutt had simply run away from their homes under the cover of night! We can scarcely realise in these days the risks and the difficulties, the social and caste prohibitions, which young Hindus had to face, sixty years ago, before they could cross the sea. We have heard that the three berths in the steamer were engaged in the name of "Surendranath Banerjea and two friends," because the two friends feared to have their names published before they had effected their escape! But they were determined, all three of them, and calmly faced all the risks that lay before them, and it almost seems as if the hand of Destiny impelled them to the bold venture which shaped their future life. The name of Surendranath Banerjea is a household word to-day all over India; as a patriot, an orator, and a journalist he has nobly performed his life's duty. Bihari Lal Gupta had a distinguished career, and retired from the Indian Civil Service, full of honours, some years ago, as a Judge of the High Court of Calcutta. Romesh Chunder Dutt also retired from the same service but won fame and distinction by his varied labours in more fields than one.

All the three succeeded at the open competition of 1869. More than three hundred English candidates had appeared at that Examination, but Mr. Dutt won the third place in order of merit; and he stood second among all the English candidates in English Literature. In Sanskrit he easily stood first.

STUDY IN ENGLAND

The Indian students found easy introductions to English homes, and Mr. Romesh Dutt was welcomed by many English families. He witnessed the great Parliamentary Election of 1868 which returned the Liberals to power, and Gladstone became Prime Minister for the first time. The young Indian student had admission to the House of Commons, listened to the speeches of Gladstone and Disraeli, and had personal introductions to John Bright and

Henry Fawcett, the greatest friends of India in those days. He attended meetings where John Stuart Mill spoke or Charles Dickens gave readings from his novels; he was present at receptions at the India Office, given by the Duke of Argyle, then Secretary of State for India; and he made many friends among the eminent Englishmen of those days. Among Professors of the London University College under whom he studied, he knew Henry Morley and Theodore Goldstucker most intimately; and altogether he carried away with him very pleasant recollections of his first sojourn in England.

EARLY OFFICIAL WORK

For eleven years, from 1871 to 1882, Mr. Romesh Dutt served in various capacities in various Districts in Bengal. His first experience of famine-relief work was in the District of Nadiya in 1874; but a more arduous work was imposed upon him in 1876, when a terrible cyclone and storm-wave swept over south-eastern Bengal, and carried away over a hundred thousand people. Mr. Romesh Dutt was selected to re-organize administration in the island of Dakhin Shahbazpur in the mouths of the Ganges. The whole island was covered with dead bodies like a vast battle-field, and dead men and women hung on trees, floated on tanks, and were carried up and down by the tides. A cholera broke out almost immediately which was scarcely less fatal than the cyclone; the looting of property which had been washed away from private homes was a daily occurrence, and a famine due to the loss of crops ended the tale of disasters. Amidst all these terrible disasters the young officer of five years' standing worked almost single-handed; he rebuilt villages, restored order, relieved the sufferers and re-organized the administration. Peace and prosperity smiled once more on the island before he left.

EARLY LITERARY WORK

In the midst of official work in various Districts, Mr. Romesh Dutt's pen was not altogether idle even in those early years. He wrote small works in English about his *Three Years in Europe* and about the Literature and the Peasantry of his own Province; but his first serious work as an author began with his well-known Bengali Novels. The famous Bankim Chandra Chatterjea, the greatest Bengali writer of the 19th century, was an intimate friend of Mr. Romesh Dutt. They met one day in Calcutta, and Bankim Chandra urged his young friend to try his hand at Bengali. "Write in Bengali!—exclaimed the latter,—"but I hardly know the Bengali literary style!" "Style!" "—rejoined Bankim,—" why, whatever a cultured man like you will write will be style. If you have the gift in you the style will come of itself!" Mr. Dutt remembered this conversation and between 1874 and 1880, he produced his four historical Novels in Bengali which are now a part of the permanent literature of Bengal. One of them, *The Slave Girl of Agra*, has since appeared in English.

DISTRICT MAGISTRATE

Eleven years had passed since Mr. Romesh Dutt had commenced service. Within this time he had twice acted as District Magistrate for short periods, and other Bengali officers had also acted in such capacity for a few months. Was it safe to place Indians in charge of Districts for long periods? Was it safe to make Indian officers permanent District Magistrates? These uneasy thoughts rose in the minds of many English administrators, and many Anglo-Indian journals scoffed at the idea! Fortunately the question was solved, not by angry controversy, but by fair trial; and Mr. Romesh Dutt was the first Indian officer who held executive charge of a District for a prolonged time. From April 1883 to April 1885, (with a very short interval) he was kept in charge of Barisal, (Backergunj,) the most turbulent and difficult District in Bengal. The time, too, was unfavourable, and race-feelings ran high during the Ilbert-Bill controversy. But the experiment ended in complete and marked success. The Indian Magistrate worked in perfect harmony with his English subordinates,—Joint and Assistant Magistrates, the Civil Surgeon and the Police Superintendent. He secured peace, and cases of rioting and disturbance in that turbulent District were fewer under his administration than they had been for many years. He won the love and respect of the people, and the Annual Resolutions published in the Government *Gazette* commended in high terms the results of his rule.

The Marquis of Ripon was then Viceroy of India. He was pleased to send for the Indian Magistrate, and expressed his high approval of his work in a difficult District, and during a time of great tension of race feelings. "I sent for you,"—Lord Ripon was pleased to remark,—"as I wished to see you and know you before leaving India. Your work should be known in England; the fitness of Indians for high administrative posts would not then be questioned." It is a pleasure to record that the fitness of Indians to hold charge of Districts has never been questioned since 1885.

THE BENGAL TENANCY ACT

Perhaps it was a higher gratification to Mr. Romesh Dutt that he was able to render some help towards the final triumph of a cause for which he had laboured for years. Very early in his career, he had written on the condition of the Peasantry of Bengal, and had pointed out the need for some security of their tenures and some fixity of their rents. The book had little influence at the time, and had been scoffed at by Zemindars and ignored by Government, but the writer never lost heart. Many years had not passed, before Government awoke to the necessity of the reforms and Mr. Dutt had many opportunities of reiterating his arguments and passing for legislation. Sir Anthony Macdonnell (later Lord Macdonnell,) then Revenue Secretary of Bengal, at last took up the work of drafting a Bill. No reports were more valuable to him than those of the young

Magistrate of Barisal; no help was more cordially acknowledged by him in the Government *Gazette* than that of Mr. Romesh Dutt. The Bill was at last passed by Lord Dufferin in the Legislative Council of India; and the protection needed by cultivators was secured by the Bengal Tenancy Act of 1885.

THE RIG-VEDA CONTROVERSY

After fourteen years of service, Mr. Romesh Dutt took two years' furlough, 1885 to 1887, and the first of these years he spent in India. He at once plunged into literary work, and produced a social Novel which has since been rendered into English under the title of *The Lake of Palms*. But this was mere literary pastime; he entered on a more formidable undertaking when, with the help of some Sanskrit Pundits, he began a Bengali translation of the ancient Hymns of the Rig-Veda. Orthodoxy took alarm at the prospect of the sacred hymns being laid open to laymen: and the idea of a non-Brahman like Mr. Dutt laying sacrilegious hands on the holiest of holy books raised a perfect storm of opposition. Furious articles appeared week after week in Vernacular newspapers, sarcasm or invective was poured on the devoted head of the daring translator; and the translation itself was condemned and vilified before it had appeared in print! Mr. Dutt faced this opposition in the way in which he faced all other opposition through life. And before the year 1885 was out, his first volume astonished all orthodox world. The very attacks on his book had added to the list of his subscribers; and before he sailed for Europe, early in 1886, the complete translation of the work was in the Press. It is the only complete translation of Rig-Veda hymns published in the Bengali language.

SECOND VISIT TO EUROPE

Early in 1886, Mr. Romesh Dutt, accompanied by his wife and children, and also by his elder brother Jogesh Chunder, the laborious translator of the Sanskrit History of Kashmir, sailed for Europe. His old friend Bihari Lal Gupta had preceded him and received him in London.

The English summer was passed in a quiet sea-side place, but Mr. Romesh Dutt wished to see more of the world. First he made a trip to the North Cape, and travelled through the delightful countries of Norway and Sweden; and later on he made a prolonged tour through the Continent.

HISTORICAL WORK ON ANCIENT INDIA

On rejoining work after leave, Mr. Romesh Dutt was posted for a short time to Pubna, where he was reminded of the days of his boyhood; and then was transferred to Mymensingh, perhaps the heaviest District in Bengal. It is a vast District with a population of nearly four millions; and Mr. Dutt was sent there when the indiscreet acts of a senior English Collector had embittered feelings between Hindus and Mahomedans. Within a few months the breach was healed, and peace was restored.

For two years and-a-half, Mr. Romesh Dutt worked in this heavy District. His administration was marked by repression of crime, increase of prosperity among the people, and by a great development of roads and communications,—the new District Boards and Sub-District Boards working satisfactorily under his sympathetic guidance. One would think such heavy work would suffice for any officer, but Mr. Romesh Dutt undertook and completed, in this District, what is perhaps his greatest literary work.

The translation of the Rig-Veda hymns had first inspired him with the idea of writing a History of Ancient India, based on Sanskrit Literature and the researches of European scholars. A few essays from his pen had already appeared, but it was now that he fairly began the Herculean task and the book at last appeared in three volumes, between 1888 and 1890. It is called *Civilisation in Ancient India*, and remains to this day a complete and comprehensive history of Ancient India. An edition appeared in London a few years later, and several editions have been published and sold in India.

DECORATION

In 1890, Mr. Romesh Dutt was transferred to Burdwan; and as the Maharaja of Burdwan was then a minor, the Collector had to look after his education and his estate. From Burdwan he went to Dinajpur, and thence to the heavy District of Midnapore, of which he remained in charge for nearly two years. His long and meritorious service in some of the most important Districts in Bengal, as well as his brilliant literary work, was known to Government, and in 1892, Mr. Romesh Dutt was made a Companion of the Indian Empire.

But his arduous work at Mymensingh and Midnapore, as well as the malarial climate of Burdwan and Dinajpur, had told on his health; and in the autumn of 1892 he was compelled to take furlough again.

THIRD VISIT TO EUROPE

During that autumn and winter, he visited Kashmir and Mussourie and Hurdwar and other places in Northern India with his friend Mr. Bihari Lal Gupta; and early in 1893 he sailed for Europe.

The inclement spring of England brought about a fresh attack of the malaria he had contracted in Burdwan, and for weeks he was confined to his room in the seaside place of Bournemouth. Recovering from this attack, he proceeded to Germany, and went through a course of mineral baths and mineral drinks at Wiesbaden.

DIVISIONAL COMMISSIONER

Restored to his usual strength and health Mr. Romesh Dutt returned to India in 1893. And it was about this time that he founded the *Bangiya Sahitya Parishad*, or the Academy of Bengali Literature, now one of the most flourishing and useful literary institutions in India. But it was his administrative career which excited intense interest at this period. He had done 22 years' service, and established his reputation as a strong, sound, and thoroughly efficient officer. His opinion and judgment were valued by Government on large questions of administration; his sympathies with the cultivating and labouring classes were known; his work in difficult Districts under difficult circumstances had been uniformly successful. "He is perilously near a Commissionership!"—remarked many an Englishman with bated breath. "Will he be passed over for a Commissionership?"—asked his countrymen in their own circles. The question went up, in some shape or other, to the India Council at Whitehall, and it was the view held there that the Indian Officer should not be passed over if he was fit. Accordingly, when the time came, Mr. Romesh Dutt was appointed Commissioner of the Burdwan Division in April 1894; and he was the only Indian who rose to the rank of a Commissioner of a Division, in all India, in the nineteenth century.

It was when he was Commissioner of Burdwan that Mr. Romesh Dutt was appointed a Member of the Bengal Legislative Council. His great experience in District work enabled him to render much help in District questions, which the then Lieutenant-Governor of Bengal, Sir Charles Elliott, gracefully acknowledged on more than one occasion. But he had to resign his Membership when he went to the more distant Division of Orissa, as there was no railway connection then between Orissa and Calcutta.

The Commissioner of Orissa is also *ex-officio* Superintendent of some twenty Native States called the Orissa Tributary Mahals. And Mr. Romesh

Dutt was appointed to the *quasi*-political appointment over the head of a senior English Officer who was not considered quite fit for the work.

Both in Burdwan and in Orissa, the first Indian Commissioner maintained the high reputation he had won by his long previous work. Early in 1897 he went again on furlough; and in October of the same year, after a service of 26 years, he retired from the Indian Civil Service.

RETIREMENT FROM SERVICE

Much surprise was felt at Mr. Romesh Dutt's retirement after 26 years' service, when under the rules of the service he might have continued nine years more.

The fact is he wished to devote himself wholeheartedly to literary pursuits which he always called his "first love." He had formed the ambition of leaving some durable works behind him, which his countrymen would value, even after his death. He was in the fiftieth year of his life and had earned his pension; and he decided to devote the remaining years of his life to earning literary fame rather than to earning a fortune.

In the second place he wished for greater independence and larger opportunities to strive for that progress in self-government and those liberal Reforms for which the time was ripe. His long experience in administration had convinced him that British Rule in India could be more efficient and more popular by the admission of the people to a share in the control and direction of that administration. And he felt an irresistible impulse to take part in the national endeavour to secure this share for his countrymen.

Those who had watched his career, since 1897 till the last day of his death in 1909 will admit that he decided rightly in obeying the impulses which he felt within himself.

PROLONGED STAY IN EUROPE

For seven years, from the early months of 1897 to the commencement of 1904, Mr. Romesh Dutt was mostly in England. Twice within this period he came to India, once to the Lucknow Congress of 1899, and again in 1902; but most of his work during these seven years, literary and political, was done in England.

Mr. Romesh Dutt's wife and youngest daughter accompanied him to England in 1897; his only son had preceded him in the previous year. The young man was admitted to Christ Church, Oxford, where he eventually took his degree, and afterwards came out to India as a Barrister. Mr. Dutt himself was appointed Lecturer on Indian History at University College, London; and he lectured on that subject for a number of years before many English students including selected candidates for the Indian Civil Service. He also co-operated with Mr. W. C. Bonnerjee in all endeavours for the reform of Indian administration; and his paper on the separation of the Judicial and Executive functions in India, published as far back as 1893, brought the question into prominence.

They and Mr. Romesh Dutt were the three leaders of the Indian party in London,—earnest, devoted men who laboured in England for the Indian cause in the closing years of the nineteenth century.

THE INDIAN EPICS

But Mr. Romesh Dutt never lost sight of his literary pursuits. Ancient Sanskrit Literature was his favourite study, and he conceived the bold idea of presenting the two ancient Epics of India, the *Mahabharata* and the *Ramayana*, in a readable form to the modern world. His plan was not to give a condensed version, but to make a full and literal translation of the essential portions of the epics, and to link them together by short explanatory notes. He tried several English metres, till he hit on the one most closely resembling the Sanskrit *Anustubh* metre; and he laboured for years together till he completed this self-imposed task. He consulted Professor Max Muller while his work was still in progress; and the venerable Oxford scholar wrote back that it was scarcely possible to present within readable limits even the main story of the *Mahabharata* an epic of ninety-thousand verses! Mr. Dutt, however, quietly went on with his work, and when the *Mahabharata* was completed, he presented a copy of it to the Oxford Professor. Dr. Max Muller was so charmed and astonished with the result, that he readily consented to write an Introduction. It is a valuable little eassy, all the more valuable because it was one of the last things that Professor Max Muller lived to write.

Mr. Romesh Dutt had wisely arranged to issue his metrical translations in the well-known Temple Classics series. They were much appreciated in England and America, and 15,000 copies of the *Mahabharata* and 10,000 copies of the *Ramayana* were sold in a few years. Mr. Dutt's purpose was fulfilled; the ancient Indian Epics were made known to the modern world.

THE CONGRESS OF 1899

Throughout the years 1898 and 1899 Mr. Romesh Dutt was invited to speak on Indian subjects on many English platforms; and he succeeded to some extent, in arousing an interest in the state of India, then in the throes of a famine, a plague, and a frontier war. Mr. Dutt's speeches were valued, more for their lucid and vigorous exposition of facts and arguments, than for any flights of eloquence or rhetoric; and he established a reputation as a safe and trustworthy and sound exponent of Indian views. His countrymen read his speeches with delight, and hailed this new advocate of the Indian cause, so strong in facts, so rich in official experience and knowledge. And towards the close of 1899 they bestowed upon him the highest honour in their power by electing him President of the Congress which was to be held at Lucknow.

Thousands of his countrymen, who had only known him by name or by his works, saw him for

Page 256.

ROMESH CHUNDER DUTT

the first time when he stood on the Congress platform in December 1899. He had passed the age of fifty, but his tall figure and vigorous erect form struck his audience. He did not belie their expectations; and he gave almost a new turn to Congress politics when he pleaded vigorously for the cultivators and landed classes of India, exposing the excessive and uncertain assessments on land which necessarily led to chronic agricultural poverty and accentuated frequent famines. Mr. Dutt's Congress speech was a virtual declaration of war against excessive land assessments in India; and those who knew him felt that he meant to fight.

CONTROVERSY WITH LORD CURZON

Mr. Romesh Dutt had a long audience with Lord Curzon on his return to Calcutta, and he pressed two points before the Viceroy. In the first place he pleaded for some reasonable limits to the Government demand from land, both in Ryotwari and in Zemindari tracts,—limits which would control the operations of Settlement Officers, and could be enforced by impartial tribunals. Lord Curzon listened courteously to the facts and arguments urged, promised to give them consideration, but was not prepared to give an immediate reply. In the second place Mr. Dutt pleaded for some share for his countrymen in the control and direction of the administration, some room in the Executive Councils of the Viceroy and of the Provinces, in fact all those reforms which have since become of such momentous importance in the scheme of Self-Government for India. There was some debate on this point, and Lord Curzon ended the debate by asking the question which he has often asked since:—"After all, is not the rule of *one man* the best form of rule for India?"

Mr. Dutt was not to be ousted in a field in which he was master. He followed up his verbal representations with those *Open Letters* on Land Assessments in India which have now become historic. Returning to England, he published these *Open Letters* in the shape of a book, with a vast deal of additional information compiled from Blue Books which was a revelation to most readers in India. Furthermore, he associated himself with a number of high Anglo-Indian administrators who had retired from India rich in renown and experience, and on the 20th December, 1900, they jointly presented a Memorial to the Secretary of State for India demanding reasonable restrictions on land assessments in India.

The India Government was thus forced to make a reply. The reply came in Lord Curzon's famous Resolution on the Land Revenue Policy of India in January, 1902. It admitted certain definite principles in the matter of Land Assessments for which Mr. Dutt and his colleagues had contended. It laid down certain authoritative rules regulating future assessments. It was a document which could henceforth be appealed to for fulfilment of the pledges it contained. So far the result of the controversy was satisfactory.

ECONOMIC HISTORY OF BRITISH INDIA

But if Lord Curzon had hoped to have the last word in this famous controversy, he had mistaken his opponent. Mr. Romesh Dutt had not been idle after the publication of his *Open Letters* and the submission of the Memorial. He had put forth all his energies on the task he had undertaken. He had collected a vast library of Indian Blue Books, dating from the commencement of British Rule in India, and consisting of over two-hundred bound bulky volumes. He had ransacked these invaluable records, and studied the history of Land Settlements and Industries, and the Finances of India. And he prepared an exhaustive *Economic History of India* from the date of the Battle of Plassey to the dawn of the 20th century. The great work appeared in two volumes, the first in 1902 and the second in 1904. It was the crowning work of Mr. Romesh Dutt's patience, industry, and literary ability. It was a lucid history of the industries, trades and manufactures of India. It was the last word on the history of Land Settlements. Lord Curzon's Land Resolution is scarcely read to-day except for official reference. Mr. Romesh Dutt's *Economic History* has already passed through two or three Editions, and is studied by every Indian desirous of knowing the economic condition and history of the people of India.

BARODA ADMINISTRATION

After seven years of arduous and incessant work, done mostly in England, Mr. Romesh Dutt returned to India early in 1904. He had passed the age of 55 years, but rest is not for such as he. One of the most enlightened Princes of India, the Gaekwar of Baroda had watched the career of this earnest worker, had studied his books, and on more than one occasion had welcomed him to the Palace of Baroda as his guest. And now, when Mr. Dutt returned to Calcutta, he received a message from the Gaekwar inviting him to take a share in the administration of Baroda. Such an invitation,—to help in the administration of one of the foremost Native States,—Mr. Dutt could not refuse. And from August 1904 to July 1907,—for three years,—Mr. Romesh Dutt was Revenue Minister of Baroda. He took charge of his new office with evident enthusiasm for the new opportunities opened out for him to do in a small scale all that he wished to realise in British India. He sketched out the plan of his future labours in glowing colours and followed it up with unflagging diligence. Thus he wrote to Sister Nivedita a letter remarkable for its tone of confidence and enthusiasm :—

> I am trying to strike out new lines of progress, to develop new policies and reforms, and am determined to move forward and to carry the State forward. I am trying to gather together the scattered forces which were present here, to encourage enterprise and talent in younger men, to welcome new ideas and new schemes, to initiate progress in all lines, and to make Baroda a richer and happier State. I go among the people, print and publish my schemes, face the Maharaja with my proposals, and manage to have my way in a manner which old officers of this State pronounce quite 'unconventional'! I am trying to relieve the agriculturists of excessive taxation on their land, I am endeavouring to get together capitalists to

start new mills and industries, and if I can build up the Legislative Council I will make the work of the state proceed in the interest of the people and in touch with the people. Everything shall be open and above-board,—nothing done in dark, torturous, secret, autocratic ways. Dreams! dreams!! some will exclaim. Well, let them be so,—it is better to dream of work and progress than to wake to inaction and stagnation. This last shall never be my vocation, it is not in my nature.

The reformer was as good as his word. The results of his three years' administration are shown in the Annual Reports of the State, but some of them will bear recapitulation. It was on Mr. Romesh Dutt's advice that the Gaekwar made large remissions of outstanding arrears of land revenue, to the extent of over thirty lakhs; and a vast burden which had weighed down the cultivators was thus removed. Taxes on various professions, paid mostly by poor artisans, traders and even labourers, were abolished; and an Income-Tax, payable by the richer classes was imposed. The minimum of taxable income was proposed to be Rs. 150 a year; but it was raised successively to Rs. 300, Rs. 500, and then to Rs. 750, before Mr. Dutt left Baroda. The rate of tax was one pice in the rupee for every class of income, and assessments were made by Government servants with the help of a Panchayet in the town or village concerned. The advantages of this new system were that—

(1) It made a clean sweep of all the numerous and oppressive Veros, except rent for homestead lands and the pilgrim tax. (2) It exempted the poor from taxation. (3) It imposed on the richer classes a proportionate burden which they had evaded before. (4) It imposed on official classes their fair share of the burden which they had escaped.

A whole series of customs duties, harassing to trade, were done away with, and duties were limited to a few principal articles which brought a substantial income without detriment to trade. Octroi duties were abolished in all small towns in the State. And it is remarkable that in Baroda, as in larger countries this reduction of duties actually brought in an enlarged revenue, as it led to an expansion of business and trade.

In the important department of Land Revenue Assessments he showed the same anxiety for the tiller of the soil as he had done while criticising the system prevailing in British India. He recommended that—

(1) The Land Revenue demand of a Taluka should be fixed after considering what the Taluka had paid in the past taking good years with bad, and can pay in the future without detriment to agricultural prosperity.

(2) No enhancement should be made unless there had been a rise in prices, or there are other reasons, like the increase of produce or of cultivation, justifying an enhancement.

(3) No cultivator should be asked to pay more than one-half of the net produce of his field.

Great encouragement was given to industries and industrial enterprises, and State competition with private companies was abolished. The State Cotton Mill of Baroda was sold to a private company, and two other cotton mills sprang up within a short time. A great number of new cotton-ginning factories and various other factories also rose under the impetus given by the new administration. The demand for labour increased accordingly; wages rose and the condition of the labouring classes was thus improved.

The revenue and judicial services were improved and graded, and none but graduates were ordinarily admitted to these gazetted services. But by far the most outstanding reform that he effected in the State was the complete separation of the Judicial and Executive services. The policy was cautiously and gradually carried out. First the bulk of the criminal work was transferred to trained judicial officers with no executive authority. The work of revenue and executive officers was gradually increased till at last they were relieved of all criminal work. Finally complete separation was effected. This important reform naturally attracted the attention of the Government of India more particularly because it was one of the constant themes of Congress agitation.

He built up a complete system of Self-Government from the bottom to the top. Village Boards were re-organised in all villages in the State, and were entrusted with powers of Village Administration. Groups of these Village Boards elected Members for the Taluka Boards, and the Taluka Boards returned Members to the District Boards. The proceeds of the Local Cess were handed over to these Boards, and local public works, small primary schools, and other duties were entrusted to them. Numerous wells for drinking water were constructed, year after year from this fund by the Village Boards themselves; and the success with which the villagers constructed such works for themselves surpassed the expectations of the officers, and showed the fitness of villagers when they were trusted. From the Village to the Taluk, from the Taluk to the District from the District to the State as a whole—thus was built up a chain of institutions linking the whole fabric from bottom to top. The last superstructure of this edifice was not long in coming. An Executive Council supervised the entire administration of the State; and an Advisory Legislative Council, consisting partly of elected members, has since been formed.

Lastly the great idea of free and compulsory Primary Education throughout the State was initiated by the Gaekwar himself, by orders issued by him from Europe, where he saw such education established. These orders were faithfully carried out. In 1905 free and compulsory education was ordered to be extended over the whole State; and to-day there are schools in almost all villages in the State, and boys and girls within certain ages are compelled to attend under penalty for absence.

The annual grant necessary for this purpose was increased to nearly five lakhs of rupees, and was divided between the Education Department, which looked after towns and large villages, and the Local Boards, which looked after ordinary villages. The rule adopted was that all boys between seven and twelve, and all girls between seven and ten, should go to schools under penalties for non-attendance, and receive instruction in reading, writing, and arithmetic in the first three standards. In that year there were over two thousand Village Boards constituted by the Local Self-Government Act of 1904, and the idea was to establish a Village School or Gramyashala under each Village Board. The total number of such schools already established up to that year (excluding those in towns) exceeded fourteen hundred.

Thus it will be seen that there was not a single department of the State which was left untouched. And Mr. Romesh Chunder Dutt touched nothing which he did not adorn. The administrative, judicial, revenue departments and local self-government, education and industries—every one of these—came in for re-organization and improvement. When, after his labours of three years, Mr. Romesh Dutt left Baroda in July 1907, all classes felt that they were losing a friend, a friend of the poor *(Daridra ka Dost)* as he was called.

DECENTRALIZATION COMMISSION

If Mr. Romesh Dutt hoped for retirement when he left Baroda on long leave, he was disappointed. He was spending a few days quietly with his friend Mr. Bihari Lal Gupta at Simultala, when he was appointed a Member of the Royal Commission on Decentralization. Mr. Dutt had however already planned a tour in Southern India; and he visited the interesting Native States of Mysore, Cochin and Travancore, receiving the utmost kindness and hospitality from the Rulers and Officers of those States. He then pursued his tour as far as Rameswaram. Hundreds of young men at Trichinopoly and Madura, Tanjore and Kumbakonam heard him speak; and a thousand assembled at the Pachaiyappa's College, Madras, when he made his great speech there on the "Study of Indian History." Mr. Dutt then hurried to Bombay, and met his colleagues on the Commission in November 1907.

The Commission came from Bombay to Madras, and commenced their arduous labours. From Madras they went to Burma, and thence to Bengal, the Central Provinces and the United Provinces. After a brief rest they proceeded to Bombay, Sindh, Baluchistan and the N. W. Frontier Province, and finished with Simla and the Punjab. Everywhere they took voluminous evidence, both of official and non-official witnesses; and in April 1908 they proceeded to England to discuss and deliberate, and to frame their Report.

The Commission made many excellent suggestions for improving the administration and broadening the basis of Government; they at the same time, made some retrograde and very undesirable recommendations, tending to increase the autocratic and almost irresponsible powers of Commissioners and Collectors. Mr. Romesh Dutt cordially agreed with his colleagues in all liberal recommendations, and vigorously dissented from them in those that were illiberal.

LORD MORLEY'S REFORMS

It was a fortunate circumstance that Mr. Romesh Dutt was in London all through the summer and autumn of 1908; and his labours on the Commission did not prevent him from taking an active interest in the scheme of Reforms which Lord Morley was preparing for India. Lord Morley himself was ever ready to see and consult all well-informed men, Englishmen or Indians, who could speak from personal experience on Indian questions and Indian administration.

Mr. Dutt kept up a constant and valuable correspondence with Lord Morley. In one of his letters to the noble Lord dated Calcutta, 20th January, 1908, Mr. Dutt pointed out :—

Large changes in the policy of the administration are effected by executive orders, and in such matters the people are kept aloof. Important details in the Land Revenue and Irrigation departments, and in matters concerning the Police, Public Works, Education, Medicine, and Forests, are settled by the Executive Councils of India, Madras, and Bombay, and by the Lieutenant-Governors and Chief Commissioners in other Provinces where there are no Executive Councils. We may run our eye over all this vast executive machinery in this great empire, and we shall not find a single Indian anywhere who is trusted to take a share in shaping the policy of administration. How much is lost by an alien government both in popularity and in the adaptability of its measures through this needless exclusiveness is known only to those who are of the people, and who feel the pulse of the people

Why should not the British rule be a popular rule in this loyal country, British officers consenting to share with the leaders of the people the task of settling the policy and the details of administration? Why should not Indian leaders proudly stand by the side of devoted British administrators, and work for the great Empire which they may then both call their own? Such questions recieve no response from officials generally. The history of the world seldom records instances of men in power consenting to share it with those over whom they rule. But it is a New Year's hope to me, as it has been my lifelong aspiration. Either such co-operation, or a widening gulf with increasing discontent and disorder is before us, there is no other alternative.

Here is another to the noble Lord under date February 22, 1908 :—

I have always thought a bold step would also be a wise step at the present juncture, and that it is possible to crush discontent and disaffection under foot by one or two acts of real and tangible concession. The present time is most appropriate. For two years, ever since the Partition of Bengal, the country has undergone local disorders, alarms, coercive measures and prosecutions. It is time now that a pacific remedy was tried. The nations of India recall the fact that this is the fiftieth anniversary of the late Queen's gracious Proclamation : may not some

real acts of grace in this year once more obliterate bitter memories?

Mr. Dutt also interviewed some Members of the House of Lords, including Lord Courtney and Lord Macdonnell whom he had known for many years. He discussed reform proposals with the Members of the India Council; and he was in close touch with several Members of the House of Commons who took an active interest in Indian affairs. All through the summer and autumn of 1908 he exerted himself personally, and through friends, to secure some real reforms for India, some share for Indians in the control and direction of their own Administration.

In all this work Mr. Romesh Dutt laboured hand in hand with Mr. Gokhale who was doing yeoman's service in the same great cause. No two men were better suited to work together in such a cause than Mr. Romesh Dutt and Mr. Gokhale. Both moderate in their views, practical in their aims and methods, accurate and well-informed in facts, tenacious and persevering in their endeavours,—they were in complete agreement in their opinions, and were often strangely similar in their style of expression. Both of them had been Presidents of the Indian National Congress, and both were listened to with attention as to the reasonable demands of their countrymen. Mr. Romesh Dutt had now counted sixty years, Mr. Gokhale was a little over forty but the elder and the younger man worked as fast friends in 1908, as they have ever done in life, in the cause of their common country.

The Reforms came out at last. Notwithstanding the limited scope of the Morley-Minto scheme, the reforms gave general satisfaction as a first step in the right direction and though much yet remained to be done they were accepted by the Indian public as a prelude to further measures of constitutional advance. Mr. Dutt himself, in the course of an article in the January number of the *Indian Review*, was enthusiastic over the Despatch of Lord Morley. He wrote:—

> The Reforms announced by Lord Morley in his Despatch of November, and in his speech of December are solid and substantial, and are precisely in the direction in which the Indian Naional Congress has demanded Reforms during the last twenty years and more. In one word, the changes announced are calculated to give the people of India a substantial share in the control and direction of their own concerns. The voice of the people will find expression through recognised official channels; the wishes and opinions of the people will influence and shape the internal administration of the country.

In the light of subsequent history we can only say that he was generous to a fault in his appreciation of the whole scheme. Little did he imagine how the purpose of the scheme would be thwarted by stringent and restrictive regulations framed by the Bureaucracy, regulations that have nullified all prospects of the success of the scheme and which have made the tremendous agitation for Self-Government inevitable.

It is interesting to recall at this time the important interview that Mr. Dutt had with Lord

Morley, touching the TIMES' sinister reflections on Mr. Gokhale's Note on the TIMES' scheme. In explaining the real facts, Mr. Dutt said:—

But Lord Morley, what the correspondent in the TIMES suggests is absolutely untrue. Mr. Gokhale laid his suggestions before you like 200 other men of all classes and shades of opinion. You have never refused to see any one—Hindu or Moslem, Englishman or Parsi—who had any valuable suggestion to make. You have considered all opinions and framed your own conclusions.

Lord Morley: That it is. Is it to be said that I am not to see a single Hindu?

Then the question of the omission of clause 3 about Executive Councils came up. Mr. Dutt informed Lord Morley, that the people of India unanimously objected to the omission of clause 3, and that a great meeting would be held in Calcutta to protest against that omission.

Lord Morley replied: Your people need not do that, the clause will be restored.

Mr. Dutt added: And Sir Charles Stevens, who was our Lieutenant-Governor, also supports the idea of a Council Government. I saw him this morning. He submitted a note to Mr. Brodrick (now Lord Middleton); I have brought a copy of the note with me.

Lord Morley: That is very important, very valuable, where is it? And the note was given to Lord Morley.

But when Mr. Dutt mentioned that the Indian Parliamentary Committee were going to have a meeting about the matter on the following day, Lord Morley pointed out that it would be better if they "showed their teeth" when the Bill was before the House of Commons, and not just on the day when it comes to the reporting stage in the House of Lords.

Lord Morley: Mr. Gladstone used to say, 'Man is the most incomprehensible of animals and a politician is the most incomprehensible of men.' Somebody added, 'Mr. Gladstone was the most incomprehensible of politicians.' Your friends of the Indian Parliamentary Committee are incomprehensible politicians! They will add to my difficulties by holding a meeting to-morrow.

They talked about the work of the Decentralisation Commission, and when Mr. Dutt was coming away Lord Morley said:—

I am glad you were on the Commission. Good-bye, Mr. Dutt, and don't let it out that you found a Minister with many difficulties using plain words and vehement expressions.

Mr. Romesh Dutt returned to India in March 1909. On the 1st of June he rejoined work at Baroda as Prime Minister of the State and the people of Baroda rejoiced to find that able and veteran administrator once more at the head of affairs. But their joy was destined to be short-lived. As early as 1906 the disease of the heart which killed him in the end had given warnings of its fatal nature. Mr. Dutt's medical advisers had repeatedly urged him to take rest. But rest was impossible to a nature with such avidity for work. If Mr. Dutt retired from official work it was only to plunge into the more taxing yet exhilarating occupation of writing books. But since the acceptance of the Dewanship he had to be occupied with the preparation for the Baroda State Durbar in honour of Lord Minto. The physical and mental exertion was too much for an over-worked constitution and the heart disease already severe became more and more threatening till at last he succumbed to the inevitable on 30th November 1909 after "great suffering and god-like endurance."

CONCLUSION

It is impossible to give anything like a detailed account of so indefatigable a worker as Mr. Dutt within the compass of a short sketch. His many-sided endeavours and his varied successes are well-known. But perhaps we understand him best, if we regard him under the triple character of an Administrator, a Patriot, and an Author. As an Administrator, both in Bengal and in Baroda, he ranks with the highest of his generation. As a Patriot, too, he takes his stand in the esteem of his countrymen with the greatest of his contemporaries. As an Author in English he has earned for himself a peculiar *niche* in the affections of his countrymen. His *Ancient India*, his *Indian Epics*, and his *Economic History* will be valued by our posterity as they are valued by us. Works like these, written by Indians for Indians, form and mould the mind of a nation; for they inspire a legitimate pride in the past, a self-respect in the present, and a bold but not vain-glorious confidence in our destiny in the future.

Page 273.

SIR SASHIAH SASTRI

Sir Sashiah Sastri*

EARLY LIFE

SASHIAH SASTRI was born on the 22nd March 1828. He was the fifth of the six sons of a Vaidika Brahman, a priest who superintended domestic rites in the Brahman households of Amaravati and a few neighbouring villages in the Tanjore District.

When Sashiah was eight years old he, as a Brahman, received the rights of second birth, and was invested with the holy thread. One of his uncles, Gopala Aiyar by name, was, at this time, earning a decent living at Madras as a dealer in precious stones. At the suggestion of his mother, this gentleman undertook to keep the boy with him and educate him at Madras, thus relieving the growing family of a portion of its burden. Gopala Iyer was a stern disciplinarian and Sashiah was brought up in diligent and virtuous ways.

Soon after his removal to Madras, Sashiah was placed under the care of a private teacher, a Mudali, under whom he picked up some acquaintance with Tamil. This course of studies was kept up for six months.

---

* Drawn freely from an excellent biography by Mr. B. V. Kamesvara Aiyar, Pudukottah.

POWELL'S BEST BOY

After a time Sashiah, with many of his school-mates, joined the newly-established Preparatory School and passed from thence to the High School. This High School sent out in the course of a few years some of the brightest ornaments of Southern India,—Ranganadha Sastriar, Sir T. Madhava Rao, Shadagopacharlu, Ramiengar, Rangacharlu, and Sashiah—each of whom has left imperishable marks in the history of South India.

A great part of the success of the High School was due to the master-mind that ruled its destinies—Mr. E. B. Powell. With the instincts of a born teacher and a single-minded devotion to his sacred work, this gentleman dedicated his time and his extraordinary talents to the advancement of his students. As might be expected Sashiah had the fullest share of Powell's companionship and guidance and the correspondence between master and pupil throws a vivid light on the extraordinary hold that Powell had over a whole generation of South Indian youths. In after years Sashiah recalled those fruitful years with tender emotion. As a humble expression of his gratitude to his master, Sashiah contributed in 1872 Rs. 1,000 towards the statue of Mr. Powell, which now adorns the Presidency College.

Sashiah continued in the High School till May, 1848. It was a hard struggle, financially, in the early years of this period. But in a few months a change came for the better in his fortunes, and

Sashiah was able to pay his own way. He also obtained a stipend from the Government and he became further one of Pachaiyappa's Free Scholars—receiving the benefit of the charities made available for educational purposes. As a mark of his gratitude he, later on in life, provided Pachaiyappa's College with an endowment of Rs. 2,000, the interest of which is to go towards two prizes in his name—one for elocution and the other for the best essay in English.

While in the High School Sashiah carried off prizes for hand-writing year after year, till it was ruled that they should not be monopolized by the same scholar. He secured Pachaiyappa's Vernacular prize for the years 1846-47 and also Pachaiyappa's Translation prize of Rs. 70 for the best translation into the Vernacular, of a few chapters of Arnold's 'Lectures on Italy.' In 1847 he gained the Elphinstone prize for an essay on 'What is civilization? The Marquis of Tweed-dale, who succeeded Lord Elphinstone as Governor of Madras, gave him a reward of Rs. 70, for general proficiency.

IN SERVICE

Sashiah's brilliant success at School and College brought him to the notice of high officials and one Sir Henry Montgomery, Chief Secretary to the Government of Madras, was so impressed by his talents that he began to evince considerable interest in his career. At his instance Sashiah was first appointed private tutor to the sons of the then Head Sheristadar of Tanjore. This tuition, for which he was paid Rupees twenty-five a month, continued from 1846 to the end of his school-days. Money flowed in upon him from various sources and thus, even as a student, not only was he able to materially relieve his uncle, but he was in a position to send substantial aid to his family at Amaravati. His father had died soon after Sashiah's removal to Madras, and his uncle died in 1847. But by this time, as we have already seen, Sashiah was more than equal to the burden of supporting two families. In 1847 a marriage was arranged between Sashiah and Sundari, a motherless girl, brought up by her uncle Ramaswami Aiyar, a native of Konerirajapuram, a village near Kumbakonam.

On the 29th May, 1848, he took the Degree of Proficient in the First Scale of Honours, standing first among his fellows in the order of merit, and received the Ring, set with emeralds, of a Proficient of the First Class. Mr. Powell, when he sent Sashiah out into the world, wrote :—

"I have a very high idea of Sashiah's integrity and would not hesitate to place the utmost confidence in him. I trust his success in life may be commensurate with his talents, industry and good conduct."

A CLERK IN THE REVENUE BOARD

It was in September 1848 that Sashiah obtained the post of an acting clerk in the office of the Revenue Board on Rs. 25. In three months he was confirmed in his job, whereafter he was shifted from one place of responsibility to another. It was about this time too that he came in intimate contact with two men who were destined to make a mark in after years—V. Ramiengar who after a varied and uniformly meritorious service in the British Government closed his public career as Dewan of Travancore and T. Madhava Rao, the illustrious statesman.

Ramiengar was in the Mahratta Cutcherry of the Revenue Board; he induced Sashiah to get himself transferred to the same department. The transfer was accordingly effected through the kindness of Mr. Pycroft, and Sashiah came to work with Ramiengar under the Sheristadar. Kandi Narasinga Rao was at this time the Board Sheristadar, a gentleman of vast experience and fame, despite his ignorance of English. The Sheristadar wrote his reviews of the Collectors' *Jamabundy* reports in the Mahratta tongue, and Sashiah as well as Ramiengar had to translate these reports and memoranda into English, an exercise which gave them numerous opportunities of studying the history of revenue administration in the Presidency and prepared them for their future work in the Revenue Department of the Public Service.

IN A ROVING COMMISSION

In June 1849 a Commission was appointed to investigate conditions in the Northern Circars especially in the matter of revenue collections and Sashiah had the good fortune to accompany the Commissioner's Sheristadar Mr. Royappa, as a member of his own family. It was a roving Commission going up and down the Circars and Sashiah's work, of which we have accounts in his letters to Ramiengar and

Madhava Rao, are full of vivid experiences of life in the Circars.

Two years of this wandering life and varied experience served to bring out his capacity for work and endurance. He had become by this time the right-hand man of Mr. Elliot. His pay had been raised to Rupees thirty-five and later on to Rupees fifty. Trained under the immediate eye of Mr. Elliot, he had acquired correct notions of revenue work and confidence in his own powers.

AS TAHSILDAR

Sashiah was appointed Tahsildar at Masulipatam where he showed remarkable ability. In one short year he had done much for the town; corruption in the office had been put down; public security had been restored; by personal supervision he had checked the abuses that were going on in the salt pans; while assiduously guarding the interests of the Government he had at the same time made himself popular with all classes of people and earned a name for unswerving rectitude.

In January 1855 he was appointed to look after the work of both the Naib and the Head Sheristadar and was not long after posted as Head Sheristadar.

AS HEAD SHERISTADAR

As Head Sheristadar he was the confidential minister of the Collector and the virtual ruler of the District. He could now bring his influence to bear on the administration of the entire District and he now did for it what he had done in a more limited sphere as Tahsildar. Inefficient officers were gradually weeded out and replaced by younger, abler and more conscientious men. This was carried out slowly and as fair opportunities occurred—not with the indecorous haste or undue precipitancy of hot-blooded reformers whose zeal gets the better of their prudence.

THE INAM COMMISSION

Sashiah was appointed in 1860 as Special Assistant to the Commissioner on a salary of Rs. 600 and placed on a par with his early friend and schoolmate, C. Ranga Charlu. From this time, for a few years, his personal history merges into that of the Inām Commission of which he, with Ranga Charlu, had now become the guiding spirit.

To each of the Special Assistants was found work that particularly harmonized with their talents and temperament. If Ranga Charlu's labours on the Commission came, by the force of happy circumstances, more prominently into notice, Sashiah's were by no means less arduous. To him fell the responsibility of controlling the head office—an establishment of over 250 clerks, of making the wheels of the machinery move without jarring, of conciliating and dismissing with satisfied hearts the large class of Inamdars, who came with grievances to be redressed. This work demanded a deep insight into human character, a delicate appreciation of and adjustment to the motives for conduct and tactful resource in trying conditions. These requisites Sashiah Sastri possessed in abundance and they contributed in no small degree to the unhindered progress of the work.

AS DEPUTY COLLECTOR

When the Inâm Commission was winding up its work, Sashiah wished to have a little respite from hard work and besought the Government to send him as a Deputy Collector to Tanjore, his native District. The Government were pleased to grant his prayer and in 1865 he was appointed Treasury Deputy Collector of Tanjore. Of his work in this office the Collector Mr. G. L. Morris was able to write to the Government in his Fusli Report for 1866-1867 :

> Sashiah Sastry, the Treasury Deputy Collector, is a first rate officer and bears an unblemished character. His office which used to be in great confusion has been brought by him into admirable order and I consider myself most fortunate in having him in my District and at my Headquarters.

IN EXCELLENT COMPANY

In 1869, the Head Sheristadarship of the Board of Revenue having become vacant Sashiah Sastri was recommended for the place. Though unwilling to move from the comparatively peaceful atmosphere of Tanjore, Sashiah was forced to accept the new appointment on increased salary. The work in the Board was arduous and exacting ; but it was congenial. There were also some of his early school-fellows and friends who had all risen to high places and who were now, by a fortunate combination of circumstances, brought together at Madras, each filling an honoured place. T. Muthuswami Aiyar was Police Magistrate. V. Ramiengar was Superintendent of Stamps.

Chentsal Rao was Salt Deputy Collector. R. Raghunatha Rao was Deputy Collector of the City of Madras. They all lived at Mylapore, a few doors off one another.

AS DEWAN OF TRAVANCORE

This delightful period was destined to be short-lived. In April 1872 Sashiah was summoned one morning to the Government House at Guindy and the *ad interim* Governor—Sir Alexander Arbuthnot—asked him if he would accept the Dewanship of Travancore then vacant by the retirement of Sir Madhava Rao. After some hesitation Sashiah Sastri accepted the offer and his services were accordingly placed at the disposal of His Highness the Maharajah of Travancore.

Sashiah Sastri reached Trivandrum about the 20th of May 1872 and was immediately installed as Dewan. The first year was to be a period of probation. His Highness the Maharajah, before confirming Sashiah Sastri in office, wished to make sure that his relations with the Dewan would be smooth and free from friction. By his tact and judgment Sashiah Sastri made himself acceptable to the Maharaja and the Resident and the former had no hesitation in confirming him in his high office.

At the time that Sashiah Sastri took over charge of Travancore there was prospective decrease in annual receipts. What was worse the expenditure for 1871-72 exceeded the receipts. And the Government of Madras in their review hinted that the constant aim of the Sirkar "should be to maintain equilibrium and with this view to exhibit a slight surplus of income over expenditure rather than the contrary as on this occasion." Having this in view Sashiah Sastri took timely precautions to regulate outlay so as to prevent a deficit. Measures were taken for bringing up the arrears of accounts, accounting for past expenditure by submission of *completion bills*, and enforcing the system of budget and allotments for the future. Sashiah also found it necessary to moderate the outlay on public works to a certain extent. (This was not done without departmental grumbling.) By these means and by a strict supervision of all sources of outlet, a slight surplus was secured for the year and the Madras Government congratulated the Sirkar on the financial results.

In spite of an anticipated fall, the revenue had gone on steadily increasing, so that the receipts for 1051, the last year of Sashiah Sastri's régime, surpassed those of the most favourable years till then recorded. A large number (about 120) of very petty dutiable articles were struck out of the export tariff as a relief to commerce generally.

He then turned his attention to land owners and the relief he gave them needs mention. More than six lakhs of rupees remained on the Sirkar books as arrears of land revenue.

A long standing grievance of the holders of *Ain Zufti* lands (that is, those lands transferred from the British territory in exchange) was redressed in 1051. They had remained on the old Tinnevelly tenure and were liable to the payment of Ayakat grain rent commuted at the market price of Tenkasi—a taluq in the Tinnevelly District The payment of the entire rent in kind, commuted at the price of a distant market, was causing great hardship. This was now removed by placing the lands on the same footing as the more favourably assessed surrounding lands of Shencottah proper.

Next came the village officers whose scanty pay told on their power and authority in their jurisdiction besides throwing them open to questionable influences. Sashiah was a believer in adequate wages and he forthwith set about reforming the standard of pay.

The village officers, *proverties* and *maniams*, humble and low paid as they were, did a vast amount and variety of work, both important and unimportant. They constituted the groundwork of the administrative agency. They collected the land revenue, had sole charge of the Sirkar granaries, had police, maramutt and purveying work, in fact represented, within their limited sphere, almost all the functions of a well-ordered Government. Their pay was not, however, in proportion to their constant duties and never-ending responsibilities; but they had, by virtue of their multifarious powers, frequent opportunities of recompensing themselves for their trouble and worry and they seldom scrupled to take advantage of them. Formerly they had been held in great respect and their position had been recognised, not unwisely, as one of honour. A gradual change for the worse had come over them of late years. Sashiah Sastri saw that the first step towards real reformation was to better their status and he quietly prepared the way for the amelioration of this class of officers who, thus gradually taught to think better of themselves, might learn to treat their fellow-subjects with greater consideration.

One of the first things to engage Sashiah's attention was the inadequate scale of salaries that obtained in many of the departments of the state, especially the Revenue and the Judicial. He held very strong views on the subject. The tone of the administration depended not a little on the *men* in the service; and to attract talent, to exorcize all thoughts of illicit gratification and to ensure cheerful and honest work no charm was so powerful as a proper and liberal adjustment of emoluments There was little wisdom in a policy of cheese-paring economy—in effecting a small saving by retrenchment, undermanning and insufficient remuneration and offering a premium to corruption and petty tyranny. With such ideas Sashiah set his heart on a general revision of salaries and establishments.

In this the Maharajah was not quite favourable to the Dewan's proposal. But Sashiah was nothing if not persistent. For, after repeated efforts the Dewan won in the end. At last in February 1874 the Maharajah graciously yielded to the earnest solicitations of the Dewan, agreed to the scheme in principle but proposed to give effect to it with discriminating selection on the merits of each case as it individually came up.

The judicial reforms included the appointment of a European Judge and a number of pending cases were quickly disposed of. The Dewan had magisterial functions and appellate jurisdiction in criminal cases. A regulation was passed towards the close of 1872, relieving him of direct magisterial functions.

The Dewan saw that much of his valuable time was taken up with attending to petty details of administration. All communication, whether in English or Vernacular, proceeding out of the Huzur Cutcherry, could only do so under the signature of the Dewan on whom was thus imposed an amount of detail work "which had perhaps no parallel in the case of any officer holding a similar position." Sashiah Sastri wrote to the Maharajah :—

> "Working at the rate of nearly 10 hours a day I find it very difficult to overtake my work. I often feel that I am neglecting really important work for drudgery; because I have no proper assistance. I want help not for getting myself any leisure for enjoyment, but to give me time to go about the country and to do good to the state and to the people and to attend to really important matters."

It was not long before a capable Secretary was appointed in his office to look after all routine work.

Sashiah Sastri made an attempt to introduce a gold currency in Travancore. It was an experimental measure and bade fair to succeed. A small stock of gold bullion of 100 touch was bought from the Calcutta mint. A suitable mint was improvised for the purpose and pagodas and half pagodas were struck and issued from the Sirkar mint. The gold coins that were thrown into circulation were received by the public with great favour and of the number that were coined and sent out not one returned to the Treasury. But as Sashiah wrote to His Highness, the late enlightened and benevolent ruler of Travancore :—

> I believe that soon after my back was turned on Travancore His late Highness Ayilyam Tirunal, my dear Sovereign, ordered the remaining ingots to be sent to the Chellam Valai. and there I suppose they still sleep in peace.

He next dealt with the Salt Department in which great many abuses had crept in. Next came the Public Works Department. The outlay on public works was placed. on a healthy basis, consistently with other interests of the general administration. New roads, notably that of Ariankov, were opened, which tapped a large tract of country hitherto almost inaccessible and gave a fresh impetus to agriculture. New trade sprang up, where it was before unknown or exceedingly limited. The long neglect from which the irrigation works in the south had suffered attracted attention and measures were taken to repair and restore to efficiency the system of irrigation channels. Excavation of tanks was vigorously taken on hand;

All the *coils* or back-water canals were made navigable at all seasons by the unceasing attention which Sashiah paid to the back-waters which used to silt up every year with the freshes.

A piece of work that Sashiah took up *con amore* and completed under his own personal supervision deserves mention here. It was the clearing of the Padmatirtham tank and the renovation of the channel that feeds it. He gave to the town, the temple and the palace a neverfailing spring of pure water, at the moderate cost of a lakh of rupees. The tower of Sri Padmanabha Swami temple at Trivandrum, which had been long left incomplete, was completed. Finials plated with gold were set up over the topmost storey of the tower and the gilt spires of Sri Padmanabha became a landmark amid the green fields and verdant groves for forty miles around.

The system of grants-in-aid was introduced. Grants were declared open to all schools, under whatever management, which taught vernacular up to a certain standard and showed an attendance of not less than 25. It was introduced to encourage elementary education in general and to show that the Sirkar was ready to assist all bodies engaged in the education of the youths of the country, irrespective of any other consideration. This measure was very popular with the several missions established in the state.

The great famine of 1876-77 drove thousands of helpless Brahmans with their wives and children to the land of charity. Travancore herself felt to some extent the effect of the failure of the rains, but it was no time to think of her curtailed resources when thousands of half-starved men, women and children had come to her gates, for succour, drawn by her fair name for unstinted charity. The Dewan provided for them all and considerate arrangements were made to feed the numberless mouths. The arrangements met with the entire approbation of the Maharajah.

Sashiah was the first minister to take a ruler of Travancore outside the limits of the Madras Presidency. The Maharajah made his first trip to Bombay in 1872 to attend a Chapter of the Star of India and thence to Benares and other places.

In January 1875 the Maharajah undertook another tour to redeem the promise he had made to Lord Northbrooke. This trip lasted for a month and a half and covered all noteworthy places in Northern India. On this occasion Sashiah Sastri made the personal acquaintance of the Viceroy and the chief officers of the Government. They were all taken up with his culture and breadth of views. His conversation, in particular, charmed one and all of them. It was on this occasion that being invited for a Government Ball given by the Viceroy he engaged His Excellency in a conversation which lasted an hour and which so kept the Viceroy enthralled that his guests began to wonder what there could be in "a native" to fascinate him so much and even make him neglectful of his duties as a general host. Sir Charles Aitchison, then foreign Secretary, entered into a long conversation with Sashiah and is said to have remarked that he had never heard a native of India talk English so well, with such purity of accent and idiom.

In 1873 he was invited by the Madras Government to proceed to England at the public cost to give evidence before the Committee of the House of Commons on Indian finance. But he could not accept the invitation. Sashiah replied to the Chief Secretary:—

> While thankful for and proud of the honour which the Government propose conferring on me, I very much regret that the state of my health and the necessities of my social position as a Brahman are such as absolutely preclude the possibility of my undertaking a trip to England for the purpose indicated in your letter—a purpose which I certainly esteem as a duty I owe no less to my country than to my Government—and for the performance of which I should willingly travel many thousands of miles if on land, and to a more genial climate.

Sashiah's engagement with the Maharajah was for five years and was coming to a close in May 1877. During these five years he had been pulling on well enough with the ruler. A few points of difference had now and then cropped up and created a slight misunderstanding between the King and the Minister. The relation between the ruler and the Dewan was getting a little strained. Sashiah submitted a revised scheme of salaries, which should complete the good work he had inaugurated at the commencement of his *regime*. His Highness thought that the Dewan was for showing a profuse liberality at his expense. He was at no pains to conceal his displeasure.

Sashiah's term was running out by May 1877. The Maharajah, though he was perfectly satisfied with the manner in which Sashiah Sastri had conducted the affairs of the state, was loath to renew an engagement which had, he believed, placed him in a position practically subordinate to that of his minister. At the suggestion of the Resident, His Highness extended the term of office for six months to enable Sashiah to wind up his administration and, as was usually done to retiring Dewans, granted him leave on full pay for three out of the six months. In the correspondence which passed with the Madras Government in connection with Sashiah's retirement, His Highness wrote :—

> I take this opportunity of recording my high appreciation of the several distinguished services rendered by Sashiah Sastri during his five years' successful administration.

Thus closed one of the brightest chapters of Sashiah's public career. Five years is a very short period—too short for any statesman to leave landmarks that can endure for all time.

> Still the country had fared happily during his administration; the finances had prospered; the tone of the Service with its attractions had been raised; new roads had been opened and villages had sprung up where before had been the home of wild beasts; petty taxes had been abolished; abuses in the Salt Department had been checked; the Padmatirtham tank had been cleansed, the Kachar channel renewed and a never-failing supply of pure water supplied to the palace and the town; the feeding houses had been improved while waste and plunder had been checked; and during the direst famine of 1877 the refugees from over the Ghauts had been welcomed, well-housed and well-fed; the cause of charity and religion had been vigorously championed; and in the several trying situations in which he found himself by virtue of his high office he had so conducted himself that without sacrificing principle he had conciliated all, and carried out his plans with matured and discerning foresight, so that to this day he is remembered as one of the wisest and most benevolent ministers that that country ever fortunate in her rulers and ministers has had.

But work was soon found for him where he was. About the middle of September 1877 he was made the Vice-President and Secretary to the Mansion House Famine Relief Committee at Trichy. This honorary work kept his hands full. Sashiah Sastri did very good work as Vice-President of the Famine Relief Committee at Trichy. He brought the sufferings of the Gosha women of Trichy to the notice of the Central Committee.

MORE HONOURS

In recognition of his long and distinguished services Sashiah Sastri was made a Companion of the Star of India and on the 1st January 1878 the royal grant of the dignity of C.S.I. and the decoration appertaining thereto were conferred upon him at Madras. His Excellency the Governor, the Duke of Buckingham, in presenting the insignia of the order, alluded in graceful terms to the valuable services rendered by Sashiah Sastri as an official of the Government and to the enlightened assistance offered by him in the administration of the affairs of Travancore.

About November 1879 Sashiah Sastri was deputed as the Madras Member of the Viceroy's Legislative Council at Calcutta.

On the expiry of his term in the Madras Legislative Council he was appointed for a second term. And Lord Ripon also offered him a seat in the Viceregal Council a second time in November 1884; but Sashiah Sastri had to wire back :—

"Feel much honoured; but regret my health is too indifferent to allow me to accept the offer with any chance of doing justice to His Excellency's nomination. Moreover I have still important reforms to carry out here—(Pudukotah) urgently."

DEWAN OF PUDUKOTTAH

About 1878 the affairs of Pudukottah were engaging the attention of the Government of Madras. So Sashiah Sastri visited Pudukottah and saw for himself how things were. But he seems to have felt that it was a regular Augean stable—almost beyond his power to cleanse, that even if he could undertake it with any prospect of success his road to reform would be beset with obstructions and it would be unwise to risk in a hopeless task what reputation he had already earned. He wrote back to the Rajah and the Political Agent declining the offer.

The Raja himself wrote to Sashiah Sastri :—

I must again press you now that you should kindly oblige me and my state by coming here and assuming the office as my Sirkele for the good of myself and my state.

I request you again not to disappoint me. Truly it will be a great sorrow, loss and disappointment if you will not at all consent to come here as my Sirkele, which, I hope the God Almighty will avoid."

Sir Madhava Rao also urged his friend very strongly to accept the place as the following extracts from his letters show :—

".........You should by no means refuse to that state the benefit of your knowledge and experience. As natives we cannot but be the well-wishers of native states. Therefore let us do our utmost to set Pudukottah on a sound footing......

Do not, pray, say, "Why should I take any trouble in the matter?" Of course, so far as your own interests go, you are quite indifferent. But I appeal to higher motives—there is the great good to be done to the native state. Have you not taken a good deal of trouble in famine relief? When you have an opportunity to secure good government to some *lakhs* of the people of Pudukottah you will not shirk'!.........

These earnest representations and requests induced Sashiah Sastri to change his mind and he signified his willingness to accept the place. He was accordingly appointed in August 1878.

In the order of appointment signed by the Rajah and the Political Agent, he was authorized to appoint or remove all public servants below a certain grade; for a few high offices the Rajah's sanction was necessary. Whenever new reforms in the state were to be introduced a reference had to be made to the Rajah previously and carried out with his approval.

Sashiah Sastri entered on his duties at Pudukottah on the 8th August 1878 and retired on the 24th November 1894. In the first half of these 16 years he was Sirkele (the office being afterwards designated by the more familiar name of *Dewan*) and in the second he was Dewan and Regent.

The first work he did was the reform of the Amani system. This reform at one stroke converted *mere tenants-at-will* into *proprietors* and gave a *money value* to lands that in the previous system had none and which thus at one stroke created a source of tangible wealth to the agricultural classes, they being now able to mortgage, transfer or sell their lands, whereas under the previous system transfers and sales were void at law. It was however, made the subject of complaints now and then and sought to be turned to political account by interested agitators. But it must be remembered that under the *Amani* system the ryots had no *wealth in land* to speak of and it was Sashiah Sastri's change of tenure that created a substantial value in the land.

Sashiah Sastri also proposed, when funds permitted, to remedy what evils there existed, by the institution of a regular survey and settlement.

The general sense of security and freedom from the thraldom imposed by a vicious system gave a great impetus to the bringing of new lands extensively under cultivation year after year in spite of alternations of good and bad seasons. The acreage yielding land revenue was 1,03,259 in 1878. In the course of 16 years of Sashiah Sastri's administration it rose to 1,63,807 acres. The enfranchisement of the Inam lands and the resumption of the Western palace Jaghire brought more lands under assessment making the total acreage yielding land revenue 2,13,000. As a result of this increase in the acreage the revenue also rose gradually from 2·75 lakhs of rupees in 1878 to about 6 lakhs.

One or two minor measures which had a marked effect in ameliorating the condition and well-being of the ryots may be here mentioned. The village accounts exhibited large sums of arrears outstanding against the ryots for a long series of years. A scrutiny was made into these arrears and most of them were written off. This at once freed them from their thraldom to the village and other servants.

The Village Kurnam's fees payable in kind were commuted into money. This was rendered necessary to complete the emancipation of the ryot from all manner of interference with his crop.

When Sashiah Sastri came into office there were, except two regulations of recent date, no written laws in the state. Their absence often left the people and the authorities in the dark as to what the law of the state really was. The British laws and regulations were taken as their guides by the Courts and the officers; and their provisions freely administered without even a royal warrant authorising such a course. A beginning was made in 1880 and as necessity arose new regulations were made and published in the

State Gazette, all more or less modelled on British lines with such changes as the requirements of state rendered desirable.

Notorious dacoits were hunted down and most of them were convicted and imprisoned. The roads became perfectly safe and security and peace reigned everywhere within the state. What contributed most towards this happy result was the magic of Sashiah Sastri's name, which was a terror to all evil-doers.

No department of the state underwent so many changes in his time as the judicial machinery.

At first there were a few Munsiff's Courts, a Civil and Sessions Court at the capital and an Appeal Court. One of the Munsiff's Courts was abolished as it was without sufficient work. Appellate jurisdiction over the Munsiff's Courts was transferred from the Rajah's Court of Appeal to the Civil Court. The Civil Judge's place having fallen vacant, a qualified officer was brought in from the British service. Under the new Civil Judge all arrears were cleared off.

The cause of higher education in the state throve wonderfully under Sashiah Sastri's fostering and discriminating care. What was in 1878 a Lower Secondary School with a strength of about 70 students grew in a few years into a brilliant second grade college nearly 700 strong. Graduates who had won honours in their academical course were secured for the College staff. The results of the University and public examinations were uniformly creditable and sometimes even brilliant and spread the name of the College far and wide and began to attract students from out-side.

A few rules for grants-in-aid were published in 1885, and an inspecting staff was appointed to inspect and report on such pial schools as might become eligible for grants. A few schools were maintained under salary system. In 1885 there were only 13 schools that could get the grants. In 1894 there were 219 such schools.

In 1884 Sashiah Sastri succeeded by his representations in securing for the Rajah the honour of the '*Salute*' of which he had been deprived and the title of Highness.

The late Rajah died in April 1886. Sashiah Sastri was made Dewan-Regent and continued in this exalted position till the present ruler came of age and assumed the reins of government in November 1894.

RETIREMENT AND REST

On retirement Sashiah Sastri repaired to his country-house at Kumbakonam where he spent the evening of his life. The house he began to build for himself on the banks of the Cauveri, at Kumbakonam, took about three years in building and was completed about the close of 1881. To this house he retired after leaving Pudukottah; his pension of Rs. 500 a month from Travancore added to his Pudukottah pension of Rs. 400 placed him in comfortable circumstances.

Thenceforward Sashiah Sastri seldom quitted his abode. Indeed it was physically impossible for him to move from place to place; and distinguished visitors from the Governor down to the Collector of the District saw him in his beautiful mansion on the banks of the Cauvery. Sir Arthur Havelock, when about to leave these shores, wrote to him :—

I shall leave India with many regrets and with many happy memories. But, of these happy memories, there are few which hold a more conspicuous place than my acquaintance with yourself. The pleasant hour I spent with you in your house on the bank of the Cauvery will always remain fresh in my recollection. I recognised in you one of the most able and remarkable personalities of Southern India and I felt it a privilege to draw on your rich store of wisdom, of knowledge and of experience.

Lord Ampthill also paid a visit to him. Lord Elgin, when Viceroy, halted for a short while at Kumbakonam during his southern tour, on purpose to see Sashiah Sastri and grant him an interview. Lord Curzon also gave him an interview at Tanjore; and all these were uniformly impressed by the personality of the grand old man of Southern India. Sir M. E. Grant Duff wrote to Sashiah Sastri in one of his letters:—

I have again and again said to others and there seems no reason why I should not say to you, that of all the native statesmen I have come across in any part of India you were the one who impressed me most favourably.

His Majesty King Edward VII made Sashiah Sastri a Knight Commander of the Star of India. Lord Curzon, the then Viceroy, wiring the news congratulated him in these terms:—

It gives me great pleasure to inform you that His Majesty has been pleased, upon my recommendation, to appoint you to be a K. C. S. I. Permit me to congratulate you heartily upon this distinction.

The evening of his life thus passed in the peace of his home, surrounded by his relatives and friends. He died, full of years and honours, on the 29th October, 1903.

Samaldas Parmananddas

SAMALDAS Parmananddas* after whom the Arts College at Bhavnagar was named by his generous master, His Highness Maharaja Takhtasinhji —belonged to the Vadnagara Nagar community, a community that gave Gourishanker Udeshanker—the sage statesman—to Bhavnagar, Gokalji Zala— the Vedanti Administrator—to Junagadh and Dewan Bahadur Manibhai Jasabhai—politician and educationist of Baroda and Bholanath Sarabhai—the religious and social reformer—to Ahmedabad. The community takes its name from Vadnagar, a small town within the territories of His Highness the Maharaja Gækwar, a few miles distant from the well-known Mehsana Junction Station on the R. M. Railway. A few centuries back, the community migrated to other parts of Gujarat and Kathiawad, while some families went to the North and East up to Muttra and Benares. The Nagars of Bhavnagar first migrated to Gogo, then a biggish town with good harbour and large import and export trade. Samaldas's forefathers came to Bhavnagar from Gogo in the 17th century, but they did not permanently abandon Gogo, which till 1878 A. D. was the socio-religious headquarters of the community.

* A Sketch by Sir Lalubhai Samaldas

Samaldas's grandfather Ranchoddas went to Baroda in search of service and had to cross the arid and dry tract of Bhal, where for miles no drinking water is to be had even now. It was much worse in those days. There is a tradition in the family that Ranchhoddas saved a woman from death by giving away the greater portion of the food that he was carrying and the water, even at the risk of meeting such a fate himself, and that in return he got the old lady's blessings—due to which not only did Ranchhoddas get a very important post in the military department of the Baroda State, but that his son, grandson and great-grandson attained the Dewanate of Bhavnagar. On leaving Baroda service, Ranchhoddas came back to Bhavnagar and built a new home from his savings; the house which was to be the residence both of his son Parmananddas and grandson Samaldas until Samaldas was able, with the generous assistance of Maharaja Takhtasinhji, to build after one hundred years a new house more suited to altered times and circumstances.

After this house was built, the family migrated to Bhavnagar, and went to Gogo on special occasions only. Parmananddas had not to go to a distant place in search of service, but was able to carve his way up to the highest administrative post in his own native place—native by adoption and not by birth. His master, Thakore Shree Vajesinhji (the titles of His Highness and of Maharaja were given by the Government of India at a later date) had such confidence in

Parmananddas's ability and loyalty that even when he was not in service (and this happened on and off several times), he was asked to prepare drafts of all important communications to be addressed to the Political Department. When I was a boy (in my teens) and at School, the then Maharaja—Sir Takhtasinhji—had this story told me in his presence by my father Samaldas and asked me if I would stand by the State as my grandfather did even after my services were dispensed with. I naturally said "no" in reply, and when taunted with a want of regard. for the State's interests I added, more diplomatically perhaps, that my refusal to do this work would not be because of offended self-respect but because even if I did my best in the matter it might be represented to the Maharaja that I had purposely done it badly. Whether it be due to the increase in the number of men capable of doing all such work, or to the exaggerated opinion as to what is due to him, both on the part of the King and the officers, the old-time cordiality and feeling of family membership have practically disappeared in all Indian States. The commercial spirit of bargaining for the best terms has entered Indian States also, and, as a result, Indian State administration is becoming an imitation—and in many cases a bad and poor imitation—of the administration of British India. This is by the way, however.

Parmananddas retired from the State service permanently in 1847 A. D. He was succeeded by his brother-in-law, the well-known figure in the history of

Indian State administration—Gourishanker Udeshanker—who was at the head of affairs, first as Dewan and then as one of the Joint Administrators of Bhavnagar—during the minority of Maharaja Tahktasinhji—for 32 years. Parmananddas had four sons, three of whom were in State service holding fairly important posts; the fourth son being a little eccentric and whimsical was dependent on his father and brother as a member of the joint family. That eccentricity in a subdued form must have existed in the other brothers too, for even now a spark of that quality is noticeable even up to the third generation. If science had succeeded in finding out how heredity works, it would have been possible to say why one branch that is Samaldas took to administrative work and the acquisition of academical qualifications, and the other branches specialised in other lines only.

Maharaja Vajesinhji looked upon Parmananddas's death as a personal loss. As was, and is even now, the custom in Indian States, Vajesinhji paid a personal visit of condolence to his sons and told them that he would look after them in a paternal spirit and that they must look up to him for guidance and assistance as they were looking to their father in his life-time.

Samaldas was the first and the youngest of Parmananddas's sons. He was born at Gogo in 1828 A. D. his mother being Rajuba—sister of Gourishanker Udeshankar, who had succeeded Parmananddas as Dewan of Bhavnagar. In those days there were no regular vernacular schools in Kathiawar. The only education—if one can use that word for the knowledge of the three R's that was then imparted—one could get was at the village school. Greater attention was paid to good handwriting and mental arithmetic than is done at present. One almost wishes—or at least wished till the typewriting machine was invented—that much greater attention might be paid to the cultivation of good handwriting than is done at present. To a certain extent the handwriting of a man is an index to his character. It shows whether the man is careful and amenable to discipline. A person who is regardful of his reader's feelings would try his best to write a legible hand.

When Samaldas had learnt all that could be learnt in the Village School of Gogo, where, after his mother's death, he was brought up by his mother's sister, Parmananddas wanted him to come to Bhavnagar to learn Persian, of which he himself was fond, and to be initiated in the administrative work of the State and indirectly in the art of diplomacy. Just about the time that Samaldas was to leave for Bhavnagar, the Bombay Government opened a regular Vernacular School at Gogo and Samaldas was allowed by his father to continue his studies there till he had completed the prescribed vernacular course. In those days the man at the head of a Vernacular School was respected more than the headmaster of a first-class high school is done in these days. The relations between the teacher and his pupils must have been very cordial and the pupil's personal gratefulness to his teachers must have been of the Guru-Shishya type of old, for Samaldas used to show the same respect for his teacher even after he became the Dewan of Bhavnagar and when the teacher was a pensioner on barely Rs. 15 a month. There has been a change in our mentality since those good old days, and though I cannot be classed as a moderner, I remember that when I saw for the first time my father showing so much respect to an ordinary Mehtaji (school-master) as he did whenever the latter paid an annual visit to my father, even I was rather disagreeably surprised. At these annual visits the teacher was paid an annuity which was continued even to his widow after his death.

After having finished his school course at Gogo, Samaldas came to Bhavnagar and began accompanying his father in his official and social calls on Maharaja Vajesinhji as that he might get initiated into the system of administration and Statecraft. As Parmananddas was a good Persian scholar, he put Samaldas under a Munshi to study Persian. Samaldas used some of his spare time in studying Sanskrit. Although the old system of teaching these languages may appear crude and unscientific in these days, yet as a result of the training in these languages Samaldas was able to read and understand stiff books in Persian and understand the Vendanta philosophy of Shreemat Shankaracharya. Vajesinjhi used to have books like Shahnama read out and translated by Samaldas. This led to a greater personal contact between the Maharaja and Samaldas, and the former began to appreciate the intellectual capacity of the latter. One wonders if Samaldas would have had the same capacity of clear thinking and correct immediate action if he had been obliged to read up to the prescribed University standards with the bogey of examinations facing him every year. Dewan Gourishanker had still less of literary education and in spite of it—or perhaps on account of it—his intellect remained sharp and his memory so remarkable that high Government officials, Governors and others were taken aback when, during conversation, he would give his reminiscences as correctly as if he were reading out from a written diary.

Although Samaldas was a keen student of Shanker's philosophy and could argue its intellectual subtleties with learned Sanyasis, (I remember, with natural pride, one such discussion he had with that very learned Swami, Raja Rajeshwar, the then Shankaracharya of the Sharada Pith of Dwarka) he thought that it was not possible to carry out into practice the Naishkarma philosophy of the first Shankaracharya and the commentators of his Bhashya. Though the Nagar community is reputedly Shaivite, his family had some generations back adopted the Vaishnava cult. Samaldas during his whole life followed the Bhakti Marga being a devotee of Shri Ramchandraji, whose high character as depicted in the Tulasi Ramayana captivated his heart. He was a regular student of Tulasidas' Ramayana, and during his father's illness he daily read selected passages from that great Epic to help him in taking away his mind from his physical sufferings and to concentrate the same in devotion to Shri Ramchandra.

On the death of Parmananddas, Samaldas, who had joined the State service in the life-time of his father and had shown his abilities as a conciliator of the Khumans of Kundla (the original Kathi Land-holders) of that Taluka, was given the important post of the City Magistrate of Bhavnagar. The importance of the post lay in the fact that the British Government had deprived the Rulers of Bhavnagar of their jurisdiction over the new and old capitals of the State (Bhavnagar and Sihor) and of other 114 villages and placed them under the Judge at Ahmedabad. As a nominee of the State he had to look after the interests of the State and to respect the wishes of the Rulers and their advisers ; he had to carry on the judicial administration according to the statutes of the Government of India under the direct orders of the District Magistrate (the Collector) of Ahmedabad. No man however capable and honest he may be and however impartial he may try to be between such conflicting interests, can continue to win the favour of both sides. Moreover, where the officer himself believes that great injustice had been done to the Rulers of the State by the deprivation of their jurisdictionary powers, he would unconsciously sympathize with the view-points of the State and its officers, more especially as the latter happened to be his near

Page 304.

SAMALDAS PARMANANDDAS

relations as was the case with Samaldas. There are always two or more parties in Indian States, not like the parties in the elected Houses of Legislature, but parties that aspire to power to use it in the best interests of the State which term in those days was synonymous with the Ruler of the State—and also of themselves and their supporters. In a State situated as Bhavnagar then was, the party not in power very often tried to hit at the other party, not by intriguing with the Chief but by prejudicing the Judiciary of Ahmedabad and hitting at the ministry through their nominee—the Bhavnagar City Magistrate. In 1857 they took advantage of a case of robbery and shooting to mix up with it the whole administration including the Chief and his ministers. The combination of the Executive and Judicial powers in the hands of one man—the Collector and District Magistrate—made the work of that party much easier than it would otherwise have been. Warrants were issued by the District Magistrate on all persons charged with complicity in this crime, including the Ruling Prince himself. Fortunately, the Prince and his chief ministers were not in Bhavnagar and thus not within British Jurisdiction. They were touring in other parts of the State where the Jurisdiction still rested with the Chief himself. Samaldas, as the chief local officer, was in Bhavnagar and was arrested with others who were within the British Jurisdiction. They were taken to Ahmedadad and, as there were no railways at that distant date, it took about a week to reach that place. Attempts were made to give as much annoyance to Samaldas as possible during this journey, but his readings of the Tulasi Ramayana came to his assistance. The head of the Police Guard was a devotee of Shri Ramchandra and when he heard Samaldas reciting pieces from that epic poem, he felt that a man with such devotional points should not be put to any unnecessary trouble. One wonders how far the common factor of faith in the same incarnation of God Vishnu proved helpful to Samaldas. When the case went up to the District Judge it was decided in Samaldas' favour, as the Judges then as now are not as a rule influenced by the opinions of the Collectors of the District. Not only was Samaldas's arrival at Bhavnagar after an honourable acquittal greeted as that of a victorious hero's return to his native place, but it was looked upon as a great success of the party in power with the then Maharaja Jaswatsinhji.

Samaldas's persecution and trials led indirectly to two very beneficial results. The first was that it led Maharaja Jaswatsinhji and his ministers to persist in their attempts to have justice done to Bhavnagar's claims to get back the jurisdiction over the 116 villages. (The term village here includes even the City of Bhavnagar.) Due to the able manner in which the case for Bhavnagar was put before the Government of Bombay both by written representations and during interviews with the high officials of that Government, and due also to the fact that the then officers of the

Government were not power-grabbing but men with a sense of fairness and justice and having real sympathy with the chiefs of Kathiawar. Bhavnagar got back its jurisdiction over these towns and villages in 1866.

While the main portion of the credit for achieving this result belongs to Gourishanker Udeshanker, those who helped him in preparing the case and in submitting the same to the Government officials are also entitled to some credit. Maharaja Jaswatsinhji bore this in mind when he rewarded the services of his ministers and officers for getting back the jurisdiction for Bhavnagar. While Gourishanker and the then joint Dewan Santokram Sevakram Desai were given a village each as Inam in perpetuity, Samaldas and Merwanji Bhownaggree (father of Sir Muncherji Bhownaggree) were given money grants of Rs. 50,000 each.

The second good result of Samaldas's persecution was that he realized by his personal experience the evil results of combining the executive and judicial functions in one person, and consequently when he was asked to organize the Judicial Service in Bhavnagar he got the Maharaja and the Ministers to agree to a complete separation of the Executive and the Judicial Departments. Whatever opinion the Government of India or the Provincial Governments may hold in regard to this important question, Sir Bartle Frere, the then Governor of Bombay, expressed himself in favour of such separation at the time of presenting the Insignia of K. C. S. I. to Maharaja Jaswatsinhji in 1867. He said:

But what I regard as the peculiar feature of your Highness' administration, which will, I believe, be productive of most good to your people, and will, I am sure, give most pleasure to His Majesty's Government, is the care you have wisely and consistently taken to improve the administration of justice, and *to separate it from all that is purely executive.*

Samaldas was put at the head of the Judicial Department soon after the organisation of the Department on the transfer of Jurisdiction to the State. He held this important post for about three years until the death of Maharaja Jaswatsinhji in 1870. During this period he went on a pilgrimage to Benares and Gaya, for he looked upon the performance of Shraddha as a duty to the Pitris. Being not a sectarian Vaishnava, he looked upon Shiva and Vishnu as different forms typifying the two activities of One God, and he had been looking forward to the bath in the Holy Mother Ganges and to the worship of Kashi Vishvanath as a step in his spiritual growth. There being no railway from Jubbalpur to Allahabad in those days he had to do the journey in ordinary bullock carts. He had a small party of his own, inlcuding a learned Shastric—Narbheran (Jani)—and a secretary or personal assistant—Jatashanker Indarji. Samaldas was able to put up with all the discomforts and inconveniences natural to bullock-cart journeys, because, though the son of a Dewan and brought up by the sister of another Dewan, he had experiences of vicissitudes of life which had removed all softness inherent in high Indian State officials' sons. Moreover, he had a deep faith that this pilgrimage was a duty he owed to the spirits of his forefathers and was necessary for his spiritual rise in future rebirths, and removed the sharp edge of such a journey's hardships. He was obliged to cut down his programme and return to Bhavnagar earlier, owing to the severe illness of the Chief, information about whose health was being conveyed to him from time to time.

When Maharaja Jaswatsinhji died after a prolonged illness in 1870, an attempt was made by the then Political Agent to place the administration in the hands of a British officer during the minority of the young Maharaja Takhtasinhji, and to make Dewan Gourishanker his assistant. This proposal was strongly opposed by the Dowager Ranis, the Ministers of Jaswatsinhji and the people of Bhavnagar, who had full confidence in the then ministers and who wanted them to carry on the administration on the same lines until Takhtasinhji attained his majority and took over the administration in his own hands. As Dewan Gourishanker was put in charge of the State by the Political Agent till final arrangements for the future administration of the State were made, he was not able to leave Bhavnagar, and Samaldas was deputed by the Ranis and the existing administration to put their views before the Governor and the members of Government. He first went to Matheran, to see the Hon'ble Member in charge, who told him that he had approved the Political Agent's proposals and had recommended its acceptance to Government. Samaldas explained the whole position to the Hon'ble Member, who was satisfied that it would be wrong in principle and unfair to the existing administration to say that they could not be trusted to carry on the administration after having declared publicly a few months ago that it was very satisfactory; and as a mark of Government's approbation bestowed the then very much coveted title of K. C. S. I., to the Ruling Chief. Samaldas's arguments convinced the Hon'ble Member that he had taken a hurried action on hearing one side only, and as a fair-minded and straight officer he wired to the Governor to give a hearing to Samaldas and not to issue any orders till then. This spirit of fairness and sympathy towards the members of the family of a deceased Ruling Prince were very effective in keeping the rulers and the Dewans of Indian States attached both of Government and to individual members as Government. The Governor, after hearing Samaldas at Mahableshwar, expressed a desire to see Gourishanker to satisfy himself about his physical capacity to carry on the onerous duties of an administrator as it had been reported that he would not be able to do so on account of his old age. Gourishanker called on His Excellency at Poona and as a result of that interview with the Governor and of further conferences between the Political Secretary and the Ministers, Government decided to have a joint administration during the minority of Maharaja Takhtasinhji, consisting of one British official and

Dewan Gourishanker. The idea underlying this decision was to combine the best of the modern and the indigenous systems of administration. The chief credit for arriving at this solution, though a reasonable compromise, belonged to Sir William Wedderburn, the then Political Secretary, who was later on President of the Indian National Congress. The first British officer selected for this purpose was Mr. Percival, the father of Mr. P. E. Percival, now Judge of the High Court of Bombay, who it may be mentioned was born in Bhavnagar. Mr. Percival, as well as his two successors, Col. Watson and Col. Parr, worked harmoniously with Gourishanker and not only hailed him as an equal but did not fail to show him the respect that was his due as the ablest Indian-State Administrator in the Province. Owing to this co-operation between the two schools of thought, reforms in the mode of administration were introduced slowly and cautiously, and were so adapted to the local circumstances that they did not lead to any unnecessary disturbance in the existing machinery but were accepted by the public and loyally put into execution by the officers of the State. These reforms were more in the nature of the evolution of the old system than the introduction of an exotic unsuitable to existing conditions of administration. There has hardly been any minority administration so successful as that of Bhavnagar, and the credit thereof belongs as much to the British officers of the joint administration as to Gourishanker and also to Samaldas, who worked as Assistant to the Joint Administration from the time of its inception.

This rise in the official status of Samaldas was his due, both because of his meritorious service to the State in connection with the organisation of the Judicial Administration of the State and also on account of the fact that, as both the Joint Administrators were connected with the Executive side of the administration, they needed the assistance of an officer who had practical personal experience of the judicial branch.

Samaldas soon won the confidence and regard of Mr. Percival, and as he had the full confidence of Dewan Gourishanker he was able to influence to a great extent the administration of the State, as he had to study the various proposals of reform and submit the same to the administrators with his opinion. By his careful study of questions affecting the common interests of the States of Kathiawar, he had achieved a very high position in Kathiawar affairs. When there was any conflict of opinion between Kathiawar States and the then Political Agent as regards the powers of interference of the British Government in the disputes between the States and their Land-holders (Mulgrasseas), the work of approaching Bombay officials and of preparing representations on behalf of the States was entrusted to Samaldas. He prepared the case for the States in the Vernacular, which was translated into English by an Englishman who had become a convert to Mahomedanism and was employed in Bhavnagar as the commanding officer of the irregular cavalry of the State. This Mahomedan officer was personally devoted to Samaldas and more to his son Vithaldas, and as he was a good English writer he proved very useful to the State in preparing English memorials from the materials supplied to him, which were finally settled by eminent counsel of Bombay or Rajkot.

Samaldas came in great personal contact with the then minor Maharaja, who took very kindly to his advice and looked upon him almost as a Guru. In later days, the Maharajah used to compare his relationship with Samaldas to that of Arjuna (the hero of Mahabharata with that of Drona Acharya). This friendship (if one may use that term in connection with the relations of a Ruling Prince and his minister) continued till the death of Samaldas. Soon after the installation on the *Gadi* of Maharajah Takhtasinhji with full powers, Gourishanker, who had reverted to the position of the Dewan, expressed his desire to retire from the ministership on account of advanced age. He suggested the name of Samaldas as his successor and his proposal met with the cordial approval of the young Maharajah, and in January 1879 Samaldas was made Dewan of Bhavnagar,—thus following in his father's footsteps after 32 years.

At the Durbar held by H. H. The Maharajah Sahib to confer on Samaldas the dignity of a Dewan and the Dewan's Poshak, Samaldas announced his own policy which he said he hoped to be able to carry out with the support of his Ruler, who had evinced full confidence in him till then. The difficulties of a Dewan of an Indian State since the advent of the British are much greater than those of the minister of old Indian States, for while the latter had to serve two masters—the Ruler and the people—the former had to serve one more master—namely the Political officer of the Province who, in those days, wielded much greater power of interference in the affairs of Indian States under his charge than is wielded by the Governor of a Province at present. The people of the State had no constitutional powers of control over legislation or administration but the Mahajan * of the Capital and of District Towns had their own methods of making their voice heard by the Ruler and his advisers,—the chief and the final of these being the observance of Hartal † a sort of general strike. On one occasion the shooting of a monkey by a Parsi municipal officer in the City of Bhavnagar created so much excitement amongst the leading Hindu residents of the City that Samaldas had to use all his persuasive powers to pacify them and to prevent a *Hartal.*

The credit of constructing the first Railway in Kathiawar belongs to Maharajah Takhtasinhji—though that Railway was financed by two States, Bhavnagar and Gondal, and was called the Bhavnagar-Gondal Railway. Gondal, whose ruler was a minor, was administered by a political officer under

---

* Literally the great men—leaders of public opinion.

† Etymologically locking (closing) the shops.

the orders of the Government of Bombay, and that officer agreed to the proposal of the Railway not because he believed in it but because the Governor of the Presidency ordered him to go in for the construction of a Railway. It is a well-known fact that the young Maharajah took his lead from Samaldas. I very well remember my father being blamed for giving his advice in support of the proposal. Dewans of other neighbouring States when consulted by Maharajah Takhtasinhji had frankly told him that he was jeopardising the customs revenue and that the Railway would lead his State in a grave financial crisis. Samaldas stood firm and strongly advised the Maharajah to go ahead, and though this is old history I cannot help saying that, proud as I am of my father on account of his many qualities of head and heart and his acts of statesmanship, I am proudest of him for the splendid work he did in introducing Railways in Kathiawar in spite of strong opposition on all sides.

Samaldas's career as a Dewan was of a very shot duration—about five years and a half. During all that period he had to curtail public works and other expenses, to be able to find money for the capital and work of the railway. Without having a regular system of budgets he kept control of expenditure in such a manner that never had the State Treasury to delay payment to the Railway Administration. At the same time, he had to see that not only was there no curtailment but a little increase in expenditure on what are now known as nation-building departments. Two outstanding acts of his administration were (1) the Salt Treaty with Government and (2) The Settlement of very important Kathi original land-holders of the district of Kundla. While the first showed his capacity of arguing important State questions with Imperialistic officers of Government, the latter showed his persuasive powers and the confidence this turbulent class of independent land-holders of the Province had in his sense of fairness and justice. All through his administrative career it was his policy to see that no Grassias (original land-holders) had any cause of serious complaint of injustice being done to their lawful claims. Possibly, the judicial training he had in his early days unfitted him for any unjust attacks on the existing rights of these land-holders. Both my elder brother, who succeeded him as Dewan, and myself learnt this lesson from him, and I can say without any exaggeration that even now, after some 25 years, the Grassias remember our fair dealings with them and speak of us in terms of affection and respect.

Samaldas looked far ahead in his dealings with large administrative questions. Years before the Viramgam-Mehsana Branch was constructed he visualized the great advantage likely to accrue to the Bhavnagar port and the Bhavnagar Railway if goods imported through Bhavnagar could go direct without break of guage to Rajputana and Northern India. With the sanction of Maharajah Takhtasinhji he made a definite proposal on behalf of his State to the Government of Bombay to construct the Railway from Viramgam to Mehsana and to pay interest and maintenance of a third rail being laid on the Broad Gauge (5' 6") line from Wadhwan to Viramgam, so that there might be direct connection between Bhavnagar and the Northern parts of the country. As the port of Bhavnagar did not provide facilities for large steamers to come into the Creek of Bhavnagar, he, in consultation with the then State Engineer, Mr. Proctor-Sims, submitted a proposal to the Maharajah for developing a new port at Kathiwadar. He did not live to see any of these undertakings carried out. While the railway connections had been made, the new port—called Port Albert Victor—had not been fully developed.

Samaldas believed in spreading education—primary, secondary and higher—in the State. When the first Girls' School was started in Bhavnagar and when there was a prejudice against giving education to girls, Samaldas took a lead in the matter by sending his daughter to the Girls' School. What was good for the public was, in his opinion, good for his children. He gave to his eldest son as much education in English as it was possible at the time to give in Bhavnagar. He did not, however, send him out to Rajkot or Bombay to receive higher education, because there was no railway communication between these places and Bhavnagar; and he did not like to send his eldest son to such a distance without the facilities of speedy travelling. When I passed my Matriculation Examination he sent me to the Elphinstone College, as he thought a higher knowledge of English and other subjects under English professors and a rubbing of shoulders with young men from other parts of the Presidency would prove useful to me. Owing to my not keeping good health and to His Highness the Maharaja Takhtasinhji's desire to train me up in administrative work early in life, I was withdrawn from the College before I finished my degree course. I realize even now what great advantage it was for me to mix with some of the best students of the Presidency and to study under well-known English professors.

Though a keen student of the Vedanta philosophy, Samaldas did not think himself fit to accept it in its entirety and consequently he did not give up the devotional side of Hindu religion. During his last illness he was having the great Hindu Epic—the Mahabharat—read out to him. These readings and the recitals of Sanskrit hymns helped him to bear his physical sufferings in the last days of his life with great equanimity of mind. He had disciplined himself from his early age to control his feelings, and even when he had justifiable cause for anger his reproach was always couched in gentle terms. In spite of this discipline he found the physical sufferings and insomnia too trying to be borne with courage and fortitude. On such occasions, he took outside help in the shape of recitals of sacred Mantras so that he might be able to divert his mind from the physical to the spiritual plane.

In his will he had predicted that Maharajah Takhtasinhji would give the Dewanate to his eldest son, but he was quite sure that the relations between the Maharajah and the new Dewan would not remain very cordial for long. He almost feared that Vithaldas might have to resign service and so he laid down a condition that in such a contingency his sons (Vithaldas and myself) should never swerve from our loyalty to the Ruler and the State and should not intrigue within the State or have pressure brought from outside to get back our posts. Although the relations between Maharajah Takhtasinhji and Vithaldas were strained the former did not part from his Dewan though he did curtail some of his powers. The separation of Vithaldas and myself from the State service came in the time of Maharajah Bhavsinhji. After we left State service we carried out the instructions of our respected father, and as a result our relations with the Maharajah and his officials have remained cordial ever since. Samaldas's giving such instructions in his Will, written out in his own hand, a few months before his death, shows his far-sightedness even during physical sufferings, which very often affect a man's mental condition.

After some months' serious illness, during which Maharaja Takhtasinhji showed him all possible kindness, Samaldas died in harness in August, 1884, at the age of 56 full of honour if not of years.

A word may here be said in addition to the foregoing sketch of Samaldas.. Samaldas was a pious Hindu imbued with the true spirit of the Vedant. But as Mr. K. Natarajan justly points out in his foreword to a biography of the great statesman, he was one of those Indians "who combine in themselves a belief in Maya and a life of strenuous action." His activities were varied—social, religious, administrative. But against the kaleidoscopic background of his multifarious activities "stands out in easy prominence the figure of Samaldas, ready of resource, patient and painstaking, energetic but not precipitous, firm in the assertion of authority, but always inclined to temper justice with mercy. He is undoubtedly entitled to a high place in the distinguished galaxy of Indian Statesmen to whom it is chiefly due that the Native States enjoy to-day a recognised and honourable position in the Imperial system."

DEWAN RAGHOONATH RAO

RAGHOONATH RAO

DEWAN BAHADUR ROOBGOONDAY RAGHOO-NATH RAO, C. S. I., to give him his full name and title, came of an ancient and well-connected Mahratta Brahmin family long settled in what is now the Tanjore District. The Roobgoondays had their family seat centuries ago in the picturesque hilly country round Poona. They were men as much known even in those days for their ready wit and readier valour as for their gentle manners and keen sense of justice. Many are the stories that have come down to us of the good that the first founders of the family did in Sivaji's father's service in Bijapur and elsewhere. Among the men who made Shahji great and his son greater still, was the family of the Roobgoondays and a whole host of Mahratta Brahmin houses whose names are now altogether forgotten, if not lost. The Roobgoondays, in the dissensions that followed the death of Shahji, followed the fortunes of Eccoji—Venkoji—who laid the foundations for a Southern Mahratta Empire at Tanjore in the stormy times of the seventeenth century. It is not possible to go here into the circumstances that led to the foundation of this principality. It should suffice to note that the new kingdom took the place of the old Nayak Kings of Tanjore and in the wake of the new conquerers, a whole army of civil and military officers descended south and settled down in Tanjore and the country round about. Among these were the Roobgoondays from whom was descended Raghoonath Rao, the subject of our sketch.

Raghoonath Rao was born at Kumbakonam on 7th February 1831. His father Rai Raya Rao Roobgoonday Venkat Rao was one of the most noted Indians of his times in Southern India. He had been Dewan of Travancore, and had won a name for himself while there as a capable Revenue Minister. When Mysore passed under the British in 1834 they found they wanted a person who, while being an Indian, possessed sufficient capacity and experience to overhaul the whole revenue system of the country. Sir Mark Cubbon in his search for men espied in Rai Raya Rao Venkat Rao the man he stood most in need of. He was requisitioned for without delay and his work as Revenue Commissioner in Mysore won general approbation. Rai Raya Rao Venkat Rao is still remembered in Bangalore, where he lived. A *chattram* (charitable feeding house) still goes in his name, having been founded by him. He belonged to the old orthodox type of Indians, now fast passing away. His wife Lakshmi Bai was a lady of rare merits. To a knowledge of Hindu sacred lore, she combined all that goes to make up the true Hindu mother. Both husband and wife loved Sanskrit too well to miss even for a day the exposition in their house of the great Epics of India. Young Raghoonath slowly but surely imbibed his love for the "Aryan" faith as he termed it, in his later life, to this patient hearing of the recital of the ancient epics by the best pandits of the time.

EDUCATION

While his father was still in the Mysore service, Raghoonath began his three R's. He began his English alphabets in a small Mission School which in those days had its habitat in what is now termed Bangalore Fort. He then passed on to the Madras High School, the precursor of the modern Presidency College at Madras, into which he entered as a student in 1845. Here he came into contact with some young men who in later life became well-known in Indian society. To name only a few, here were Sir T. Madhava Rao, Raghoonath's cousin (paternal uncle's son), Dewan Rangacharlu of Mysore, Sir Amaravati Seshayya and Sir T. Muthusami Ayyar just completing their English education under Eyre Burton Powell, the famous Irish Educationist of Madras. Eyre Burton Powell's name is still remembered in Southern India. Young Raghoonath could not but profit by such association. He not merely added to his fund of knowledge but also underwent the discipline of an English public school in Powell's High School, as it was affectionately styled in those days.

EARLY CAREER

Raghoonath did not wait for his proficient's degree, the highest obtainable in pre-University days in Southern India. He left school to manage his vast paternal estates in Kumbakonam in 1850. There he stayed for four years or so. This gave him an insight into the revenue system of the country. If he became a champion of the ryot in later days, it was partially due to this early intimate and first-hand knowledge of his difficulties. However, he had no idea of continuing in estate management. He privately read up law and qualified for the bar. In 1856 he obtained a pleader's diploma with Sir T. Muthusami Ayyar, afterwards famous as the first Indian Judge of the Madras High Court.

IN THE PUBLIC SERVICE

Though he qualified for the bar, Raghoonath Rao had no real liking for it. Government service offered a peculiarly attractive field to one like him. He joined service as Translator in the Collector's Office at Tanjore with his friend Muthusami Ayyar and the late Rai Bahadur T. Gopal Rao, afterwards well-known as Principal of the Kumbakonam College. He next became Sheristadar (Chief Ministerial Officer) of the Sub-Court at Kumbakonam, then presided over by Mr. L. C. Innes, afterwards a Judge of the Madras High Court. Innes was so much struck by the uprightness, the intelligence and sense of duty of Raghoonath Rao that he ever afterwards spoke of him as one of the best Indians he had come across with in his service. When, in 1859, the new scheme sanctioning the entertainment of Indians as Deputy Collectors was introduced, Raghoonath Rao was selected for one of the first posts created. He was appointed by Sir Charles Trevelyan, then Governor of Madras, and a warm friend of Indians, to his own native district of Tanjore. Raghoonath Rao wished for a change, but so great was the trust placed in him by the Government that they refused to reconsider their decision. The trust reposed in him was fully reciprocated. The Mutiny had given an impetus to railway construction in India. In Southern India, a large railway project had to be pushed through. This project would have covered, if it had been finished as originally conceived, the whole of the country now traversed roughly by the S. I. and M. & S. M. Railway systems. The project was known as the Great Southern Railway and land had to be acquired for it without delay for laying the line. The line started from Negapatam and was at first to come up to Trichinopoly. To this part—the first part of the great project—Raghoonath Rao was posted to acquire the necessary lands. There were no proper legal facilities in those days for acquiring private lands for public purposes; the Land Acquisition Act had not yet been dreamt of. By a rare degree of prudence and tactfulness Raghoonath Rao succeeded at last in discharging the difficult task entrusted to him to the entire satisfaction of all parties concerned. Sir Charles Trevelyan, the then Governor of Madras, was so much pleased with his work that when troubles arose later on in connection with the acquisition of lands for the Tungabhadra Canal Project, he sent for Raghoonath Rao and requested him, as a personal favour, to proceed to Kurnool to set matters right there. On his consenting to do as desired, Sir Charles authorised him to draw direct upon the Treasury and invested him with full plenary powers in all other respects. Thus armed, Raghoonath Rao proceeded to Kurnool at once and succeeded, by a series of conciliatory measures, in acquiring the lands required for the Canal Project. Meanwhile, a change in the Governorship of Madras had occurred. Sir Charles Trevelyan resigned office in consequence of difference over the question of income-tax and had been succeeded by Sir William Denison. Sir William was as much satisfied with Raghoonath Rao's work as Sir Charles Trevelyan had been, more especially as the work in Kurnool was expected to end even in bloodshed.

On his return from Kurnool, Raghoonath Rao was posted to Trichinopoly as Treasury Deputy Collector and as Land Commission Officer. In the latter capacity he did much useful work on behalf of the great Srirangam temple. This work endeared him to the people and to the Collector of the district Mr. Agnew. Meanwhile, Mr. Raghoonath Rao was, at his own request, transferred to Coimbatore as Deputy Collector and District Registrar of Assurances. He, however, did not long remain at Coimbatore. The Government of Lord Napier and Ettrick saw through a conspiracy hatched up against so dutiful and honest an officer of Government as Raghoonath Rao, and to mark their appreciation of his conduct transferred him to Madras as Head-quarters Deputy Collector. The Income-tax Act had just been passed and come into operation for the first time in Madras. To Raghoonath Rao was entrusted the work of assessing and collecting it in Madras city—a work as difficult as it was delicate. Mostly taxes are disliked and perhaps no tax is more cordially disliked for its highly inquisitional character as the income-tax. Raghoonath Rao, however, succeeded in the task to the entire satisfaction of both the tax-payers and the Government. A grateful Government showed its approbation of his conduct by appointing him to the Head Sheristadarship of the Madras Board of Revenue, the highest post then open to an Indian in the metropolis of Madras. Lord Napier himself personally liked him so much that on the eve of his departure he gave him his newly arrived copy of Ruskin's *Seven Lamps of Architecture* with his autograph signature in it. Lord Hobart, his successor, made him a Presidency Magistrate for the City of Madras and a J. P. and would have done more for him in the years to come if Raghoonath Rao had not been called away for work elsewhere.

DEWANSHIP OF INDORE

By this time Raghoonath Rao had attained to something more than mere local celebrity. In fact, he had come to be recognized as one of the ablest Indian officials in the Southern Presidency. His fame had preceded him to Northern India which he toured through in 1873. He visited *en route* Calcutta,

Delhi, Agra and Bombay. At Poona he was introduced to the late Maharajah Tukoji Holkar of Indore by his cousin the late Sir T. Madhava Rao, then Prime Minister of that State. The Maharajah, though peculiar in his temperament was so well impressed with him that he appointed him in 1875, with the approval of the Government of India, as Revenue Minister of Indore. And when Sir T. Madhava Rao vacated the Dewanship of Indore in order to assume the Regency of Baroda (in 1875), the then Maharajah selected Mr. Raghoonath Rao for the Dewanship of his State, which at that time was by no means a sinecure or a bed of roses. The then Holkar was a man of strong character, and had certain very definite notions about his dignity and powers as Ruler of Indore; and relations were not always as cordial as they might have been with the Governor-General's Agent in Central India, Sir Hugh Daly. But Mr. Raghoonath Rao won the confidence of the latter, and did as much as his position could to make matters run smoothly.

Mr. Raghoonath Rao's administration of Indore was marked by much ability, zeal and firmness. He was above board in his transactions and was recognised on all sides to be a thoroughly honourable minister. When King Edward VII visited Indore as Prince of Wales he had a long interview with Mr. Raghoonath Rao, and freely exchanged political views with regard to Native States, and presented the Dewan with a gold medal. In 1881 Mr. Raghoonath Rao reverted to the Madras Government Service, and in 1887, when the late Maharajah Holkar ascended the *musnad,* he requested Mr. Raghoonath Rao once more to assume the Dewanship of Indore. Mr. Raghoonath Rao was now in an even more trying and delicate position than on the occasion of his previous Dewanship. The late Holkar—to put it mildly—was a Prince of peculiar temperament. He also held some very distinct views as to his powers and dignity, and at times would assume an impossible attitude. The Government of India naturally did not view many of his proceedings with approval, and frequently relations became strained with Sir Lepel Griffin, the Governor-General's Agent in Central India. Raghoonath Rao's tact and ability were now severely taxed. Sir Lepel Griffin entertained a high opinion of him and reposed great confidence in him; and Mr. Raghoonath Rao was able to conduct political business and internal State affairs as well as was possible under the circumstances. In 1888, however, he relinquished his Dewanship, and declined to re-accept it on subsequent offers being made to him by the Maharajah. Among the many reforms he introduced into the administration of Indore may be mentioned the introduction of a Penal Code, a Code of Criminal Procedure and a Code of Civil Procedure, all of which are still in force.

PUBLIC WORK AT MADRAS

Raghoonath Rao shortly afterwards reverted to the service of the Madras Government but he did not long remain in his old office of Head Sheristadar. In April 1888, he retired from the service on a pension of Rs. 5,000 *per annum*, the highest then allowed to an uncovenanted officer. At this time he was only 57 years of age, and had still much strength and vigour left in him. He settled down first at Mylapore—Madras—and then about 1894 removed himself to Kumbakonam, his family seat, from whence he unceasingly worked for the public good. His work during the next thirty years or so may be described as the work of a man who loved his country. It proved invaluable to its progress in almost every direction. In social matters as in political, in religious as in temporal affairs, he stood for advance. Though a Hindu of Hindus, he was no crude believer in effete dogmas and superstitions. Learned himself in Sanskrit, he probed rampant social evils and found remedies for them in consonance with the received opinions of orthodoxy. Therein he differed from reformers who stand for radical changes of the root and branch type. He was, however, not merely a "national" reformer but also a "rational" reformer. He stood out for commonsense in reform matters, while making every allowance for the orthodox to come, if they chose, by the back door of Shastraic texts and formulæ. He, however, believed in what he said and did. He was not a radical, if by radical we mean a revolutionary. He was no friend of uprooters of Hindu society or the foundations on which it is built. At the same time, he was not a reactionary of that strange type who loves a thing because it is sacrosanct with age. As a pioneer in the field of social reform Raghoonath Rao found it both right and necessary to keep as far as possible to the society to which he belonged. That was why he was gentle in his methods, and in fact he quoted chapter and verse to his opponents. His opponents were of the orthodox type, and it is noteworthy, he retained their respect if he did not always win their approval or adhesion to the cause that lay nearest to his heart. But his spirit was far too indomitable to yield to mere clamour or to interested opposition. The position he took in connection with the Age of Consent Bill shows this in an unmistakable fashion. There he had to meet not merely orthodox opposition but the opposition as well of genuine leaders of conservative Hindu society. The heated controversy which took place over this simple measure shows how far the attitude taken up generally by Raghoonath Rao in regard to Hindu social reform was just in his days. It also shows how cautious he was in his methods as a pioneer. For this the Hindu community owes him a deep debt of gratitude. Raghoonath Rao was convinced of the justice of the Bill. He was opposed by men of greater standing, of greater dialectical skill than himself, and even greater standing as well in Hindu society, but nothing daunted he held to his position as only *he* could. That was the man as a reformer. Come what may, he said; he would not yield in a matter of that kind. Though his cousin, the great

Sir T. Madhava Rao, took a different view, he agreed to differ even from him. It is this attitude that endeared him to progressive India.

RELIGIOUS REFORM

Raghoonath Rao was as anxious for religious as for social reform. He lived the life of a typically religious Hindu. He read the holy scriptures of the Hindus and wrote up small catechisms and books for children. He compiled short story books based on the *Bhagavata* for boys and girls. He called his religion the "Aryan" religion. He believed that Hinduism was an all-embracing religion; and that in its fold all persons of every nationality could easily come in. He held too that the fundamental concepts of Hinduism were quite in keeping with science, and that the religious philosophy of the Hindus was something unknown to Europe. He was also of opinion that Chiristianity, great religion as it is, is at best only one aspect of Hinduism. This, he said, in a philosophical sense. He was no doubt thinking of the personal relationship between God and man when he made this remark. He not only believed these things, but had the boldness to frankly put forward these things again and again in his public utterances. The occasions for public speaking were many for him. Not a day passed without his presiding at some function—religious or social, political or educational—and at these he spoke straight to the hearts of the people what he thought and believed.

POLITICAL REFORM

In politics he was, in modern terminology, a "Moderate." But he was no stickler at old things because they were old in politics any more than in religious or social matters and where he felt a change was necessary, he made people in power know it. He was one of the originators not only of the Indian Social Conference but also of the Indian National Congress, in both of which he took an active part for a long time. He wrote on the questions of the day in the papers. Not a day passed, in fact, without a letter from him. In this he resembled his cousin Sir T. Madhava Rao. Both believed in propagandistic work. Both gave out freely their views and experiences for the benefit of their countrymen and the Government. Questions of every kind attracted Raghoonath Rao's attention from single stalk plantation of paddy seedlings to the proposed reforms of Lord Morley and on each of these he wrote to the Press. He wrote briefly, clearly and concisely. He was an ideal newspaper writer. There was little verbosity in what he wrote; what he wrote was to the point and went straight to the heart of the reader. That was one reason why no newspaper editor rejected his letters, and why few, if any at all, missed the attention of the reading public.

LAND REVENUE PROBLEMS

Though he wrote on almost every subject of any current interest, he had specialised, so to speak, in some particular subjects. These were briefly—the

Land Revenue Policy of the Government of India, the economic condition of the country, the education of the people, establishment of agricultural banks, the organisation by the people themselves of their talents and resources for their own political advance, the separation of the judicial from the executive functions, etc. On these he spoke and wrote with a sanity which won for him approbation even from Government. It is not possible to go into all these matters here at length, but it is necessary to refer to a few at least of these to indicate the tenacity of purpose with which Raghoonath Rao fought for progress in the political sphere. His interest in the agrarian question was great. It started with his career and stood unabated till his death. When still a young man, he rendered signal service by exposing the use of torture in the Southern Presidency and to prevent the spoliation of minor inams in the Tanjore district. He was a true friend of the ryot and fought for justice for him all through his strenuous life. On the eve of the departure of Sir Charles Trevelyan (June 1860) he wrote a long and admirable letter to him on the land tenure of Tanjore and the *mirasidars'* right in the land. This pamphlet he reprinted in 1890 for free circulation. It is a pamphlet full of quaint information drawn up in a historical and argumentative fashion. Raghoonath Rao develops his position in a masterly fashion and shows that *mirasi* right in Tanjore is vested in the *mirasidar* and not in the sovereign. The genesis of this letter is rather curious. Sir

Charles wanted to introduce, if he had continued in office, a settlement in Tanjore by which landed property might be rendered secure, interference of Government servants with the *mirasidars* avoided and just opportunity for augmenting the Government revenues lost. He asked Raghoonath Rao for his views. The result was the letter referred to herein. In this letter, which is of great interest even now, he proposed a full scheme of settlement which (is it necessary to state ?) has not so far received the attention it deserves. That is one reason why Tanjore has been losing its name—and what is worse its tenantry as well. "I beg to assure Your Excellency," said Raghoonath Rao in 1860, "that my proposal, if carried out would not tend to lower the Government revenue, would make it certain and permanent, would make the landlords wealthy and independent and of great assistance to Government." Sir Charles unhappily left the Presidency immediately after the despatch of this letter to him. He got himself stranded over the Income-tax Bill. On his way home, he wrote to Raghoonath Rao a letter which shows what he would have done if he had continued at the helm of affairs at Madras for some time longer. "On your main point," he wrote from Galle on 27th June, 1860, "I entirely agree with you. Where landed property is found to exist I would do all I could to confirm and develop it. And where it does not exist every necessary means should be taken to create it. I see no objection to the arrangements proposed by you for the completion of the land revenue settlement of Tanjore." If Raghoonath Rao's views had been adopted, Tanjore would have fared differently in recent years.

LAND ASSESSMENTS IN MADRAS

In later days Raghoonath Rao returned again and again to the agrarian question. In the controversy over land assessments in Madras, during Lord Curzon's time, he figured prominently. The letters he published on this subject in the Madras newspapers are typical of the clear thinking and close reasoning he always displayed in his polemical efforts. He convinced the Madras Government of the utter impossibility of their sticking strictly to the theory of their settlement. Even so stout a champion of official figures and ways as the *Pioneer* found it impossible to defend Government.

Raghoonath Rao returned to this subject again. In 1908, as President of the Tanjore District Association, he thus referred to it in a public address presented to Sir Arthur Lawley then Governor of Madras :—

> While the India Government has relied upon the statement of the Madras reports that the land-tax represents one half of the twenty per cent. of the gross produce, the settlement records show that for wet lands it amounts to not less than 16 per cent. thereof. Owing to the incorrectness of the estimate of gross outturns of land, the profit calculated is raised considerably higher leaving very little to the agriculturist and disabling him and reducing his staying power whenever there is a failure of rains.

He referred to the same question in his evidence before the Decentralisation Commission. He there explained his position briefly by saying that the share taken by Government in Tanjore, according to the Re-settlement record, was proved to be 28 per cent. " In reality, " he added " it is not less than 50 per cent. of the gross produce for, if the gross produce was over-estimated, cultivation expenses were under-estimated and the net profit thereby rose to a fictitious figure and half of it was fixed as the Government share or assessment or land-tax."

Raghoonath Rao did not leave matters there. He went into the question as to how this had happened. How came this to be? What contributed to this juggling with figures? Mr. Raghoonath Rao tried to probe this question. He set it down to the Secretariat system. He thought it was becoming more and more the fashion in the Secretariats to view public questions apart from the interests and feelings of the people whom they vitally affected. "They very often," he said solemnly, " consider matters, irrespective of the consideration of the results affecting the good feeling and happiness of the people. The Government is certainly impersonal. The result of the administration is judged upon its capacity to raise larger revenues." Raghoonath Rao attacked this soulless, impersonal sytem of Government—call it what you will. He was so true a friend of India that he wished the Government of India to be not a mere machine but a true King in the land—a King endowed with eyes to see and ears to hear so that it may act rightly, justly and equitably with the masses of the country, who are among the poorest of the poor in the world.

INDIAN FAMINES

Closely connected with land assessment is the question of famines. Raghoonath Rao held the view that "a fixed land tenure and remunerative public works will alone save India from the occurrence of future famines." This view he came to after a wide and varied experience of thirty years' work as a revenue officer in some of the best districts of Madras. To this subject he had devoted a pamphlet of some 26 pages, in which he set out his theme in his own simple but striking manner. He wrote this pamphlet on the eve of the great famine of 1876, from the effects of which some parts of India have not yet recovered. Twenty-three years later India experienced another famine. Then he turned his thoughts once more to the subject.

In discussing the question at length, Raghoonath Rao reverted to the question of land assessments and showed its bearing on the famine problem. He developed his position in the following paragraphs which we have reproduced here :—

I hold that until property in land is acknowledged and upheld by Government, the Indian soil will *not* be improved, despite the model farms, the Agricultural Department of the Government of India, Agricultural Gazettes and similar works. On this point, an eminent English nobleman, Sir Charles Trevelyan, says "Where landed property is found to exist, I would do all I could to confirm and develop it; and where it does not exist, every necessary means should be taken to create it." What has been the practice? The Anglo-Indian Government has been systematically destroying every right in connection with property in land, notwithstanding the repeated orders of the Home authorities to the contrary.

The process of extinction of property in land, successfully commenced in the beginning of the nineteenth century, has been steadily progressing and many of the settlements which had been considered permanent, with or without evidence, has been declared non-permanent. Hence the apathy of every one having anything to do with cultivation, to give back to the soil what is taken from it and the charge against the past generations of "ignorance and recklessness" is not deserved by them. They fully knew, and the present generation fully understands, the theory of the exhaustion of the soil. They certainly know how to manure their field and why they should do so; but they would not apply the remedy, for they do not expect to be benefited thereby.

To remedy this evil, we must strike at the root. The largest source of revenue in India has always been and still unfortunately is land. It should be most openly and solemnly declared to be private property subject only to payment of tax to Government.

The tax should be declared to consist of a fixed proportion of its net produce, that is, a fixed quantity of grain. This fixed proportion should not exceed 1/3 of the net produce, the other 2/3rds being left to the landlord. The market value of this 1/3 should be collected as the land-tax. Convert the value of the *fixed* portion of the *fixed* net produce at the average of the market rates of the past as many years as you please, provided you exclude the extraordinary years Fix the average rate thus obtained, as the rate of commutation for the coming year. Omit the first year's rate of the last series of years, and add in its place the rate of the last year. Then, again, find out the average. If this average does not considerably differ from the last average, make no alteration in the commutation rate for the coming year; but if it materially differ, then adopt the average rate as the rate for the next year. This done, the ryot will know what he has to pay to the Government and will feel a desire to increase the produce of the land in hopes of appropriating all the increase to himself which he obtains by his labour and investment. Inconsiderable fluctuations in the market price should be omitted from calculation. What is inconsiderable should be once for all declared by Government. I would declare any fluctuation within 25 per cent. either way as inconsiderable."

If this is so, why do natives of India invest their money in land? To that Raghoonath Rao has his answer to give. They invest in land not for profit but simply to secure it against robbery. Investment in stocks and shares is still foreign to this country and the reason for it is the want of credit facilities, which, again, is due to want of a sense of security in the people in anything other than land, which is tangibly immovable and cannot be lost. If this reasoning is not correct, "why," asks Raghoonath Rao, " is not British capital expended in the purchase of large tracts of land in Madras and Bombay?" If assessments were really as light as stated this would have been the case, but as they are not, the thing has never come to pass. Coffee and tea lands, it is needless to add, stand on an altogether different footing.

FOREST ADMINISTRATION

Still another subject in which Raghoonath Rao took much interest was forest administration. Times without number he referred to this subject in his letters to the Press. He held the view—the view promulgated by the Government of India—that minor forests are intended for communal and agricultural purposes and ought to be conserved by the Revenue Department quite independently of the Forest Department as such. This simple and just rule has not been maintained in most districts much to the detriment to the rights of the agricultural community. Its rights and privileges have been, he says in one place, systematically ignored, its pasture lands and its cultivation implements have been taken away and its communal property denied to it. The result has been, he adds in another pathetic sentence, very great injury to the agricultural population in the shape of loss of cattle, fuel, grass, green manures, etc. A juster view has prevailed in Madras, and the Forest Panchayat system has been the result of the persistent agitation carried on in the matter by Raghoonath Rao and men of his stamp in the years gone by.

MISCELLANEOUS MATTERS

Upon other subjects he held views equally definite. The following sums up many letters of his to the public Press during half of a century of his retired life :—

> The land assessment is too heavy. The penal provisions of the salt-tax are cruel to the poorest of the people. For the sake of the Abkari revenue, drunkenness is increased. The income-tax is badly administered. The water-rate laws are not just and are enforced unduly harshly. The Land Encroachment Act is a piece of legislation believed by all people to be perfectly unnecessary and subversive of all the rights of people long enjoyed by them. The rules for the management of Hindu religious institutions require modification as shown by the experience of the past half a century.

One other thing deserves to be noted in this conection. Both study and habit had made him a constructive critic. He never tried to pull down for the mere fun of doing so; he also tried to build on the vacant spot. If he said that desire for increased Abkari revenue increased drunkenness, he also pointed that the revenue might be got without recourse to heroic remedies. He held that customs and excise duties may be raised as much to prevent drunkenness as to augment revenue, while local option may be allowed to the people. He strongly held to the view that shops near places of worship and public instruction should not be allowed. These are yet far too common, and if that is so, there seems to be point in his observation that local option is necessary to check this unfortunate tendency of allowing the haphazard location of shops. Before leaving this subject, it might be well to add that Raghoonath Rao's letters and correspondence show that he felt fairly often that the British Government in India ran its machinery on absolutely safe lines, though always timid and afraid, in consequence, of change. It is inferable also that he felt that it somewhat partook of the character of a " soulless bureaucracy " so much so that he often sighed for the good old ways of the " defunct East India Company. " He was no " impatient idealist " of the modern type. He felt far too keenly all the same that things must change fast enough for progress all round, if Government was to keep abreast of the growth of public opinion in the country.

GOVERNMENT BY THE PEOPLE

This brings us to a rather important point. How far did Raghoonath Rao believe in representative institutions? Did he believe in anything like " a democratic Government for India ? " Did he think that the educated classes did not represent the masses? Did he want class or communal representation or a representation based on wider grounds or principles, such as a high property qualification, etc. ? Did he think that Christians and Mohammedans should be swamped by Hindus or the latter should invariably yield to the clamours of the minorities? These are all interesting questions for the simple reason that answers to them would show what an old world Indian friend of the British Government and an unsparing critic of his own countrymen thought of them of all. Raghoonath Rao, to start with, never thought that the Government of his time was caring as much for the opinion of respected Indian leaders as he thought they should. On one occasion he said:—

> At present, the Government of India has great difficulty in making their measures and motives generally understood and in correcting erroneous opinions of people thereon, a fact well known to the people as well as to the rulers. It is absolutely necessary that this difficulty should be removed as speedily as possible. The best means to remove it, is no doubt, to obtain the opinions on administrative measures and proposals for action of those qualified to advise Government. Government used to do so invariably about 30 years ago. This process has fallen into disuse of late. The formality of this process may have continued partially, but the weight which used to be attached to the opinions elicited has been vanishing. Hence the difficulty above referred to has been on the increase. I entirely agree with the sentiment expressed in paragraph 4 of the said letter, *viz.* "Such advice and opinion as are thus obtained are the indispensable foundation upon which good administration is built up, and the regular consultation of persons qualified to give them is part of the necessary procedure of Government." This is no new idea. It was the principle of the ancient Hindu rulers, well known to the people and fully appreciated by both the rulers and the ruled. With the crusade against the village governments, systematically commenced a generation ago and against the *Mirasi*, the tie which used to bind the ruled and the rulers has been loosened and they now do not know each other.

There is considerable truth in that grave complaint of his as any one who knows the ancient history of this land can bear testimony to. He criticised for the same reason the Indian National Congress organization severely for beginning at the top instead of at the bottom. He was for councils from the village upwards to the Central Government. He was not for communal or class representation as such, though he was for "making liberal concessions to Mohammedans and Christians". He was for a high property qualification and he favoured the election of "specially literate" men. So high a value he set on education that he was prepared to declare a graduate of any University qualified for voting, irrespective of property qualification.

In the highest council of all, namely the Legislative Council, he did not favour an official majority. He was one of the few who severely criticised paragraph 20 in Sir Harold Stuart's (Secretary to the Government of India) letter on Lord Morley's Reform proposals to the local Governments. In that paragraph the Government of India's view is thus expressed:—

> The general principle to be borne in mind is, as already stated, that the widest representation should be given to classes, races and interests, subject to the condition that an official majority must be maintained.

This paragraph caught the eye of Raghoonath Rao, who thus cauterized it:—

> I am unable to understand the principle, the necessity and the wisdom of the official majority in the Legislative Councils. Rather than maintain it and make the Council a farce, it is better to make a rule that in cases in which the Government may not have a majority of votes, it shall carry out the views of the minority on the responsibility of the head of Government. Such a rule would be a valuable one releasing several important officers of Government from attendance at the Council, neglecting their own duties for which the people pay them handsome remunerations, and sitting in the Council room, imprisoned and directed to hold up their hands when called upon by the

Government to do so. We have no party government in India. The majority do not get the plums of service. The declaration now made that a law was passed by the Legislature is a misnomer and is really not true.

Later on in the same letter he adds :—

The Governor may have the option to adopt the views of the majority or of the minority as he thinks fit. In this scheme, the contrivance for having an official majority disappears and the stigmas that Legislative Councils are nothing but a farce will disappear.

INTRREST IN EDUCATION

Raghoonath Rao's interest in education was great. He was the friend of the aspiring student. He was the guide of the helplesss youth who knew none in the city to guide him. He was the monitor of many a promising boy. When he saw a boy on the beach, at school or at play, he tarried a while and spoke to him. That was a habit he shared with his great cousin Raja Sir T. Madhava Rao. He was the founder in reality of what is now the Kumbakonam College. It grew out of a small class which was opened by Raghoonath Rao for giving instruction in English to the sons of his friends and neighbours. An English public hospital was also established at Kumbakonam, mainly through his exertions. In after life, he never declined an invitation to preside at a school function. He religiously accepted such duty and discharged it faithfully and conscientiously. He preached the gospel of duty for duty's sake even to the young. He described it as the highest ideal to be striven for in this world ; the highest religion that the Indo-Aryans had evolved. The boy that passed under his eye never forgot him. His spell was cast on him for ever; it never broke. Such was his influence on successive generations of the youth of Southern India that it might, with justice be said that he moulded it to no small extent. Much of the social advance that Madras has seen during the past thirty years may be set down to some extent at least to Raghoonath Rao's influence on its youth.

GOVERNMENT'S APPRECIATION

One like Raghoonath Rao could not but catch the eye of the rulers of the land. They showed marked regard for him and his opinions. Special interviews were accorded to him; special visits were paid to him and special requisitions for his views on current questions were sent to him by the highest in the land almost throughout the whole period of his retired life. He was made a "Dewan Bahadur" a title which fitted him admirably and stuck to him admirably too. For once the title fitted the man and the man the title. He was invited to give evidence before the Royal Commission on Decentralisation, which he did in a strikingly original manner. The distinction of C. S. I. was then conferred on him.

Sir Arthur Lawley at the investiture ceremony, unhesitatingly described him as, in the opinion of European and Indian, official and non-official, "the true friend of India."

He was also nominated a member of the Madras Legislative Council. As a legislator, he did in a short while much useful work by drawing the attention of

Government to certain anomalies, for which due attention was secured, if not exactly promised. His colleagues in Council treated him with the utmost respect and the Government felt that in him they had a true friend of the people and an honourable critic of Government.

GENERAL TRAITS AND CHARACTERISTICS

Kind and courteous, accessible alike to the rich and the poor, the cultured and the uncultured, Raghoonath Rao led a simple and unostentatious life. Rising at 3 A.M. every day, he performed his self-appointed tasks with a regularity which, perhaps more than any other, kept up the vigour of his body and mind practically unimpaired to the last day of his life. Besides discharging his various public duties—including in later days the duties of President of the District Association of Tanjore, Vice-President of the Agricultural Association at Kumbakonam, etc.—he managed a large estate on which he paid Rs. 10,000 annually to Government, besides a large number of charitable institutions, some founded by his father, and some by himself and consisting of *chattrams*, travellers' bungalows, temples and *agraharams*. He spent annually a large amount on public and charitable purposes. His charity was non-sectarian. He was the true friend of the needy and the indigent of every caste, creed and community. He was, in a word, mindful alike of the interests of the Hindu, Mahommedan, Panchama and the poor.

AS PREACHER, TEACHER AND CITIZEN

Raghoonath Rao preached as he went and taught as he spoke. He was a true citizen of the world. Though he said hard things, there was no rancour behind his words. There was the true spirit of sincerity about what fell from him. Throughout his long career, there was never the slightest suspicion against his integrity. His private life was a simple, unblemished one, and he was held in the highest esteem by people everywhere in Southern India. He had age, experience and wealth at his command, and his habits of life gave him ample opportunities to be of benefit to his fellow-beings. He fought their battles for them in the social, religious and political fields. He stood for their rights with a tenacity of purpose which surprised those who had known him only in his gentler moments. And he argued the case for them with a wealth of detail and a richness of illustration that anticipitated the objections of their adversaries. One like him could not but be the beloved of his people. He was their "Grand Old Man of Southern India."

"Perhaps few of you have been privileged to see Dewan Bahadur Raghoonath Rao," said the late Mr. Ranade in his address to the Social Conference at Lahore in December 1893. "He is the father and the patriarch of this movement. The respect due to age and rank and education is sanctified in his case by the charm of a highly spiritual life, a temper so sweet, a heart so warm and sympathetic, that I am not exaggerating when I say that many of you might well undertake a pilgrimage all the way to Madras to see him once in your life."

AS PUBLICIST AND AUTHOR

Raghoonath Rao could never sit idle when there was need to act. He spoke, wrote, and acted as and when required. Early in life he cultivated the habit of writing what he thought worth keeping a record of. Some of his pamphlets contain shrewd observations, some others show the close reasoning he employed in fighting his case. One on *Organization* is a most impressive one. On the religious side, he wrote commentaries on the *Bhagavad Gita*, the *Bhagavata* and the *Rig Veda*. Pamphlets on social reform he wrote many. One of these on *Hindu Marriages* attained more than local fame. Others on sea voyage, widow re-marriage, infant marriage, etc., created great stir. His connection with the Madras Press was an honourable one. He was one of the first to start a weekly newspaper in that town. It was the one that in later days developed into the *Hindu* of to-day. He wrote in a simple, chaste and crisp style. He hit hard when the occasion required it. When on the contrary praise was deserved, he never denied it to any one—no, not even to Government. He wrote daily, nay hourly, to the Madras Press on every conceivable topic. He was one of the most hard working, thinking politicians that India possessed in recent years. He was never wearied of work. He would have been most miserable if he had nothing to do. But that was a contingency that never occurred in his case. For he worked as he sat, walked or talked. In conversation, he was wise, witty and polite. Wilfrid Blunt in his Reminiscences wrote admiringly of his wit and his conversational powers: "His conversation might have been that of a Socrates whom in person he much resembled." Recalling the interesting interview he had with Raghoonath Rao, Blunt wrote: "I wish I could recall all his good stories, all his wise opinions and illustrations. There are not a dozen men in the House of Commons who could hold their own with him in talk." He could give a point to any one in any walk of life. He was ready with shrewd observations. He was rarely outwitted. Though frank himself to a degree, he never could be taken in by the pretended frankness of an opponent. He could see through such game quickly and make short work of him by a few sharp questions going to the root of the matter. As a magistrate he was as much feared as respected and loved.

HOME LIFE

In his home life, he was simple. A more loving husband there could not have been in Hindu India during his time. Mrs. Raghoonath Rao was a lady rich in resource, full of the gentleness of her sect, and equal to the best that was expected of her by her husband. They were a couple universally liked. They both lived to a long age and both died universally mourned. The wife predeceased the husband by a year or so. Raghoonath Rao, though he lost in her his help-mate, took the event as became a true Indian. He himself continued in his customary mode of life till he was called away at Kumbakonam on the 3rd May 1912. He died, full of honours and years, in the plenitude of his fame, universally respected and deeply mourned by all who knew him.

Gourishanker Oodeshanker

JUDGED by any standard the name of Gourishanker Oodeshanker deserves an honoured place among indigenous statesmen. Men like Sir Salar Jung and Sir T. Madhava Rao found their opportunities in such first class Indian States like Hyderabad, Mysore or Travancore and their operations on an extensive scale naturally attracted wide attention and they worked more or less in a blaze of public recognition. But in the minor States of Feudatory India there were not wanting men whose labours on behalf of their States were no less arduous. They were destined to work quietly and unostentatiously without attracting that notice which is sometimes the prerogative of sheer magnitude. But both in the complexity of their problems and in the need for delicate handling of situations, big and small States are alike. Gourishanker found the State of Bhavnagar in chaos when he entered service in the twenties of the last century, and he left it after fifty-seven years of unbroken service, a well ordered and prosperous State. Such devoted service to a State coupled with great tact in management of affairs deserves to be recorded in any book of Indian Statesmen.

Page 352.

GOURISHANKER OODESHANKER

his native place and received the usual education of those days. At the age of seventeen he entered the service of the Bhavnagar Durbar, being employed in the Political Department on a salary of Rs. 25 a month. It was not long before he attracted the notice of the head of the department, Desai Shevakaram Rajaram who was so impressed with the work and ability of Gourishanker that he appointed him as his confidential assistant. In this office practically the whole revenue management of a division came into his hands. As good luck would have it he had not to wait long to prove his mettle. The story of his brilliant career and his successive achievements is told with engaging vividness in Mr. Sorabji Jihangir's "Representative Men of India." About this time, says Mr. Sorabji,

> Some disputes arose amongst the Kathi Kermans, a lawless tribe inhabiting the Kundla Pergunna, and, as a result, the country was laid waste, villages were destroyed, and the peaceable peasant population of the country put to the sword. Those were days when the duties of officials were not confined to mere routine labour, but when every man was obliged to carry arms, and to know how to use them if occasion required. At this critical juncture Mr. Gourishanker was not found wanting. He connected himself with the *Sebandi*, the military force of the State, kept watch night and day, and acted so vigorously against the disturbers of the peace that quiet was soon restored and the collection of the revenue was secured.

The services he rendered on this occasion recommended him to the notice of the then reigning Chief, H. H. Vijayashingji, who directly appointed him to conduct an important appeal in the British Court at Surat. The facts of the case are worth noting as they have an important bearing on the future of the State. They may be narrated thus in the words of Mr. Sorabji himself:—

> In the declining years of Vakatasingbji, the father of His Highness Vijayasbingji, the British Government had deprived the State of its civil and criminal jurisdiction over tho villages, including the capital itself, which paid tribute to the Peshwa; and in 1816 a regulation was passed by which the Chief himself was made amenable to the civil and criminal laws of the British Government. This change in the status of the Chief seriously affected his influence with his subjects, and involved him in troubles which were most galling to a man in his position. One effect of the loss of jurisdiction was, that he was compelled to defend suits brought against him in British Courts by his own subjects Those who are acquainted with the value attached by Native Chiefs to personal dignity, will readily understand how irritating this provision must have been, and how reluctantly the Chief must have acknowledged the power of the British authorities to try matters in which he was concerned. But his feelings had to give way to the force of circumstances, and thus it happened that a Bhavnagar merchant brought an action against him in the Civil Court at Ahmedabad for the sum of Rs. 11,77,500, alleged to have been lent to the Maharaja Vakatasingbji. The case was heard in 1825 before Mr. Jones, the Zillah Judge of Ahmedabad, who passed a decree in favour of the Chief. Against this decision the plaintiff in the case appealed in the Saddar Adaulat at Surat, and when the question of jurisdiction was minutely gone into, the Chief's case was so ably advocated by Mr. Gourishanker, that in the end the British Government was compelled to pass a special Regulation by virtue of which the suit was dismissed.

In this connection Gourishanker had to stay in Surat for three years, during which time he looked after the interests of Bhavnagar in various other ways as well. Apart from the proceedings in court he had also to settle some disputes which had arisen regarding the relations of the Bhavnagar State with the British Government; and he was employed by the Thakore Saheb to conduct the correspondence in this matter. He was also entrusted with the revenue management of the Daskroi Mahal and he filled this office with distinction for four years from 1830.

Amongst other matters he was charged with the settlement of some troubles which had arisen owing to the ravages of the Khasia Kolis of the Mahawa Pergunna. The Bhavnagar Durbar was desirous of expelling these turbulent individuals from the State, and with that end in view Mr. Gourishanker was despatched to Bombay to seek the aid and co-operation of the British Government. He stayed in Bombay for about six months, and so well fulfilled his mission that soon after his return to Bhavnagar, towards the close of 1839, he was appointed Assistant Karbhari or Dewan of the State, which position he occupied until 1846, being principally engaged during the time in settling disputes arising between the political and regulation districts. In 1847 he was appointed Dewan.

As Dewan of Bhavnagar Gourishanker had to deal with a multitude of cases each demanding his immediate attention. They are all told with vivid impressiveness by Mr. Sorabji from whose sketch of Gourishanker we have taken the liberty to draw at some length. As was the case with many Indian States of those days the Bhavnagar Durbar maintained a large force of Arab mercenaries for the protection of its territories. These troops were a source of great expense and contributed in no small degree to the financial embarrassment which called for Gourishanker's attention when he assumed office.

Some years previously, the Thakore Vakatsinghji had passed a guarantee to Nasir, the *jemadar* of the force, for a very large sum of money, and the pay of the troops being also greatly in arrears owing to the want of funds, an enormous debt had accumulated. In 1836 the descendants of Nasir, finding that there was no chance of the debt being liquidated, adopted the bold course of seizing by force the Mhowa district, one of the fairest portions of the State, as security for their claim. The Durbár was too much in the power of Arab adventurers to offer any effectual resistance to this lawless proceeding; and the usurpers were enabled to establish their supremacy so effectually, that even the State officer located in the district was continually subjected to all kinds of irritation and insult at their hands.

Nor were the Arabs the only persons to whom the State was indebted.

For years the Durbar had been incurring debts to various people, until at length the solvency of the State became seriously affected. In addition to the claim of the Arabs, which amounted to an enormous sum, as much as Rs. 16,00,000 was due in other quarters, principally to money-lenders and merchants who had made advances to the rulers of Bhavnagar.

Amongst many things which tended to increase the financial embarrassments under which the province laboured, there was a drain of about Rs. 1,500 a month from the State Exchequer on account of no less than seventy mohosuls, or summonses, served upon it by the Political Agent for as many claims and suits, which were either pending or had been adjudged against the State. The payment of these fees was not only an indignity, but in the impecunious condition of the territory it was a real hardship. No sooner had Mr. Gourishanker assumed the reins of office than he directed his attention to these and other evils under which the administration suffered.

The formidable claims of the Arabs were examined, and immediate steps were taken to relieve the State of a difficulty which at one time threatened its very existence, beside being a tanding menace to the Thakore's authority. By degrees this large debt was paid off, and in 1851 Mr. Gourishanker had the satisfaction of seeing the Mhowa district restored to the uninterrupted authority of the Prince. The other creditors of the Government were also dealt with, and in the course of a few years their claims were all either paid off or amicably settled, and thus the State was rescued from a very serious pecuniary position, which if it had been allowed to continue might have resulted in the interference of the British Government.

While engaged in all these transactions Gourishanker did not lose sight of the important question of the Mohosul fees which were a constant source of anxiety. Colonel Lang, the then Political Agent of Kathiawar, was officially addressed on the subject, and he was so impressed with the justice of the application made to him, that he withdrew all the mohosuls, and the State was thenceforth permanently freed from a distasteful and vexatious levy, which had given rise to much annoyance and difficulty.

These settlements were important achievements tending to free the State from the serious complications into which it had fallen. There was another matter more important still. Kathiawar, as Mr. Sorabji rightly points out, is an aggregation of petty principalities, the territories of which overlap and mingle with one another in a way often difficult to know where one State begins and the other ends. The Bhavnagar State, for instance " is surrounded by seven hundred different boundaries and boundary questions have ever formed a fruitful subject of dispute in the history of the State." Gourishanker after great trouble and years of toil succeeded in the end in obtaining a clear and permanent definition of the boundaries.

Yet another matter which called for Gourishanker's immediate attention was with reference to the claim prepared by H. H. The Nawab of Junagad of certain villages, seventy six in number, which are in absolute possession of Bhavnagar. After lengthened investigations Major le Grand Jacob reported in favour of Junagad. Bhavnagar was ordered to restore some of the villages, but subsequently the Bombay Government—deeming it inadvisable to compel Bhavnagar to give up the jurisdiction which it had so long enjoyed over this territory—directed the Political Agent to make a valuation of the revenue of the villages, with a view to the payment of a subsidy of an equal amount by Bhavnagar to Junagad. Gourishanker represented the Bhavnagar state in the making of this valuation and succeeded in convincing Col. Lang, the Political Agent, that Junagad's claim was inadmissible.

Eventually, through Colonel Lang's mediation, the subject was referred to arbitration, and a subsidy of Rs. 9,000 only was adjudged in favor of Junagad, and the Junagad's claim for the said villages was finally disallowed. By this transaction, mainly through Mr. Gourishankar's exertions, territory at present yielding a revenue of three lakhs of rupees was preserved to Bhavnagar.

Another and even more successful achievement was carried through by Gourishanker in a similar matter. This question referred to a large portion of the Bhavnagar State, comprising 116 villages, which had been taken under British protection in 1815, owing to a misunderstanding of the act committed by a former Chief, through his over-zeal in the cause of the Hindu religion. Some years after his accession to office, the Dewan directed his efforts to the recovery of this territory, and with that end in view addressed repeated representations to the British authorities. The claims of the Bhavnagar Durbar for years met with no satisfactory response, but ultimately in 1866, during the Governorship of Sir Bartle Frere, this tract of country was restored to the Bhavnagar jurisdiction.

Gourishanker was mainly responsible for the many improvements effected in the State. Previous to 1856 there was not a school in the whole of Kathiawar worth the name. Over a dozen schools in the city of Bhavnagar itself and over a hundred in the whole State were started in his regime.

Other improvements effected in his regime deserve mention.

The Dewan also greatly improved the revenue system, and rendered eminent service to the poorer class of cultivators by doing away with many of the imposts which are exacted from cultivators in Native States under different pretences, and which, in the hands of unscrupulous officials, are a powerful means of oppression. A Survey establishment has been introduced under the superintendence of an able officer, and a survey of all the land in the State has been made on the British Government system. The judicial administration was also reconstituted during Mr. Gourishanker's tenure of office. A complete code of laws, constructed on the lines of the British Penal Code, but adapted to local customs and requirements, was modelled, and regular Courts were established. The police force was likewise put in an efficient condition, and dacoits, who had formerly defied the law with impunity, were run down and brought to justice. To Mr. Gourishanker was also due the establishment of an efficient and well organized gaol in Bhavnagar, the system of discipline observed being based on that in vogue in the gaols of the Presidency Town.

Mr. Sorabji, writes in high terms of Gourishanker's services to the City of Bhavnagar in particular which rapidly rose in importance as a commercial centre equipped with every advantage that the best modern city administration should give.

An efficient Public Works Department, established some years since by Mr. Gourishanker, and placed under the superintendence of a competent European engineer, was directed to provide the city with urgent requirements. One of the principal of these requirements was the provision of a plentiful water supply. This is brought from a river sixteen miles distant, by means of a canal, and it is stored in a large reservoir in the heart of the City, whence it is distributed to all quarters of the place. The department has also been employed in the construction of handsome and commodious buildings for the transaction of public business, of sewers, roads, and bridges, and of tanks, wells, bazaar, travellers' bungalows, and dharmsalas Dispensaries have also been established in the capital and principal district towns, which have done much towards improving the public health and alleviating suffering humanity.

Gourishanker's ability and integrity were duly appreciated by the British Government and on the death of H. H. Sir Juswuntsingji he was appointed joint administrator with a British Officer. For many years he was working in this office with marked success, securing the approbation of the Imperial Government as well as the subjects of the State.

In 1877 he was created a Companion of the Star of India, in recognition of his meritorious services. In handing the decoration to Mr. Gourishanker, the Political Agent, Mr. Peile, expressed his gratification that the insignia should be delivered at his hands "to a Minister whose ability and independence I have observed with respect during an official intercourse f more than eighteen years, and whose character, in its strength and sagacity, is a worthy object of study and emulation to the men of his order." Mr. Gourishanker also received a silver medal at the time of the Delhi Imperial Assemblage.

When, in 1879, increasing age and infirmities necessitated his retirement from the service of the State, he handed over his duties to his nephew, the late Mr. Samaldas Parmanandas, with the satisfaction of knowing that, mainly through his own exertions, the State had been, a generation before, rescued from a position of difficulty and no small danger, and placed on the firmest basis. He had been in the service of the Principality for over 57 years, and was associated with the reigns of four Chiefs.

Shortly before his death Gourishanker renounced the world in the way of orthodox Hindus and adopted the habit of a Sadhoo or Sanyasin.

Maharaja Sir Pratap Singh.*

A RAJPUT PRINCE

HIS HIGHNESS MAHARAJAHDHIRAJ Lieutenant-General Sir Pratap Singhji Saheb Bahadur, G.C.S.I., G.C.V.O., G.C.B., Knight of St. John of Jerusalem, L.L.D., D.C.L., A.D.C., to His Imperial Majesty the King-Emperor, Regent and President of the Regency Council, Marwar State Jodhpur, was the second son of Maharaja Takhat Singh and was born in the historic fort of Jodhpur in 1846. From his early boyhood he showed signs of uncommon courage, and was always fond of manly sports. He received his first education in Hindi, Urdu and Persian, and later cultivated a knowledge of English.

IN JAIPUR AND JODHPUR

At the age of thirty-one he went to Jaipur and there learned the work of administration under the able guidance of his brother-in-law Maharaja Rama Singh. At the age of thirty-three he was appointed as the Prime Minister of Jodhpur, the largest State in Rajaputana "which is more than three times the size of Belgium and has about as many inhabitants as Denmark."

---

* Adapted from an article in the *Indian Review*, by Mr. N. Gupta, B. A.

A SOLDIER-STATESMAN

Sir Pratap proved himself as great an administrator as he was a soldier. Before his appointment the State was heavily in debt, its expenditure exceeded its revenue, and there was much unrest due to the constant depredations of the wild hill-tribes of Minas, Bhils, Baories and Ladhkhanis.

REFORMS IN JODHPUR

Within six years after his appointment he not only paid off the debts amounting to over 50 lacs, but raised the revenue to 40 lacs, and afterwards to 50 lacs. He established a State Treasury and by regulating the income and the expenditure established a proper control over the finances.

He introduced many other reforms in the State, and a brief summary of them is given below:—

(1) Establishment of the State Treasury in place of the Banias or Bankers who formerly used to receive and disburse money on behalf of the State.

(2) Introduction of cash system in place of the Batayi (kind).

(3) Systematic collection of revenues.

(4) Establishment of Courts of Justice and introduction of Written Codes of Law.

(5) Introduction of Forest Conservation.

(6) Suppression of Criminal Tribes.

(7) Establishment of a college and schools for boys and girls where education is free.

(8) Establishment of free State dispensaries and introduction of European medicines.

(9) Establishment of Municipal Committees.

(10) Improvement of Jails.

(11) Construction of large Bundhs and Water-reservoirs for irrigation purpose.

(12) Opening up of railway lines.

(13) Re-organisation of the Military Department and establishment of the famous Jodhpur Imperial Service Lancers.

He was the Prime Minister of Jodhpur from 1878—1902.

In 1902 he became the Maharaja of Idar State and received an addition of two guns to his personal salute.

AS A WARRIOR

The British Government had, from the first, recognised the statesmanship and administrative qualities of this gallant soldier and statesman. But he was a warrior of no mean repute—and he proved his mettle on more than one field of battle. He was an Honorary Lieutenant-General in His Imperial Majesty's Army, an Honorary Colonel of the Poona Horse, and Honorary Commandant of the Imperial Cadet Corps. He was specially deputed to accompany His Imperial Majesty when he toured through India as the Prince of Wales, and he was likewise attached to the staff of the Prince of Wales during his recent tour in India.

MISSION TO AFGHANISTAN

In 1880 he accompanied the mission to Afghanistan, and in recognition of his services he was appointed a Companion of the Star of India. He was promoted to the Knight Commandership in the same order on 1st January 1886.

IN TIRAH AND CHINA

He served on the staff of Generals Ellis and Sir William Lockhart in the Mohmand and Tirah Campaigns, and was favourably noticed in the despatches. For this he was appointed a C. B. and an Honorary Colonel in the British Army. He was also awarded the Frontier Medal with two clasps. In 1900-1901 he again served in China and on his return in August 1901 was made a K. C. B.

AS REGENT OF MARWAR

On the demise of his nephew Maharaja Sir Sardar Singhji, K. C. S. I. in March 1911, he abdicated the Idar "*gadi*" in favour of his adopted son, Maharaj Kumar Dowlat Singh, at a great personal sacrifice in order to become the Regent of Marwar State so as to see the fruition of those reform schemes which he had inaugurated when Prime Minister of Marwar. The Supreme Government allowed him to retain the title of "H. H. Maharaja" and the personal salute of 17 guns so long as he remained the Regent of Marwar. At the Delhi Durbar in 1911 His Imperial Majesty was pleased to create him a G. C. V. O.

VISITS TO ENGLAND

(2) On the occasion of the Diamond Jubilee of Queen Victoria in 1897, when he was created a Grand Commander of the Star of India. The degree of L.L.D. (Honoris Causa) was also conferred on him then by the Cambridge University.

(3) On the occasion of the Coronation of His Imperial Majesty King George V, when the Oxford University honoured him by conferring the degree of D. C. L. (Honoris Causa.)

(4) During the Great European War he accompanied his late Highness Maharaja Sir Sumer Singhji when he with the famous Jodhpur Lancers proceeded to the Front in 1914, and again went there in 1916, and contributed not a little to the triumph of Indian arms in the European War. For his meritorious services he received the title of Knight of St. John of Jerusalem in 1916, and was also made a Lieutenant-General. On 1st January 1918, His Imperial Majesty made him a G. C. B. in appreciation of his services in the Great European War. He went from Europe to Egypt and Mesopotamia in 1918.

During the minority of the present Chief, His Highness Maharaja Captain Sir Umed Singhji Bahadur, K. B. E., he was again appointed Regent of Marwar and President of the Regency Council, and he exercised a general control over the administration of the State. He expired on 4th September 1922 at the ripe old age of 76 years.

Looking back on the life of this soldier-statesman one is impressed by the volume of his work and the variety of his experiences. But even apart from his achievements there were traits in his character which marked him out as a man among men. His heroism and chivalry were in every way worthy of a descendent of the great warriors of Jodhpur.

SIR PRATAP AND LORD ROBERTS

There is an interesting incident in the life of Lord Roberts which the Commander-in-Chief described in his volume of Experiences in India. The incident reveals the intimate relationship of the two great generals and sets out the character of the Indian hero in its true perspective. We cannot do better than quote the words of Lord Roberts himself:

> At Jodhpur my friend the Maharaja Sir Pratap Singh gave us a signal proof that the ancient valour of the Rajputs has not deteriorated in the present day. I had wounded a fine boar, and on his making for some rocky ground where I could hardly have followed him on horseback, I shouted to Sir Pratap to get between him and the rocks, and turn him in my direction. The Maharaja promptly responded, but just as he came face to face with the boar his horse put his foot into a hole and fell, the infuriated animal rushed on the fallen rider, and before the latter could extricate himself, gave him a severe wound in the leg with his formidable tusks. On going to his assistance I found Sir Pratap bleeding profusely, but standing erect, facing the boar and holding the creature (who was upright on his hind legs) at arm's length by his mouth. The spear without the impetus given by the horse at full speed is not a very effective weapon against the tough hide of a boar's back, and on realising that mine did not make much impression, Pratap Singh, letting go his hold of the boar's mouth, quickly seized his hind-legs, and turned him on his back, crying '*maro, Sahib, maro,*' which I instantly did and killed him. Any one who is able to realise the strength and weight of a wild boar will appreciate the pluck and presence of mind of Sir Pratap Singh in this performance. Fortunately my wife and daughter, who had been following the pig-stickers in a light cart, were close at hand and we were able

to drive my friend home at once. The wound was found to be rather a bad one, but it did not prevent Sir Pratap from attending some tent-pegging and other amusements in the afternoon, though he had to be carried to the scene."

Of such stuff was Sir Pratap Singh made.

Page 368.

MAHARAJAH SIR PRATAP SINGH

Page 369

MAHARAJA SIR KISHEN PERSHAD

Maharaja Sir Kishen Pershad

THE NIZAM'S STATE

THE great State of Hyderabad is a polygonal tract in the centre of the Deccan occupying an area of over 82,000 square miles and was founded by the House of the illustrious Asaf Jah, Nizam-ul-Mulk, a distinguished General of Aurangzib, of Turcoman descent. He had long been the Subhadar of the Deccan; but his practical independence of the Delhi Power dates from 1724 when he triumphed over Mubariz Khan who was sent out from Delhi to oust him. Throughout his long career of activity and assertion, he maintained his dignity; and by the time of his death at an advanced age in 1748, he was firmly established as the independent sovereign of a kingdom which was almost co-extensive with the present State and also included Berar. The Dynasty of the Nizams has almost uniformly been closely attached to the British Power ever since the Third Anglo-French War in the Carnatic which ended with the fall of Pondicherry in 1761. The Nizam has been consequently termed as "Our Faithful Ally the Nizam." Nawab Mohsin-ul-Mulk, Secretary to the Government of Hyderabad, writing in his learned and voluminous *History of*

Hyderabad Affairs (1883, for private circulation) tells us of the great name and character of the Founder of the State and also of how

> **" impartial estimates of his character can hardly begrudge his descendants a pride in the founder of their name and renown, for his politic compass and tenacious hold of independent power were unstained by treachery or cruelty and *the later annals of the family are similarly clear of* the grosser incidents of conquests." (quoted in Sir R. Lethbridge's *The Golden Book of India* ; 1893 ; p. 180).**

THE EARLY MINISTERS OF THE STATE

The first treaty between the British Power and the Nizam was concluded in 1766 ; and it was supplemented by more important and more permanent treaties in 1798 and 1800. According to these and other engagements, the Nizam received large accessions of territory including Berar, from the conquests from Tippu and from the Marathas. Nizam Ali, the last of the sons of the Founder to occupy the throne, died in 1803 ; and he was succeeded by his son, the Nizam Sikandar Jah, who was served by three Prime Ministers of ability, Mir Alam, Munir-ul-Mulk and Maharaja Chandu Lal. Munir-ul-Mulk was the son-in-law of Mir Alam and succeeded him as Minister. He was the father of Suraj-ul-Mulk who became Minister after Chandu Lal and the grandfather of the great Nawab Sir Salar Jang I. who was Minister from 1853 for over 30 years.

CHANDU LAL, PESHKAR AND MINISTER

Chandu Lal, the ancestor of Maharaja Sir Kishen Pershad Bahadur, was descended from one of the most distinguished Hindu families settled in the Deccan. The original home of the family was Hindustan ; and its most illustrious ancestor was the famous Raja Todar Mal, the great finance minister of the Emperor Akbar. Rai Mal Chand who was fifth in descent from Todar Mal accompanied the great Asaf Jah, Nizam-ul-Mulk, to the Deccan and rose to high distinction under him, holding the office of *Karrora* or the head of the customs and excise department. Rai Mal Chand was followed in that office by his son, Rai Luchchi Ram ; and he in turn gave place to his elder son Rai Nanak Ram. Chandu Lal was a grandson of Rai Luchchi Ram ; and he raised the family " to that pitch of eminence in the Deccan which it had occupied in Northern India during the time of Todar Mal. " (*Who is Who in India*—Popular Edition, Lucknow (1911) p. 139).

Chandu Lal was practically the Minister even during the tenure of office of Munir-ul-Mulk and exercised all real authority. He was in theory only the deputy of the Minister, being Peshkar. In those days the Minister ranked next in dignity to the Nizam himself. His duties were to supervise the collection of general revenues, to control all branches of the army, to arrange for the administration of justice, to grant pensions and allowances and to control patronage. He was assisted by the Peshkar who was appointed by the Nizam, but was directly subordinate only to himself. The office of Peshkar was practically hereditary in the family of Chandu Lal. Chandu Lal was Peshkar from the time of Mir Alam. He was the real controller of the entire internal administration, and particularly of all revenue matters ; and he did his business so thoroughly that he received the warm commendations of the British Resident. (p. 5. Vol. II. of Kaye's *Life of Lord Metcalfe*).

CHANDU LAL'S WORK

After the death of Munir-ul-Mulk Chandu Lal became the minister in name as well as in fact, though he continued to hold the title of Peshkar merely which he never wished to change. Chandu Lal resigned his high authority only in 1843 when he was 77 years of age. Sir Henry Russell the Resident at the Nizam's Court from 1810 to 1820, was a very warm friend and supporter of Chandu Lal in whom he could not perceive any serious fault; but his successors, Sir Charles Metcalfe, afterwards Governor-General, and General Fraser were very outspoken in their criticisms of Chandu Lal's administration. Chandu Lal was generally favourable to the strengthening of the hands of the Resident and to the heeding of the wishes of the Government of India in the matter of reform. He saw the necessity of keeping up in efficient condition the British Contingent and was inclined towards a reduction in the number of the Nizam's irregular forces. He was afraid of openly going against his master who would not tolerate any reduction either in his army or in his extravagant private expenditure. He consequently found himself frequently unable to secure funds from the regular state-revenues for the Contingent and resorted to loans at great, even usurious, rates of interest. But he looked to no personal interest in such transactions. With so many opportunities of profit, and living in the midst of so much corruption Chandu Lal retired from office a poor man and died in comparatively unaffluent circumstances; and to this day Chandu Lal's family has remained, judging by the standard of the great Hyderabad nobles, a comparatively poor one. Even Metcalfe, Fraser and other Residents who did not like him and his methods have borne uniform testimony to the loyalty of Chandu Lal both to his own master and also to the Suzerain Power. In a letter written to Lord Auckland, the Governor-General, General Fraser thus speaks of Chandu Lal:—

> **Adroitly opposing the Nizam to us (the British) or us at other times to his sovereign, he (Chandu Lal) has continued to keep the Government—or rather the dictatorship—of the country in his hands for 30 years. Still whatever his motives may have been, and how far soever actuated by self-interest and determination to uphold his own authority, he has been truly and essentially our friend.**

Sir Richard Temple says in his *Journals Kept in Hyderabad, Kashmir, Sikkim and Nepal* that the financial difficulties of the State became greatly embarrassing under Chandu Lal's administration, and the old judicial arrangements were largely obliterated, giving place to a variety of usurpations of jurisdictions on the part of individuals, especially the Arab chiefs in the army and the great noblemen. Influential persons, military chiefs, power ful landholders, rich bankers and great noblemen often refused to submit to the jurisdiction of these courts.

Later Ministers

After the death of the Nizam Sikandar Jah in 1829, in the reign of the Nizam Nasir-ud-Daula, and during the Ministry of Chandu Lal there occurred a serious Wahhabi conspiracy in 1840 aiming at the overthrow of the English. It was engineered by an uncle of the Nizam and directed against the British Government as well as the Nizam himself. Nasir-ud-Daula's reign was also marked by the serious Shiah-Sunni Riot of 1847 and by the conclusion of the famous Berar Assignment Treaty of 1853. A week after the conclusion of this treaty, the Minister Suraj-ul-Mulk died; and his young nephew, the famous Salar Jang, was appointed in his place. In 1857, a new Nizam, Afzal-ud-Daula succeeded.

Sir Salar Jang I.

Both the Nizam and the Minister stood by the English with unshaken loyalty in the crisis of the Great Mutiny and were later on royally rewarded and honoured for their services. On the death of Afzal-ud-Daula, his son, Mir Mahbub Ali Khan, then only three years old, succeeded; and a Regency was constituted with Sir Salar Jang as Regent and the great premier noble Nawab Shams-ul-Umara as Co-Regent. The Regency continued till 1883 when Sir Salar Jang died; and the Nizam, coming of age in 1884, was formally installed by Lord Ripon.

The Co-Regent, Nawab Shams-ul-Umara, was the Amir Kabir, the chief noble of the court, descended from the ancient family of the saint Shaikh Farid of Pakpatan in the Punjab and closely connected by marriage with the ruling house. He was the hereditary holder of the Paigha Lands covering an area of over 4,000 square miles, and intended for the maintenance of troops known as the Nizam's Household Troops. He was Co-Regent till his death in 1877 and was succeeded by his brother the Nawab Vikar-ul-Umara who also died in 1881.

His Successors

After the death of the Nawab Salar Jang II. who was appointed Minister soon after his father's death, Sir Asman Jah, another member of this great Shamsiyah family became the Prime Minister. He had already acted in that capacity during Sir Salar Jang I.'s absence in Europe, had been appointed to the Council of Regency on the latter's death in 1883 and had represented the Nizam at the Jubilee Celebrations of Queen Victoria in 1887. He continued as the Prime Minister for several years during which two important reforms were effected. First a Code was published for the guidance of the Minister, known as the *Kanuncha-i Mubarak* (the auspicious code); and more important still, a Council was established composed of all the Ministers of State. He was succeeded in the exalted office by yet another kinsman, the Nawab Sir Vikar-ul-Umara who also proved a very capable administrator and effected several changes in the various departments of the administration.

SIR KISHEN PERSHAD, MINISTER (1901—1912)

Maharaja Sir Kishen Pershad followed in 1901 and continued to hold that office for over a decade. He is descended from Chandu Lal in a direct line of succession. The latter's grandson, Maharaja Narayan Pershad Naraindar Bahadur was appointed Senior Minister under the Council of Regency on the death of the great Salar Jang in 1883. When he died in 1888, he adopted his daughter's son, Maharaja Sir Kishen Pershad Bahadur, as his heir. Sir Kishen Pershad was born in January, 1864. He gave even as a boy great promise of future abilities. He early displayed a talent for poetical composition in Urdu; and he was soon honoured with the title of *Shagird-i-Khas Asaf Jah (i. e.,* the special pupil of His Highness) which is considered "to have a very special honour attached to it and is seldom bestowed by a sovereign on his subject."

LIFE AND WORK

In 1892 he was appointed to the hereditary post of Peshkar and was made also Military Minister. He was shortly afterwards given the title of *Rajayan-i-Raja Maharaja Bahadur Yamin-us-Sultanat,* the first portion of which has been enjoyed by his ancestors. He was appointed to act as Prime Minister in 1901 and confirmed in the place in the next year. His literary tastes are keen; and he has published some novels in Urdu and also several books of verse both in Persian and in Urdu. He has inherited all the jaghirs of Maharaja Naraindar Bahadur which yield him an annual income of several lakhs of rupees. He has also been given full civil and criminal powers over his people, which is a privilege only enjoyed by the highest nobles of the State. He received from the British Government the insignia of K.C.I.E. in 1903 and that of G.C.I.E. in 1910.

HIS ADMINISTRATION

Under the Ministry of Sir Kishen Pershad the form of administration was that which was prescribed by the original instructions issued by the Nizam in his Edict of 1893 (*Kanuncha-i-Mubarak*), subsequently modified in some important particulars. According to this scheme, the Minister was the chief controlling authority in the State; there were four subordinate Ministers assisting him, respectively in charge of the financial, military, judicial and miscellaneous departments. The Minister was known as the *Madar-ul-Maham;* and the Assistant Ministers as the *Muin-ul-Mahams.* The revenue department was directly under the Minister who controlled, land revenue, survey and settlement, customs, *inams* and *abkari*, forests, agriculture and commerce. There were six Secretaries, including the Private Secretary to the Minister. The whole State is divided into 4 *subahs*, each under a Subahdar or Commissioner, and being divided into Districts, each of which was controlled by a First Talukdar or Collector assisted by a Second and a Third (or Assistant) Talukdars. There were subordinate officials like the Tahsildar who had charge of the revenue and magisterial work of his *taluk* assisted by a *Peshkar* (assistant) and in some places by a *Girdavar* (revenue inspector). Villages were controlled by one or two *Patels* (headmen) who had charge of the revenue and police functions and were assisted by accountants known as *Patwaris, Karnams* or *Kulkarnis*. There are also the *Samasthans* and *jagirs* which cover an area of more than 24,000 square miles.

PROGRESS IN THE VARIOUS DEPARTMENTS

A Legislative Council was first established by decree in 1893 which consisted purely of high officials. In the next year a *farman* of the Nizam recognised the right of the people to share in the work of legislation and to representation on the Council. In 1900 the whole scheme was modified as Act III of Fasli 1309. According to this the Council consisted of 19 members, presided over by the Minister—the Assistant Minister whose department was concerned in the Bill before the Council, being the Vice-President for the time being. 8 of the 11 official members were nominated by the Minister. Of the 6 non-official members, 2 were elected by the *Jagirdars* and land-owners, 2 by the pleaders of the High Court and the remaining 2 were nominated by the Minister, one being chosen from the *Paigah Ilaka*. The first years of office of Sir Kishen Pershad saw the passing of the Census, the Weights and Measures and the Limitation

Acts, besides the passing of the Criminal Procedure Code, the Evidence Act, the Stamp Act, the Ferries Act, and several regulations of the High Court. Customs and Excise Revenue began to yield a profit only with Sir Kishen Pershad. In 1904, the total revenue of the State, excluding the *Sarf-i-Khas* (Crown Lands), the *Paigah* and the *Jaghirs* which together make up a third of the whole area of the Dominions, stood at 469 lakhs. The total expenses came in that year to 450 lakhs. Fortunately since 1901-2, the rate of exchange between the State rupee and the British rupee has been fairly steady "the former exchanging at about 8 per cent. above its bullion value." In 1904, the Government issued an improved rupee known as the *Mahbubia rupee* representing on one side the famous Char Minar building. Since then the minting of rupees has been so arranged as to avoid violent fluctuations in exchange. The rate now stands about 115 & 116 *Mahbubia* to 100 British rupees.

The Minister amalgamated in 1903 the two Municipalities (originally introduced in 1869) of Hyderabad and Chaderghat under a Commission of non-officials assisted by a special officer styled Secretary to the Committee. The Local Board Department first established in 1887 was also largely improved. In 1901 there were 13 District and 70 Taluk Boards, the former presided over by the First Talukdars and the latter by the Second and Third Talukdars. The local cess, originally one anna per rupee of land revenue, provides funds for the building and upkeep of roads, schools, dispensaries, rest-houses, etc. There were also arrangements for conservancy in the Divisional, District and Taluk headquarters: there were besides 21 mofussil municipalities in the State in 1901 whose expenditure was met also from the local cess. Irrigation, Public Works, Police and Jails all continued to be efficient; in the matter of Police, there were 3 distinct jurisdictions within the State, *viz.*, the *Sarf-i-Khas* the *Diwani* and the *Paigah and Jaghir* police; while the City Police Force of Hyderabad had a distinct organisation. The Education Department worked by a Director of Public Instruction and ultimately controlled by the Minister, made commendable efforts at the spread of primary and girls' education in the *regime* of Sir Kishen; while the Madrasa-i-Aliya for the education of noblemen, now known as the Nizam College, and the Dar-ul-Ulum or the Oriental College continued to flourish. Some progress was also made in the direction of providing boarding houses for the students of some of the District High Schools of which there were 16 in the State in 1901. A system of grading teachers was also introduced; while the children of the of the agriculturists were given instruction in a manner which enabled them to assist their parents in the fields in the busy seasons of the year. The girls' schools were naturally very few; but attempts were made vigorously to promote female education; and the Government High Class Zenana School at Hyderabad did very good work.

SETTLEMENT OF THE BERAR QUESTION

It was in the Ministry of Sir Kishen Pershad that the Berar question which had been hanging fire for so many years was closed by Lord Curzon in a bargain which has been described by Mr. Lovat Fraser *(India under Curzon and After*—p. 226) as being a fair one and doing reasonable justice to both parties. The Minister and the Resident Sir David Barr were largely responsible for the successful termination of the negotiations out of which the Nizam felt that he emerged, with his prestige enhanced, because firstly of the British Government remaining in Berar only as his lessees, and secondly of their consenting to reduce the number of British troops in his territories. It was Sir Kishen Pershad again that put the Finance Department of the State under the able guidance of Mr. Casson Walker who continued to be the Finance Minister till his retirement in 1911 and who succeeded in rehabilitating the entire finances of the State. He was specially honoured and decorated for his tact and skill in the negotiations connected with the Berar Settlement.

THE RECALL OF SIR KISHEN TO HIS POST

Sir Kishen Pershad retired from the Ministership in 1912 and devoted himself to the elegant luxuries of a well-deserved life of repose and quiet. His leisure hours were occupied with his favourite pastimes of versifying, photography, painting and billiards. The self-complacent attitude of the present Nizam who succeeded his father in 1911 led him first to dispense with the office of Minister and become himself his own Minister. The regular Ministership was in abeyance for a period ; and attempts were made to constitute an Executive Council with a President at its head, who would discharge some of the functions of the previous Minister. The circumstances which brought about the publication of the acute correspondence between H. E. the Viceroy and H. E. H. the Nizam, in the beginning of last year, have been followed by an attempt at re-organisation of the personnel of the higher governmental machinery of the State. Recently Nawab Wali-ud-Daula Bahadur of the noted Shamsiyah family, made over charge of the Presidentship of H. E. H. the Nizam's Executive Council to Maharaja Sir Kishen Pershad Bahadur whom therefore the Fates have summoned again to preside over the destinies of his State. The Maharajah's accession to the Prime Ministership, at a time of exceptional difficulty, was considered an event of striking significance. A descendant of Chandu Lal and a Hindu nobleman of the highest eminence, he has proved himself a loyal and capable servant of the State in years past. His statesmanship and tact in dealing with the Berar Question has been noticed: and it is believed that his handling of the situation at the present time may prove beneficial to Hyderabad. The situation, as revealed in the recent correspondence, demands exceptional statesmanship and great hopes are entertained in this illustrious descendent of Chandu Lal,—who in his own day proved himself so invaluable not only to Hyderabad but to the Suzerain Power as well. It is hoped that a similar fortune will result from the efforts of Sir Kishen Pershad. The Maharaja was, on his accession, the recipient of numerous addresses of congratulation. "All justifiable demands will be met" was the answer given by Sir Kishen Pershad in reply to the address presented to him on December 11, 1926 by the non-official members of the State Legislative Council, who demanded the introduction of Reforms. The address contained definite requests for substantial increase of the non-official element, the grant of representation on the Council to the elected representatives of every district, and powers to the members of the Legislative Councils to put interpellations, move resolutions, and discuss the State Budget. We hope that under the wise guidance of this experienced Hindu nobleman the dissatisfaction of the Hindus in the State will also be abated and the whole administration will put on a more progressive complexion than has been possible in the last decade.

One who is closely associated with the Maharaja and is therefore competent to speak with authority on the subject relates a story with which we may conclude this sketch. It is said that the late Nizam who was two years younger than Maharaja Sir Kishen Pershad remarked in his early years before his courtiers "what a remarkable likeness the young Raja bears towards Maharaja Chandu Lal!" adding with his characteristic grace and patronage, "I think he will be another bright star in his family." This prophecy, says the writer, does credit not only to the Royal eye but also shows what a promising young man the Maharaja must have been.

INDEX